ACCENTS ON SHAKESPEARE

General editor TERENCE HAWKES

Shakespeare and Appropriation

The vitality of our culture is still often measured by the status Shakespeare has within it. Contemporary readers and writers continue to exploit Shakespeare's cultural afterlife in a vivid and creative way. This fascinating collection of original essays shows how writers' efforts to imitate, contradict, compete with, and reproduce Shakespeare keep him in the cultural conversation.

The essays:

- analyze the methods and motives of Shakespearean appropriation
- investigate theoretically the return of the repressed author in discussions of Shakespeare's cultural function
- put into dialogue theoretical and literary responses to Shakespeare's cultural authority
- analyze works ranging from the nineteenth century to the present, and genres ranging from poetry and the novel to Disney movies.

Christy Desmet is Associate Professor of English at the University of Georgia, and author of *Reading Shakespeare's Characters: Rhetoric, Ethics, and Identity* (University of Massachusetts Press, 1992)

Robert Sawyer is a Robert E. Park Fellow in English at the University of Georgia.

ACCENTS ON SHAKESPEARE
General Editor: TERENCE HAWKES

It is more than twenty years since the New Accents series helped to establish "theory" as a fundamental and continuing feature of the study of literature at the undergraduate level. Since then, the need for short, powerful "cutting edge" accounts of and comments on new developments has increased sharply. In the case of Shakespeare, books with this sort of focus have not been readily available. **Accents on Shakespeare** aims to supply them.

Accents on Shakespeare volumes will either "apply" theory, or broaden and adapt it in order to connect with concrete teaching concerns. In the process, they will also reflect and engage with the major developments in Shakespeare studies of the last ten years.

The series will lead as well as follow. In pursuit of this goal it will be a two-tiered series. In addition to affordable, "adoptable" titles aimed at modular undergraduate courses, it will include a number of research-based books. Spirited and committed, these second-tier volumes advocate radical change rather than stolidly reinforcing the status quo.

IN THE SAME SERIES

Shakespeare and Appropriation
Edited by Christy Desmet and Robert Sawyer

Shakespeare Without Women
Dympna Callaghan

Shakespeare and Appropriation

Edited by
CHRISTY DESMET and ROBERT SAWYER

London and New York

First published 1999
by Routledge
11 New Fetter Lane,
London EC4P 4EE

Simultaneously published in
the USA and Canada
by Routledge
29 West 35th Street,
New York, NY 10001

Routledge is an imprint of the
Taylor & Francis Group

Typeset in Baskerville by
Ponting–Green Publishing Services,
Chesham, Buckinghamshire

British Library Cataloguing in Publication Data

A catalogue record for this book is available from the British Library

Library of Congress Cataloging in Publication Data

Shakespeare and appropriation / [edited by] Christy Desmet and Robert Sawyer
p. cm. – (Accents on Shakespeare)
Includes bibliographical references (p.) and index
1. Shakespeare, William, 1564–1616 – Adaptations. 2. Shakespeare, William, 1564–1616 – Film and video adaptations. 3. Shakespeare, William, 1564–1616 – Influence. 4. American literature – History and criticism. 5. English literature – History and criticism. 6. Influence (Literary, artistic etc.) 7. Imitation in literature.
I. Desmet, Christy, 1954– . II. Sawyer, Robert, 1953– . III. Series.
PR2880.A1S52 1999
822.3'3–dc21 99-31115
CIP

ISBN 0–415–20725–8 (hbk)
ISBN 0–415–20726–6 (pbk)

For Fran Teague and Marianne Novy

Contents

Figures

Contributors

James R. Andreas, Sr. (Professor of English, Director of the Clemson Shakespeare Festival and of the South Carolina Shakespeare Collaborative at Clemson University) has for sixteen years been editor of *The Upstart Crow: A Shakespeare Journal*. He has published extensively on medieval rhetoric, Chaucer, Shakespeare, and African American Literature.

Caroline Cakebread has published articles on Shakespeare and contemporary women's writing; her essay on Marina Warner's *Indigo* and *The Tempest* appears in Marianne Novy (ed.) *Transforming Shakespeare: Contemporary Women's Re-Visions* (St. Martin's Press 1999). She lives and works in Toronto.

Sudipto Chatterjee (Tufts University) received his Ph.D. from the Tisch School of the Arts, New York University. He is working on a book about "The Colonial Stage(d): Hybridity, Woman, and the Nation in 19th-Century Bengal" and has published essays in anthologies and journals.

Christy Desmet (University of Georgia) is the author of *Reading Shakespeare's Characters: Rhetoric, Ethics, and Identity* and of articles on Renaissance Drama and Shakespearean criticism in the nineteenth century.

Richard Finkelstein (State University of New York College at Geneseo) has published articles and reviews on Shakespeare, Jonson, and other Renaissance dramatists. He is currently working on the politics of Shakespeare's Third Folio.

Terence Hawkes is Professor of English at the University of Wales, Cardiff.

Ivo Kamps (University of Mississippi) is the author of *Historiography and Ideology in the Stuart Drama* and co-editor of *Journal x: A Journal in Culture and Criticism*. With Jyotsna G. Singh, he is currently co-editing a collection of early modern travel narratives dealing with the East.

Matt Kozusko is a Ph.D. student in English at the University of Georgia with an interest in Shakespeare.

Laurie E. Osborne (Colby College) is the author of *The Trick of Singularity: Twelfth Night and the Performance Editions*, articles on Shakespeare on film (including *Shakespeare: The Animated Tales*), and an essay on gender in Shakespeare's audiences, the subject of her next book.

Robert Sawyer (University of Georgia) has completed a dissertation entitled "Mid-Victorian Appropriations of Shakespeare: George Eliot, Robert Browning, and Algernon Charles Swinburne." He has been published in *The Upstart Crow*, and his book reviews have appeared in *Shakespeare Bulletin* and *South Atlantic Review*.

Jyotsna G. Singh (Michigan State University) is the author of *Colonial Narratives, Cultural Dialogues*, and co-author of *Weyward Sisters: Shakespeare and Feminist Politics*. She is currently co-editing (with Ivo Kamps) *Travel Knowledge: European "Witnesses" to "Navigations, Traffiques and Discoveries" in the Early Modern Period*.

Lisa S. Starks (University of South Florida) has published on Renaissance drama and film. She has also edited two special issues of the journal *Post Script* on Shakespeare and film and currently is co-editing, with Courtney Lehmann, a collection of essays entitled *Screening the Bard: Shakespearean Spectacle, Critical Theory, Film Practice*.

Gary Taylor (Director of the Hudson Strode Program in Renaissance Studies at the University of Alabama) is co-editor of the works of Shakespeare (1986) and editor of the works of Thomas Middleton (forthcoming), author of *Reinventing Shakespeare* (1989),

Cultural Selection (1996), and *What Does Castration Mean? Augustine, Middleton, Freud* (forthcoming).

Georgianna Ziegler, Reference Librarian at the Folger Shakespeare Library, has published on Shakespeare and other early modern English authors and is researching a book on nineteenth-century Shakespeare.

General editor's preface

In our century, the field of literary studies has rarely been a settled, tranquil place. Indeed, for over two decades, the clash of opposed theories, prejudices, and points of view has made it more of a battlefield. Echoing across its most beleaguered terrain, the student's weary complaint "Why can't I just pick up Shakespeare's plays and read them?" seems to demand a sympathetic response.

Nevertheless, we know that modern spectacles will always impose their own particular characteristics on the vision of those who unthinkingly don them. This must mean, at the very least, that an apparently simple confrontation with, or pious contemplation of, the text of a 400-year-old play can scarcely supply the grounding for an adequate response to its complex demands. For this reason, a transfer of emphasis from "text" toward "context" has increasingly been the concern of critics and scholars since World War II: a tendency that has perhaps reached its climax in more recent movements such as New Historicism or Cultural Materialism.

A consideration of the conditions, social, political, or economic within which the play came to exist, from which it derives, and to which it speaks will certainly make legitimate demands on the attention of any well-prepared student nowadays. Of course, the serious pursuit of those interests will also inevitably start to undermine ancient and inherited prejudices, such as the supposed distinction between "foreground" and "background" in literary studies. And even the slightest awareness of the pressures of gender or of race, or the most cursory glance at the role played by that strange creature "Shakespeare" in our cultural politics, will reinforce a similar turn toward questions that sometimes appear scandalously "non-literary." It seems clear that very different and unsettling notions of the ways in which literature might be addressed can hardly be avoided. The worrying truth is that nobody can just pick up Shakespeare's plays and read them. Perhaps – even more worrying – they never could.

The aim of *Accents on Shakespeare* is to encourage students and teachers to explore the implications of this situation by means of an engagement with the major developments in Shakespeare studies of the last ten years. It will offer a continuing and challenging reflection on those ideas through a series of multi- and single-author books which will also supply the basis for adapting or augmenting them in the light of changing concerns.

Accents on Shakespeare also intends to lead as well as follow. In pursuit of this goal, the series will operate on more than one level. In addition to titles aimed at modular undergraduate courses, it will include a number of books embodying polemical, strongly argued cases aimed at expanding the horizons of a specific aspect of the subject and at challenging the preconceptions on which it is based. These volumes will not be learned "monographs" in any traditional sense. They will, it is hoped, offer a platform for the work of the liveliest younger scholars and teachers at their most outspoken and provocative. Committed and contentious, they will be reporting from the forefront of current work and will have something new to say. The fact that each book in the series promises a Shakespeare inflected in terms of a specific urgency should ensure that, in the present as in the recent past, the accent will be on change.

Terence Hawkes

Acknowledgments

Every collection of essays is dependent on the intelligence and diligence of its contributors, and the members of this volume have been exemplary on both counts. We would like to thank them, and particularly those who were part of the two South Atlantic Modern Language Association panels on "Shakespearean appropriation" organized by Robert Sawyer (1997 and 1998). They helped to shape the volume from its beginning and remained enthusiastic through its production. Deirdre Ralston helped to facilitate those panels. We would also like to thank Terence Hawkes for his interest and guidance. The members of our families, human and canine, provided excellent support, and Kathy and Jane of the University of Georgia Freshman English Office offered encouragement on a daily basis. We would like to thank Keith O'Neill and Matt Kozusko for their help on the project, and other friends for their encouragement: Mary Anne O'Neal, George Fink, and Anne Williams. This volume is dedicated to Fran Teague and Marianne Novy, from whom we have learned much about good scholarship and collegiality.

C.D. and R.S.

Note

Unless otherwise noted, Shakespearean references are to *The Norton Shakespeare*. Excerpt from "The Hollow Men" in *Collected Poems 1909–*

1962, copyright 1936 by Harcourt, Inc., copyright © 1964, 1963 by T.S. Eliot, reprinted by permission of Harcourt, Inc. and of Faber and Faber Ltd. Excerpts from *A Thousand Acres*, by Jane Smiley, reprinted by permission of Alfred A. Knopf Inc. and the Aaron M. Priest Literary Agency, Inc. Quotations from Tom Stoppard's *Rosencrantz and Guildenstern Are Dead*, copyright 1967, reprinted by permission of Faber and Faber Ltd. and Grove/Atlantic, Inc. Excerpts from Gloria Naylor's *Mama Day*, published by Ticknor and Fields, copyright 1968, reprinted by permission of Sterling Lord Literistic, Inc.

Introduction

CHRISTY DESMET

> All your life, you live so close to truth, it becomes a permanent blur in the corner of your eye, and when something nudges it into outline it is like being ambushed by a grotesque.
>
> I'd prefer art to mirror life, if that's all the same to you.
>
> (Tom Stoppard, *Rosencrantz & Guildenstern Are Dead*)

Tom Stoppard's *Rosencrantz & Guildenstern Are Dead*, probably the best-known and most frequently quoted of all Shakespeare parodies, includes a wonderful travesty of *Hamlet*'s Nunnery scene. In Stoppard's revision, the Nunnery scene and *Mousetrap* play follow one another helter-skelter, fractured further by squabbles between the Players and Shakespeare's minor courtiers. Hamlet enters and intones the portentous line: "Nymph, in thy orisons be all my sins remembered" (Stoppard 1967: 75). "Good, my lord, how does your honour for this many a day?," Ophelia responds on cue. "It's like living in a public park!," Rosencrantz objects, as his conversation is interrupted by the inexorable demands of Shakespeare's script. The Players move on to the *Mousetrap*'s dumbshow, only to be interrupted again by Hamlet, who enters shouting at Ophelia: "I say we will have no more marriage. ... To a nunnery go!" (78).

Shakespearean appropriation begins precisely in moments like this one, when experiencing Shakespeare becomes "like living in a public park." Private interests and public situations converge, and back-stage suddenly becomes front-stage, so that truth comes into focus with the force of a "grotesque." Verisimilitude, that comforting illusion that drama holds the mirror up to nature, but from a safe distance, becomes something more, either dream or nightmare. Then Shakespearean appropriation becomes possible, perhaps even imperative.

The essays in this volume approach Shakespearean appropriation from two perspectives. They discuss what Michael Bristol (1996) has called "big-time Shakespeare," an institutionalization of the Bard that has been ongoing at least since David Garrick's early theme park venture, the Shakespeare Jubilee (1769). As Richard Finkelstein demonstrates, Shakespeare continues to be appropriated by large corporations such as Disney as a vehicle for accruing capital, power, and cultural prestige. Ivo Kamps and Terence Hawkes remind us that Shakespeare has also been used ideologically to shape the academic study of English; battles over his literary remains still help to keep the professoriate and institutions of higher education in business.

Shakespeare and Appropriation also considers what might be termed "small-time Shakespeare," individual acts of "re-vision" that arise from love or rage, or simply a desire to play with Shakespeare. As Laurie Osborne shows, contemporary romance novelists are drawn to Shakespeare, in part for the cultural prestige he confers on their devalued genre, in part for the sheer fun of playing "identify that quotation." At times, Shakespearean appropriations have a personal urgency for their creators, and might, in Adrienne Rich's words, even be considered acts of survival. Jane Smiley, as discussed in Caroline Cakebread's contribution, writes vehemently against traditional readings of *King Lear* in *A Thousand Acres*. African American writer Gloria Naylor rejects Shakespeare as a literary forebear, but as James Andreas argues, her novel *Mama Day* can be read as a productive act of resistance, a rewriting of *The Tempest* from an Africanist point of view. Productions and films of Shakespeare's plays can also be appropriations. According to Lisa S. Starks, directors from Laurence Olivier to Kenneth Branagh reformulate not only the psychology of Hamlet, but also their relation to Shakespeare and to one another, through their filmed interpretations. The same could be said for Tom Stoppard's play, *Rosencrantz & Guildenstern Are Dead*.

"Big-time Shakespeare" serves corporate goals, entrenched power structures, and conservative cultural ideologies. "Small-time Shakespeare," which emerges from local, more pointed responses to the Bard, satisfies motives ranging from play, to political commitment, to agonistic gamesmanship. But big-time and small-time Shakespeare cannot always be so easily separated from one another, for even the corporate films of Disney bear the personal stamp of its powerful leaders. In her exploration of nineteenth-century representations of Lady Macbeth, Georgianna Ziegler shows the complex way in which literary and cultural climate, the opinions of prominent actresses, and visual representations of both the Shakespearean heroine and the actresses come together to refashion Lady Macbeth as a model of Victorian femininity. Robert Sawyer's essay traces the process by which Robert Browning's personal identification with Shakespeare ends with the canonization of Browning himself as a Victorian bard. Sudipto Chatterjee and Jyotsna Singh, who remind us that Shakespearean appropriation is a world phenomenon, show how high the political stakes can be in acts of appropriation. In the collaboration between James Barry and Bustomchurn Addy to put on a Native production of *Othello* in nineteenth-century Calcutta, we can see at work the profit motive, an act of resistance against colonial definitions of the Native as Other, and finally, the possibility/impossibility of defying political power through art. The essays in *Shakespeare and Appropriation*, in their dual focus on big- and small-time Shakespeare, at once challenge the idea that Shakespeare must always already be co-opted by the dominant culture and caution against the easy assumption that Shakespeare can set us free.

Shakespeare and Appropriation is divided into two parts. Part 1, "Appropriation in Theory," considers broadly the appropriation of Shakespeare as a cultural phenomenon: the contexts for this interpretation include the current Anglo-American academic scene (Kamps); the historical interface that links the birth of English studies in British academe with Liberal politics, cultural nostalgia, and scholarly editions of Shakespeare's plays (Hawkes); the appropriation of Shakespeare's "cultural capital" by a specific class of authors working in a particular genre, the romance (Osborne); and the importance of lost historical moments from locales far away from the Avon and its swans to the understanding of Shakespeare's role within the colonialist project (Chatterjee and Singh). Part 2, "Appropriation in Practice," focuses on specific, local acts of appropriation. It describes the dynamics of appropriation in the novel (Cakebread and Andreas), in film (Starks and Finkelstein), and in poetry (Sawyer). It considers the (re)construction of Shakespeare's character and the character of his dramatic figures (Ziegler and Sawyer). While Part 1 of *Shakespeare and Appropriation* involves cultural critique, Part 2 offers explorations in literary criticism. In this way, the book introduces readers first to issues pertinent to the study of appropriation, then offers examples of practical criticism, focusing on individual works and characters that might be studied in a class on Shakespeare or Shakespearean appropriation, or might simply be read for fun. The distinctions are not hard and fast: *Shakespeare and Appropriation* simply attempts to put theory and practice into dialogue.

I Appropriation in theory

> Pragmatism? – Is that all you have to offer? You seem to have no conception of where we stand.
>
> (*Rosencrantz & Guildenstern Are Dead*)

Discussion of appropriation as an aesthetic phenomenon raises questions of individual agency and therefore demands a theory of textual relations. While authors themselves often deny literary influence, insisting on a pragmatic approach to literary relations, just evoking the term "appropriation" forces us to consider "where we stand" theoretically in relation to the signifier "Shakespeare." The word "appropriation" implies an exchange, either the theft of something valuable (such as property or ideas) or a gift, the allocation of resources for a worthy cause (such as the legislative appropriation of funds for a new school). Something happens when Shakespeare is appropriated, and both the subject (author) and object (Shakespeare) are changed in the process.

The scholarly study of Shakespearean appropriation begins with a commitment to literary and social history. As Gary Taylor reminds us in his "Afterword" to this volume, Shakespeare has a history, one that Taylor himself traces in his magisterial study, *Reinventing Shakespeare* (1989). Georgianna Ziegler's essay, in this volume, also contends that attending to nineteenth-century representations of Lady Macbeth helps us know "where we stand" by articulating our indebtedness to, as well as differences from, our Victorian ancestors and their attitudes toward gender.

The history of Shakespearean appropriation contests bardolatry by demystifying the concept of authorship. Michel Foucault's "What is an Author?," a founding text for appropriation studies, begins with the assumption that all "discourses are objects of appropriation" (1984: 108). The author, no longer regarded as the origin of writing, becomes simply a proper name by which we describe a piece of discourse. Shakespeare therefore becomes the author-function "Shakespeare." If Shakespeare is really "Shakespeare," then his name can be pried loose from the discourses he names and circulated through culture and time. Ivo Kamps explains the process by which Shakespeare accumulates what Pierre Bourdieu (1984) calls "cultural capital" with the metaphor of Jeremy Bentham's auto-icon, the stuffed body of the utilitarian philosopher who, in his present state, functions as a kind of patron saint for University College, London, as Shakespeare has functioned for several centuries as an Anglo-American literary saint. As Bentham's body is stolen and returned in a yearly ritual between rival universities, it accrues symbolic value and legendary status – in short, "cultural capital." In a comparable way, "Shakespeare" is circulated through different ages and social strata, in turn accruing and conferring symbolic value on cultural projects from both highbrow and lowbrow culture – to use Lawrence Levine's (1988) seminal construct – and sometimes both together.

When Shakespeare's name, face, and words are used to sell beer or plane tickets on British Airways, "Shakespeare" obviously participates in the kind of social economics that Michael Bristol (1996), Barbara Hodgdon (1998), and in this volume, Richard Finkelstein and Gary Taylor describe. He becomes a commodity, "an article of commerce exchanged with a view to purely economic advantage among people who remain strangers to each other" (Bristol 1996: 36). Postmodernist critiques of modernist, postmodernist, or late capital culture are concerned less with such blatant theft of Shakespeare's commercial potential than with the more subtle machinations of what, in the 1940s, Theodor Adorno and Max Horkheimer identified as the "culture industry." (See Finkelstein's essay.) Cultural critics worry specifically about the way in which technology, including the technologies by which Shakespeare is disseminated to a wide audience, eradicates the "human" – the personal, the local, the different. While appropriation may situate us in history – a consummation devoutly to be wished – it may also perform the less benign work of shaping and organizing the most private aspects of experience. In *Cultural Selection* (1996), for instance, Taylor anatomizes the ways in which memory itself is produced and reminds us that for Bourdieu, "shared artificial memories create a kind of 'cultural capital' that distinguishes social classes far more effectively than lineage or income" (Taylor 1996: 186).

It is easy to demonize popular culture and even the culture industry, but Shakespeare's ideological function looks equally suspect from the ivory towers of academe. Hugh Grady (1991) and Terence Hawkes (1996: 1–16) uncover a residue of modernism in professional Shakespeare studies and, by implication, in the university curricula supervised by professional critics; the university therefore participates in the modernist impulse to collapse historical and geographic distance into a false universality and so frustrates "truth's" effort to ambush reader/writers "like a grotesque." John Guillory (1993) argues as well that institutions exist first and foremost to reproduce themselves, and educational institutions are no exception. The syllabus or curriculum therefore becomes a "fetish," an object venerated without reference to its cultural or even institutional function. Ivo Kamps's essay testifies to the fact that the college classroom, while a place of discussion, rarely produces revolution. Finally, in *Meaning by Shakespeare*, Terence Hawkes analyzes the ways in which those of us who critique "Bardbiz" also participate in the Shakespeare industry as critics, teachers, and editors (1992: 141–53).

II Appropriation in practice

> *Ros*: What's the game?
> *Guil*: What are the rules?
>
> (*Rosencrantz & Guildenstern Are Dead*)

The recognition that the self, values, and reality are not only socially constructed, but inexorably shaped by culture at its most conservative, is a daunting one. Foucault argued that the concept of "authorship" comes into existence at that moment when writers can be punished for discourse, or when writing becomes subject to censorship and cultural surveillance. But authorship must also then be grounded in the belief that discourse can be transgressive. The notion of transgression and its rhetorical counterpart, communion, are the terms around which small-time Shakespeare, or local acts of appropriation, are organized.

Current accounts of literary influence are often grounded in metaphors of conflict, a dialectic between transgression and submission. Harold Bloom's (1973) quasi-Freudian account of the "anxiety of influence," although by now venerable and even hoary, still influences our understanding of literary relations of the personal kind. According to Bloom, authors, or more specifically poets, ward off death by writing against a powerful precursor. Weak poets idolize, strong poets contest the precursor. Adrienne Rich offers a feminist rethinking of Bloom's agonistic model for authorship. In Rich's polemic, women writers and critics alike must not only combat death, but also awaken their dead or sleeping consciousness to face with fortitude and rage the victimization of women by centuries of an oppressive gender-class system. For Rich, "re-vision" – looking at old texts with fresh eyes, entering them from a new direction, and therefore rewriting the history of oppression – is for women, at least, a political act of survival.

Acts of appropriation, although they articulate where the author "stands" in relation to the object of appropriation, can be intensely personal as well as political. Such is the case for Paul Robeson, the African American singer, actor, and political activist, who played Othello in London during the 1930s opposite Peggy Ashcroft and on Broadway during the 1940s with Ute Hagen. In a well-known essay published in 1945 in the *American Scholar* (Foner 1978: 163–64), Robeson uses Theodore Spencer's universalizing *Shakespeare and the Nature of Man* (1949) to characterize Othello as the Renaissance man, denied the security of identity that was enjoyed by his medieval forebears. But even as he distances himself from Othello historically, Robeson identifies with his Shakespearean counterpart, telling concert audiences that Othello's position is much like that of the twentieth-century African American, himself the descendant of slaves. Robeson describes his identification with Shakespeare's character in terms of a dialectic between performance and intimacy, or between front- and back-stage. Discussing his London performance from the distance of 1944, Robeson speaks ironically about the self-consciousness that he felt about playing a character who makes love to, then kills, a white woman: "For the first two weeks I played with Desdemona that girl couldn't get near me, I was backin' away from her all the time. I was like a plantation hand in the parlor, that clumsy" (Foner 1978: 152).

What is Othello to Paul Robeson, or he to Othello? Robeson's identification with Othello, at once political and intensely emotional, reminds us of a lesson that African American, multi-cultural, and feminist literature and theory have taught us: the literary is personal. Kenneth Burke remains the best theorist of the rhetoric of identification that informs acts of Shakespearean appropriation like the one described by Paul Robeson. In Burke's lexicon, identification works as a dialectic between "identification of" (a public naming of the Other's qualities) and "identification with" (a private desire for union with the Other through mimesis or imitation) (Burke 1969: 19–29, 55–59 and *passim*). The African American actor identifies *with* Othello as the victim of a racism that transcends time and place, and identifies Othello *as* a slave who is therefore different from himself. Robeson is not the slave in the plantation parlor, he is not the Moor, but confronted with a white actress on the public stage, he is not yet so different from either of them. Appropriation therefore becomes the arena within which the relation between Self and Other is worked out. When the Other carries with him as much cultural capital as Shakespeare does, the dynamics of identification can be highly charged, indeed. (See Desmet 1992, especially Chapter 1.)

More concretely, how does Shakespearean appropriation work in practice? Several essays in this volume find Mikhail Bakhtin's account of dialogism useful for describing a writer's relation to Shakespeare. Bakhtin's *The Dialogic Imagination* (1981) posits that not only literary works, but language itself, is constituted from multiple, often competing voices. A novelist like Dostoyevsky, Bakhtin's epitome of the dialogic writer, not only produces a text rich in dialogue and employs all of the dialects, verbal styles, and forms at his command, but he also attends to the rich array of meanings implicit in those utterances. Bakhtin's concept of dialogism contains within it the paradoxical intersection between conflict and community that was implicit in Rich's reworking of Bloom's "anxiety of influence" and in Burke's rhetoric of identification. In *The Dialogic Imagination*, Bakhtin writes that: "The word is born in a dialogue as a living rejoinder within it; the word is shaped in dialogic interaction with an alien word that is already in the object" (Bakhtin 1981: 279). Metaphorically, at least, discourse involves dialogue with the alien.

Within the tradition of Shakespearean appropriation, as both a creative and critical practice, dialogue with the alien manifests itself in a variety of literary forms and practices. The simplest, and yet most enigmatic, forms of appropriation are quotation (or citation) and simple reading. In *I Know Why the Caged Bird Sings* (1970), Maya Angelou tells how, as a child, she was reduced to silence by sexual abuse. When Angelou started to speak again, an episode not recounted in that book, she recited Portia's "quality of mercy" speech for her church congregation. Quite literally, Shakespeare returns to Angelou her voice (discussed in Lootens 1996: 96). Recitation, of course, can turn citation into parody. Prince Charles's rewriting of Hamlet's "To Be or Not To Be," discussed by Kamps, may be unintentionally comic in its effect, but Stoppard's "Fifteen-Minute Hamlet," a brilliant parody, is based on nothing but a ruthlessly trimmed version of Shakespeare's now very incomplete text. Quotation and interpretation of Shakespeare can also be agonistic or compensatory. George and Cocoa, in Naylor's *Mama Day*, use *King Lear* to argue about their relationship. The father from one of Osborne's romances, *The Lady Who Hated Shakespeare*, combats grief by reading Shakespeare to his unreceptive daughter.

On a larger scale, Shakespearean appropriation can involve, as Rich says, entering a text from a new angle. Margaret Atwood's very short story, "Gertrude Talks Back," is a monologue that rewrites *Hamlet*'s closet scene from the perspective of Gertrude, its passive auditor, and ends with a witty twist: "Oh! You think what? You think Claudius murdered your Dad? ... It wasn't Claudius, darling. It was me" (Atwood 1994: 19). Dialogic encounters with Shakespeare, of course, can also involve larger revisions of plot and literary form. *Mama Day*'s experimental form, Robert Browning's dramatic monologue, the change of protagonists in *A Thousand Acres* – all emerge at least in part from the dynamics of appropriation. Even the smallest revision can be significant. In a recorded version of a concert performance of Othello's last speech, for instance, Paul Robeson (Robeson 1992) talks about the dignity of the Moor's culture, then – in the role of Othello – asks that this audience speak of him as one who "loved full wisely, but too well." The line makes no sense theatrically, but it speaks volumes about Robeson's relation to Shakespeare and his investment in Othello as a character.

Often appropriation involves what Bloom would call a strong misprision or misreading of the parent text. It may also involve a kind of simplification that sets appropriation and the study of it apart from other forms of Shakespearean criticism, particularly historicizing criticism. While recent readings of *Othello*, for instance, explore the multiplicity of racial identities imposed on the Moor (see Neill 1998), Robeson's reading of the character narrows that array of identities down to the one that explains best his alienation, that of the African American slave. The same is true for Naylor's

Africanist reading of *The Tempest.* Acts of appropriation, as they put the rhetoric of identification into the service of the personal, become what Kenneth Burke would call a "representative anecdote," a stylized answer to the questions they pose (1973: 1). Appropriations, then, make a strong statement in a bold way. To this extent, Shakespearean appropriation often comes close to that least valued form of literary appreciation, character criticism (Desmet 1992). Yet acts of appropriation are also responsive, in the sense intended by Bakhtin (1990) when he calls the ethical dimension among dialogic texts "answerability," so that every "response" of one text to another also renders that discourse "responsible."

On the other hand, as Lisa S. Starks shows when she subjects Kenneth Branagh and his version of *Hamlet* to the hermeneutics of suspicion, the most resolutely a-theoretical statements are subject to the most interesting theoretical readings. Starks's finely nuanced account of the literary genealogy that links the filmed *Hamlet*s of Kenneth Branagh, Franco Zeffirelli, and Laurence Olivier points to the complex relation between theory and practice in Shakespearean appropriation. Because Branagh's film records his resistance to Olivier's placement of Shakespeare's play within psychoanalytic discourse, Branagh's ironically becomes the most repressed of the filmed *Hamlet*s.

Although performance and film criticism have emerged as scholarly fields in their own right, it is important to recognize performance as a form of appropriation. Chatterjee and Singh point to the fact that identity is always derived, but also performed (Butler 1990). In the case of the Bengali actor Addy, the formulation of a "hybrid" identity offered, at least momentarily, a "way out" of cultural fantasies about the Moor and his relation to the rhetoric of empire. To the extent that appropriation is a performance of identity, it offers possibilities for cracking the codes of ideology and provides glimpses of realities that as yet have no name.

III Shakespeare's future

Gary Taylor's "Afterword" to *Shakespeare and Appropriation* predicts the demise of big-time Shakespeare. Taylor does not think that the diminution of Shakespeare's cultural influence is a bad thing: it makes room for other writers, other forms of entertainment, other takes on life. But "Shakespeare" and "Appropriation," at least as a small-time activity, remain closely linked by more than the weak conjunction "and" in this book's title.

Probably the most vigorous trading in Shakespeare's cultural capital still goes on in schools and universities; and despite the intransigence of institutions, the promise of small-time Shakespeare, specifically as an antidote to the ills of big-time Shakespeare, lies within the educational system. Students have always found a way to circumvent the reigning wisdom. Back in 1887, *The Girl's Own Paper* sponsored a contest, asking its young readers to submit essays about "My Favorite Heroine from Shakespeare." In reporting the results, the contest organizers admitted that Portia, "the lady Lawyer," was hands-down the girls' own favorite. To their chagrin, Shakespeare's "exquisite" tragic heroines had far fewer partisans ("Essay Writing" 1888: 381). Should it come as a surprise that young girls would vote for long life, success, and happy marriages over an early death and a gold commemorative statue, which is the fate of Shakespeare's Juliet? The contest organizers also complained about the number of essayists who strayed from the topic, using Portia as a pretext for feminist pronouncements. This, however, is the kind of activity that Martha Rozett (1994) calls "talking back to Shakespeare," a pedagogical practice that takes shape as both a challenge to tradition and a conversation among peers.

Shakespeare and Appropriation takes as its premise the usefulness of talking back to Shakespeare. It includes students as well as Shakespeareans in the audience that it attempts to reach, and either grounds its discussion in texts that we hope will remain readily available or makes available texts and readings to which students would probably lack access. References to Shakespeare's plays are marked in the essays and generally keyed to the *Norton Shakespeare*, which is rapidly becoming the classroom standard for post-secondary Shakespeare courses, at least in the United States. As Martin Orkin's (1998) recent essay on Shakespeare's continued influence in the educational system of South Africa might suggest, we not only need to talk back to Shakespeare, but also to widen the conversation to include more discussants from beyond the shores of England and North America.

The importance of Shakespearean appropriation in the classroom, perhaps the smallest of small-time Shakespeare, is suggested by Tom Stoppard and Marc Norman's *Shakespeare in Love* (1998). There are some jokes aimed at Shakespeare scholars, but others that anyone who has survived the ninth grade in the United States can enjoy. Gwyneth Paltrow's nurse seems to have stepped right out of Franco Zeffirelli's *Romeo and Juliet*, which despite its brief moment of nudity, has become a school staple in the U.S. In one of the film's cleverest scenes, Viola and Shakespeare meet at her balcony to parody not just the balcony scene from *Romeo and Juliet*, but specifically Zeffirelli's staging of the scene. *Shakespeare in Love* offers a useful lesson in literary influence. In a puckish nod to Anti-Stratfordian zealots, we see that everyone, from Christopher Marlowe to the lovely Viola herself, writes Shakespeare's plays for him. Worse, the immortal Bard's beauties go through the same kind of painful revision that every student's essay must undergo. The first draft of Romeo and Juliet's farewell includes, after all, the anguished exchange: "It is the rooster. No, it is the owl" (parodying *Romeo and Juliet* 3.5.1–35). Finally, we see Shakespeare creating *ex nihilo* the worst of clichés when, after the boy actor who plays Juliet can no longer voice the part, Philip Henslowe counsels Shakespeare: "The show must ... you know. ..." "Go on!" is Shakespeare's profound rejoinder.

The small-time Shakespeare show also goes on. Terence Hawkes (1992), in a misunderstood phrase, says that Shakespeare does not mean; rather, "*we* mean *by* Shakespeare" (1992: 3). The point is not that Shakespeare has no meaning, but that because meaning changes with context, he has, if anything, more meanings than we can yet imagine. If big-time Shakespeare is in decline, his plays will continue to provide occasions for the impersonations and improvisations of small-time Shakespeare. *Shakespeare in Love* is not a radical film. Next to the intense responses to Shakespeare of a Paul Robeson, a Gloria Naylor, a Robert Browning, or a Sarah Siddons, it will seem trivial. But the film does remind us that culture is not sacrosanct. Playing (around with) Shakespeare can still be done for fun, as well as for profit.

Part 1

Appropriation in theory

1

Alas, poor Shakespeare! I knew him well

IVO KAMPS

Not all the water in the rough rude sea
Can wash the balm from an anointed king.

(William Shakespeare, *Richard II*)

Mistah Kurtz – he dead.

(T. S. Eliot, "The Hollow Men")

Sometime in 1790, William Cowper composed his "Stanzas on the Late Indecent Liberties Taken with the Remains of the Great Milton." "Ill fare the hands," Cowper writes, "that heav'd the stones / Where Milton's ashes lay! / That trembled not to grasp his bones, / And steal his dust away" (1926: 399). A small stone in St. Giles, Cripplegate, still marks the spot where Milton was buried. But the poet's body is no longer there:

> In the eighteenth century, drunk after a party, some "gay young blades" dug up the body and pulled it to bits. Hair, teeth, fingers, ribs, and leg-bones were said to have been peddled by relic-mongers. So, the last remains of [England's most famous Puritan poet] suffered the fate of a Catholic saint.
>
> (Wilson 1983: 259)

Six years later, in 1796, a group of workmen dug a vault next to the grave of Shakespeare in Holy Trinity and reported that when they accidentally "opened one side of the poet's tomb," they "found nothing except a hollow space where the coffin may have lain" (Hamilton 1985: 4).[1] Had Shakespeare fallen victim to grave robbers as well? "Cvrst be he that moves my bones" – so reads the playwright's gravestone. Did he fear grave robbers and relic mongers, or was he trying to ward off the sexton, who would occasionally remove skeletons to the "bone house" to make room for fresh corpses? We may never know, but that Shakespeare was acutely aware of the ironic and violent fate a poet's body might suffer is certain. In *Julius Caesar*, for instance, Cinna the Poet is torn to shreds by an angry mob, first because the crowd believes him to be one of the conspirators, but ultimately for his bad verses. In the current debate over critical appropriations of Shakespeare, the connection between the poet's body and the reception of his verses is quite suggestive because the anxiety over the mutilation and destruction of the literal body has its corollary in today's anxiety over the appropriation of the literary body.

In 1990, Alvin Kernan, a distinguished and widely respected Renaissance scholar, announced the death of literature in a book that received favorable reviews in the *Times Literary Supplement*, the *New York Times*, and other publications with wide circulation. From the reactions to *The Death of Literature*, it appears that many share its author's apprehension that literature, which was once the proud repository of much that was held sacred, valuable, and universal in society, has lost its viability in our present-day culture. Kernan points to several factors contributing to literature's demise in the postmodern era – television, a crumbling educational system, rampant relativism, and multiculturalism, to name just a few – but he also holds the current generation of literary critics responsible for literature's passing. The problem, as he sees it, is that structuralists, deconstructionists, cultural materialists, new historicists, Marxists, and feminists have "emptied out" literature "in the service of social and political causes that are considered more important than the texts themselves, to which the texts are, in fact, only means to a greater end" (Kernan 1990: 212). Like Richard Levin, Brian Vickers, Edward Pechter, Graham Bradshaw, and others who have taken issue with recent critical developments, Kernan does not deny that literary texts contain traces of past cultures, such as the oppression of women and class inequality. But he finds it impossible to envision how literature, when "stripped of any positive value" and viewed as "the instrument of oppression, furthering imperialism and colonialism, establishing male hegemony, suppressing any movement toward freedom from authority," can "be considered worth reading and interpreting" (213). Literature is dead, and all that is left are the type of "relic mongers" who sold Milton's hair, bones, and teeth for profit, or, in the uplifting words of Kernan, a bunch of Marxists, feminists, and other radicals who "fight" over "the right to identify the smells arising from the literary corpse" (5).

Has literature been emptied out of meaning and "positive value," only to be pressed into the service of what Graham Bradshaw demeaningly calls "ideological critique" (1993: 6–7)? Are today's critics irresponsible, self-absorbed "gay young blades" who pull the poet's body to bits and sell the remains? These kinds of questions are misleading: they misconstrue the locus of literary value and *modus operandi* of educational institutions. But they are asked so often by influential people reaching large audiences that we do well to entertain them seriously.[2] An American pundit like George Will, for instance, gets to announce in *Newsweek*, a publication that reaches an audience far beyond the sphere of academia, that "[c]riticism displaces literature and critics displace authors as bestowers of meaning" (1991: 72). The study of literature, Will promulgates, is reduced to sociology, and sociology "to mere ideological assertion." The ultimate goal of the radicals, as he sees it, is to discredit "the books and ideas that gave birth" to "Western Civilization." And because Will sees the ideas contained in literature as those that shape the "national mind" of the United States – what Will calls our nation's "real Constitution" – it is easy for anxious minds to link the death of literature to total anarchy and the end of civilization as we know it. George Will's panicked hyperbole goes so far as to announce that Lynne Cheney (then chairman of the National Endowment of the Humanities) had a more crucial role in our "domestic defense" than did her husband Dick Cheney, then Secretary of Defense. For, so says Will, the "foreign adversaries her husband, Dick, must keep at bay are less dangerous, in the long run, than the domestic forces with which she must deal" (72). What is more, this type of alarmist language is not unique to the far right. Harold Bloom, for instance, loudly echoed Will and, to a lesser extent, Kernan when he recently condemned political critics as "worse than the enemy [and as] desecraters of Shakespeare" (Bloom 1998a).

On the other hand, most of us would agree with George Will, and in fact insist, that there is an indisputable relationship between literature and society, and that critics and teachers play an integral role in the dynamic of that relationship. In the national mind, it seems that teachers and literary scholars are still revered. What is more, whatever respect accrues to those who teach against the critical and cultural grain is probably misplaced because much of it stems from university administrators and non-academics who still believe professors of literature to be time-honored guardians of transcendent wisdom and knowledge – they just do not know what we really do. But how long will even this misplaced trust continue if people start listening to Will, Kernan, Vickers, and like-minded voices who portray radical teachers as enemies of the people? Now it should be clear that Levin, Kernan, Pechter, and Bradshaw are well to the political left of Will. Their criticisms of the various new approaches are, for the most part, also more local, subtle, fair-minded, and sophisticated than Will's uninformed, wholesale condemnation of seemingly all members of the Modern Language Association. But their work is highly receptive to appropriation by anyone with an ax to grind against "dangerous" critical approaches and the current trends in English departments and universities.[3] For anxious minds, it is easy to (mis)read Richard Levin's attack on certain aspects of feminist criticism as an attack on feminism in general.[4] How big a step is it from there to Kernan's death of literature and from there to Will's decline of the national mind? A giant leap for some but only a teensy step for the George Wills, William Bennetts, and Allan Blooms – all of whom address vast audiences – of this world. How long will we last if we are portrayed as "killers of literature," as "grave robbers," and "desecraters of Shakespeare" in politically conservative election platforms? How long will literature last in institutions of higher education?

Depending on which conservative critics you read, radical critics are charged with interrogating, torturing, mutilating, and "distort[ing]" (Levin 1988: 136; see also Will 1991; Vickers 1993: 415) texts until they yield meanings that confirm the critics' political proclivities. In these accounts, enough violence is perpetrated to kill or, at the very least, to maim beyond recognition, the literary text of old. But that is of course only half the story. While Kernan brings to view literature's death, Vickers, Bradshaw, Will, and Levin insist that when the radical critics are done butchering the text, they reanimate it, not with the original life with which the author first infused his creation but with a false, ideological life (see also Levin 1990: 501 and 1997: 533; Vickers 1993: 415–16; Bradshaw 1993: 34–124; Will 1991). The radical critic thus emerges not merely as the mutilator and relic monger of literary bodies, but as a literary Dr. Frankenstein who stitches the mangled body back together and resuscitates it with political lightning to produce a counterfeit life.

Neither the grave-robber metaphor nor the Frankenstein metaphor is quite apt here because not even Kernan really believes that literature is teetering on the edge of the grave. (He is far too astute a scholar to waste his time on a corpse.)[5] What *is* dying is a brand of literary interpretation that has installed literature as the record of the greatest accomplishments of Western civilization. Kernan, it is clear, uses his "death of literature" rhetoric to create a sense of alarm, a feeling that unless right-minded people do something about those radical critical approaches now, we will soon have to do without literature. George Will amplifies this point to absurdity when he dubs radical critics the new enemy within. Kernan, therefore, is not so much giving the literary corpse its last rites as he is prematurely eulogizing literature in order to re-appropriate it for an out-of-fashion critical sensibility.

In the context of critical appropriation, Shakespeare's corpse/corpus therefore more closely resembles the corpse of philosopher and inventor Jeremy Bentham (1748–1832) than it does the mutilated body of Milton or the patched-up creature of Frankenstein. Bentham's bodily remains, which he donated to science when he died, are still on display in the foyer of University College, London (Bentham 1999a). The "skeleton is seated, wearing Bentham's everyday clothes, his wide-brimmed straw hat upon his [stuffed] head, and the faithful Dapple in his hand" (Costigan 1967: 25). He sits there, a stuffed and constant reminder of his own greatness and, by extension, of the greatness of the college that he helped found and that proudly displays him. What is more, according to one story, a video camera is permanently pointed at Bentham, so that every few minutes an image of his current state is posted on the World Wide Web. That Bentham's body is lifeless and relatively unchanging apparently does not eliminate the need to make it continuously available for mass appropriation. Indeed, this appears to be the point of a Website about Bentham (Bentham 1999b), which notes the irony that the inventor of the panopticon (a glass prison that allows for the continuous and complete surveillance of the inmate) could himself be the most closely observed person in the world. Now the story goes that as a yearly prank, students from a rival college steal Bentham's corpse, temporarily hide it, and claim it, and its cultural legacy, as their own. The body becomes temporarily unavailable. University College reclaims the body, which is returned in time, and so Bentham's corpse and legacy are passed back and forth with definite regularity. This passing back and forth, this annual reappropriation of the corpse, though it may be partly apocryphal, is nonetheless an apt metaphor for the Left–Right debate over who owns Shakespeare. Leftist criticism may not actually be agreeable to returning the stolen Shakespearean body to the traditionalists, nor may the traditionalists agree to the theft, but every time Jonathan Goldberg or Catherine Belsey goes after Levin, or Bradshaw goes after Greenblatt, or Levin goes after feminists, or Pechter goes after the Left and the Right, or Vickers goes after everybody, the Shakespearean body is circulated – is passed around freely – among the most fierce rival critics. Such circulation constitutes literary life.

Traditionalists could not be further off the mark when they accuse radical critics of killing Shakespeare, but it could make some sense if they were right. It requires no explanation why Shakespeare, who has been the property of a conservative intellectual elite for most of this century, should attract traditional scholars. But we may wonder why critics dedicated to profound social change would waste their time on an author who, in the work of some new historicists, is portrayed as an extension of the state apparatus and reproducer of the socio-political status quo. Clearly, if ideology is the central concern, then bourgeois, patriarchal, authoritarian Shakespeare promotes the wrong values. What is more, as Terry Eagleton has conceded on several occasions, a new reading of a Shakespeare play – no matter how radical – is not going to bring about the revolution. Why, then, not remove Shakespeare from the curriculum and replace him with authors who better suit radical agendas?

The question is naive, and the answer is simple: because Shakespeare serves radical critics just as well as he serves conservative ones. Shakespeare has accrued so much cultural capital over the years that all sides have equal need of him – professionally, politically, and financially.[6] To let conservatives "have" Shakespeare would be strategically stupid. A competent Marxist or feminist reading of his work instantly situates the critic at the heart of academic debate, in a place where not only Shakespeareans but literary scholars of all fields converge. Likewise, a conservative critic who wishes his or her views disseminated among the largest possible literary audience is most likely to achieve that aim with a study connected to Shakespeare, who remains the most widely read author. The list of scholars – radical and non-radical – who boast Shakespeare as the centerpiece of their career is long and growing longer every day. Shakespeare is where the "money" is – sometimes quite literally. When, as an ambitious graduate student, I edited *Shakespeare Left and Right* for Routledge Press, one of my professors was quite taken aback by the size of my advance. He wrote to Oxford University Press and asked why he was getting less for his new book on Oscar Wilde than his student was getting for a mere essay collection. I thought it was a good question. The Oxford editor answered simply: Shakespeare.

Shakespeare's centrality in our universities is, of course, partly driven by his centrality in our culture, where his name carries tremendous weight and where he is still held up as an icon of good taste, cultural refinement, and intellectual ability (see Bristol 1990 and 1996; Taylor 1989). In 1989, to use a particularly silly yet instructive example, the Prince of Wales used Hamlet's "To be or not to be" soliloquy to demonstrate the appalling decline of the English language from Shakespeare's day to the present. In an Associated Press article, the Prince rewrites the soliloquy in what (he thinks) is modern slang:

> Well, frankly, the problem as I see it
> At this moment is whether I
> Should just lie down under all this hassle
> And let them walk all over me,
> Or, whether I should just say: "OK,
> I get the message," and do myself in.
> I mean, let's face it, I'm in a no-win
> Situation, and quite honestly,
> I'm so stuffed up to here with the whole
> Stupid mess that, I can tell you, I've just
> Got a good mind to take the quick way out.
> That's the bottom line. The only problem is:
> What happens if I find that when I've bumped
> Myself off, there's some kind of a, you know,
> All that mystical stuff about when you die,
> You might find you're still – know what I mean?
> (Charles 1989)

We may wonder in precisely what part of the British Empire Charles's rendition of Shakespeare passes for "slang," but the more important point is that the Prince of Wales can call on Shakespeare to chastise young people's speech. It apparently eludes Charles entirely that no one in Shakespeare's time – including Shakespeare himself – would have expressed him or herself in daily life as Hamlet does.

Indeed, Shakespeare is called on to underwrite all types of projects, even those that already bear his name. On the back of the box of Kenneth Branagh's production of *Hamlet*, the film is advertised as "Shakespeare's greatest creation in its entirety." The claim is, of course, false because Branagh's script is a conflation of the quarto and folio texts and is therefore not "Shakespeare's creation" as such. However, the need to have Shakespeare authorize the Hollywood film is powerful: it simply sounds much better to speak of "Shakespeare's greatest creation" than of Branagh's conflation.

The cultural power that sustains the type of claim made for Branagh's video and by Prince Charles in the newspaper beguiles many readers, including academics who have otherwise learned to resist unabashed bardolatry.[7] We could discuss here the incredible number of books published on Shakespeare each year, the number of journals solely devoted to Shakespeare criticism, the number of English departments that still require a class in Shakespeare for all their majors, or the fact that Terry Eagleton, although a Marxist critic, fully understands that even a slight book on Shakespeare is far more marketable than a tome on the politically more radical Brecht or Milton. Even those who would argue against Shakespeare's centrality and special status cannot help but bask in his cultural aura. A fictional story illustrates the significance of Shakespeare's name best. In his novel *Changing Places*, David Lodge has a group of academics play a game, which goes as follows: everyone has to confess before the group the most canonical work he or she has not read, and the player who names the most canonical text wins the game. Of course, the contest pits against one another two extremely potent academic impulses: the desire to appear well-read before one's peers and the desire to outdo one's peers. One particularly competitive untenured Assistant Professor confesses that he has not read *Hamlet*. Needless to say, he wins the game, but shortly thereafter is turned down for tenure. The point of the story is that in the body of canonical literature no text is more canonical than *Hamlet*, and to confess ignorance of it disqualifies the Assistant Professor in the eyes of his tenured colleagues from a permanent position among the academic initiated. He has not claimed the requisite portion or relic of the Shakespearean body; he has not partaken of the academic Eucharist and is not privy to the mysteries of transubstantiation, of turning the literary body into academic capital. As Harold Bloom observes in his brand new tome on Shakespeare, Hamlet's "effect upon the world's culture is incalculable. After Jesus, Hamlet is the most cited figure in Western consciousness; no one prays to him, but no one evades him for long either" (1998b: xix). As Bloom concludes, "If any author has become a mortal God, it must be Shakespeare" (3). Lodge's Assistant Professor learns this the hard way.

To study Shakespeare professionally is to become initiated; it is to learn the secret handshake, to join the old boys' club (which now counts a significant number of powerful women among its members), to become associated with our culture's most potent literary name, and to have access instantly to the vast network of institutions and people that have been created around the name of Shakespeare. In time this may change, but I do not see any evidence of it changing just yet; feminists, Marxists, and cultural materialists seem very much at home these days in the reading rooms of the Folger Shakespeare Library – and I do not see any of them trying to tear the place down, the way Protestant reformers smashed Catholic icons, nor close it down as Stalin did the churches. At four o'clock you might see radical critics sipping their tea without so much as a word about plots to finish off literature and destroy the national mind. In fact, they might be discussing the new Norton edition of the collected works of Shakespeare, a text designed specifically for classroom use by a small group of Marxists, feminists, and new historicists, which – the truth be told – is a monument to the playwright's staying power and cultural cachet. Clearly, the name Shakespeare has such resonance and potency, such power to enhance whatever agenda or product we are pushing (be it the revolution or Starkist Tuna),[8] that it cannot be left unexploited, unappropriated – by the Left or the Right.

Is literary studies, then, simply the *Kampfplatz* in which only the fittest critics will stand after the war? Probably not, though there will be some casualties. Every reading of a Shakespeare play, we need to keep reminding ourselves, is already an appropriation, an interpretation that is limited only by the constraints that our academic institutions, journals, and university presses place on it. And the interpretive models we use are so varied, so inconsistent, so incomplete, and so contradictory, that in and of themselves they do not drive academic readers of Shakespeare into any compelling direction when trying to determine the meaning of the plays. Though at times literary criticism has aspired to scientific status, protocols for reading do not even begin to resemble the rules of scientific experimentation. There is no indication that literary criticism is moving any closer to "the" meaning(s) of Shakespeare, nor is there an indication that this is criticism's goal (to have such a goal could spell professional suicide). In other words, at any given historical moment we are working within a certain range of academically and culturally possible and acceptable interpretations. There is no doubt that as institutions, journals, presses, and our culture change, there will be no future interpretation of Shakespeare so at odds with the text that it would be unacceptable in some as yet unimaginable context. The other side of that coin is, of course, that whatever interpretations of Shakespeare are currently imaginable and acceptable are, necessarily, just that: currently imaginable readings of Shakespeare. It probably will not be of much comfort to conservatives today, but there is no doubt in my mind that the wisdom of Greenblatt, Eagleton, Belsey, Dollimore, and Howard will some day – if they are lucky – have the same status now afforded to A. C. Bradley, E. M. W. Tillyard, Cleanth Brooks, and Muriel Bradbrook.

What becomes clear here is that in the long run the body of Shakespeare – his *corpus*, and what it means or does not mean – is not particularly important. It is more important *that* one writes about Shakespeare than *what* one writes about him. This is not to say that critics at any given moment do not argue with a degree of sincerity about the meaning of the Shakespearean text. They do, for this is a necessary part of the convenient fiction that meaning matters. But over time, Shakespeare is far more important to criticism as a conduit, as a uniquely powerful academic interface, as that part of the academic body through which the most theoretical innovation and political energy course. Shakespeare's name provides the critic with a forum; it is the occasion for literary criticism. The literary body has become largely inconsequential: it is present but often goes unnoticed; it is, as Kernan suggests, a means to something else – and it *always* was.

Reading the current Shakespeare wars, therefore, is a lot like watching Hamlet and Laertes struggling in the grave to prove who loved Ophelia most (*Hamlet* 5.1). Or it is like watching Lucrece's father and Collatine "weep with equal strife / Who should weep most, for daughter or for wife" (*Rape of Lucrece* 1791–92); "The one doth call her his, the other his, / Yet neither may possess the claim they lay" (1793–94). Dead Ophelia and dead Lucrece lie by as the men rage on, and the women's presence is incidental to the drama at best; Ophelia's corpse is the occasion upon which Hamlet and Laertes try to reclaim their reputations as honorable and loving gentlemen; and the corpse of selfless Lucrece, in death, is primed for appropriation by father and husband because her unselfish suicide goes a long way toward cleansing *their* reputations, which were tarnished by her rape.[9] In death, both women have tremendous exchange value; like the supposedly dead Hero in *Much Ado About Nothing*, they will appear "[m]ore moving-delicate, and full of life, / ... / Than when [they] lived indeed" (*Much Ado* 4.1.227, 229). Material bodies have become pure exchange value, markers of cultural capital, opportunities for meaningful appropriation. Shakespeare may serve as the single most powerful signifier in literary culture, but it is culture that inscribes and reinscribes his name – that *names* and *re*names his name – and that gives local habitation and a name to his corpus.

Shakespeare's literary body, therefore, is neither the desecrated body of Milton nor the stuffed head and dressed-up skeleton of Bentham; rather, it resembles the chaste but absent bodies of Ophelia and Lucrece and the chaste body-in-hiding of Hero. In a twisted reading of Donne's "Holy Sonnet 14", we might suggest that, like Donne's speaker, Shakespeare's text must be battered, broken, ravished, and violated if it is to be "chaste" and "free." Many scholars have observed that the scarcity of information about the historical Shakespeare (who apparently is absent from his grave), as well as his "absence" from the moral universe of his plays, make Shakespeare supremely receptive to interpretation and appropriation. Indeed, as Michael Bristol puts it, it is "Shakespeare's radically disembodied and culturally promiscuous character" that assures his privileged place in our world today (1996: 90). Shakespeare's promiscuity, however, does not appear to affect the "chastity" of his reputation. On this point, the similarity between Shakespeare and his female characters breaks down. When physically violated (Lucrece), thought to have been violated (Hero), or might-as-well-have-been violated (Ophelia), each female character loses her reputation as chaste. Circulation amounts to loss of chastity. Lucrece understands that if she is to minimize the damage done to Collatine's name, she must irrevocably remove herself from circulation. The only way to "prove" her chastity is to kill herself. Likewise, Ophelia, though she may not have slept with Hamlet, is no longer fit for social circulation because her intense emotional commitment to the prince has left her severely damaged. She withdraws from Elsinore society, first through her madness, and then through suicide. Even Hero, who is falsely accused, must temporarily be taken out of social circulation and proclaimed dead if her chastity is to be (re)proven. The body of Shakespeare's text, on the other hand, seems to circulate endlessly without the playwright losing his reputation, no matter how unwholesome the meanings his texts seem to yield. No matter how many hands ravish it, the poet's name remains chaste. The reason for the continued "chastity" of Shakespeare's reputation is, of course, that in our competitive or adversarial climate critics overwhelmingly hold each other responsible for meanings "found" in the plays. Curiously, no one blames Shakespeare for yielding so many meanings; no one blames Shakespeare for meaning so much.[10]

Despite this elusiveness and the eclectic character of literary criticism, I do not mean to suggest that whatever is, is right; rather, that whatever is, is – and will be as long as it falls within the current academic or professional paradigm. When the paradigm shifts, what is will be no more, although it may continue as literary history, as fodder for new generations of critics to discover how previous generations were shaped by history. What critical paradigm are we currently living in? If we believe Kernan, we are entering literature's twilight; he speaks of literature's imminent "[c]ultural obsolescence" (1990: 10). Why does a preoccupation with feminist or Marxist or psychoanalytic issues spell the doom of literature as a "positive value"? When Kernan refers to critics who conceive of literature "as suppressing any movement toward freedom from authority" (213), he is talking about a narrow, Greenblattian version of "containment" that has been under severe attack from cultural materialists, feminists, and even from some of Greenblatt's own new historicist followers.[11] In truth, few critics today view literature as a simple extension of the state apparatus, though Kernan implies that most of them do. Surely, most radical critics would insist that they teach Shakespeare in a way that leads toward freedom and away from authority. Indeed, if, as Kernan admits, literature "often treated women in at times contemptuous, nearly always a patronizing fashion" (212), then how can it be harmful when scholars, teachers, and students discuss the texts in those terms to learn about the history of gender relations? Why does this, as Kernan claims, put Shakespeare and literature in general "out of business" (212)?

What is more, my experience in the classroom suggests that no critical movement has done more than feminism to save Shakespeare from obsolescence. How can Shakespeare possibly stay vital to new generations of students unless his name can be invoked powerfully in the context of current concerns? For, as I suggested earlier, it is not the "ideological content" of Shakespeare's works, but their "symbolic capital" (to borrow a phrase from John Guillory) that makes them so well suited to the reproduction of institutional and social relations – and, of course, to the succession of professional careers that flourish in our institutions of higher learning (see Guillory 1993: ix).

It is ironic and self-serving that some conservatives who have seen their own careers and standing in the profession weakened by new methods of interpretation should accuse those who made their mark in the 1970s, 1980s, and 1990s of "rampant careerism" (Sabin 1997: 86; Kernan 1997 quotes Sabin: 5; Vickers 1993). Indeed, if they could look past their longing for the past, they might see more clearly that it is not literature's obsolescence, but their own, that is at stake here. Indeed, if the traditionalists wish to postpone their professional obsolescence, they should not focus so much on the imminent demise of literature, tradition, Western Civilization, and Shakespeare. They should not cry foul when new generations of academics invent new Shakespeares and appropriate his name for *their* causes. Nor should they pretend that new generations of critics are killing or dismembering the Shakespeare who once upon a time we all supposedly shared and loved. Instead they should realize that if they want to continue to claim for a little while longer a viable place in the current critical paradigm, they must, in the final analysis, make their Shakespeares compete in the academic marketplace with all the alternative Shakespeares out there – because this is the tradition of Shakespeare criticism, a tradition of competition and appropriation, one of newfangledness and inevitable obsolescence.

But it is not merely personal and professional bitterness over where English studies may be heading that grieves traditionalists. They do not seem to understand what literary "value" is and how it functions in the university and in society. They appear to believe that literary works possess values in and of themselves, and that those values can be taught in the universities to successive generations of students in direct support of a process of social and cultural reproduction. Value, in turn, is based on literary meaning, which, they believe, is pretty much fixed (by authorial intention, notions of universal truth, human nature, and what have you), though it may be open to subtle interpretations by well-educated, sensitive, commonsensical, generally like-minded critics who can reasonably differ – as gentlemen sometimes do. Moreover, it is the critic's solemn task and professional duty to teach meanings and their value in such a way that they aid in the reproduction of social relations and, in the words of George Will, the "constitution" of the "national mind." What they do not grasp is that literary value is "not a property of the work itself but of its transmission" (within the social/educational system), and that "[t]he real social process [at work here] is the reproduction not of values but of *social* relations" (Guillory 1993: 55–56). What actual "value" or "meaning" a critic might locate in a literary text does not really change the way the school or university operates in society. To argue that the witches are the heroines of *Macbeth*, that *The Tempest* participates in discourses of imperialism, or that *King Lear* dramatizes the decline of feudalism and the emergence of a vicious middle class does not constitute an intervention in the structural operations of the institution. The most deconstructive reading of Shakespeare does *not* alter the university hierarchy or the tenure process in North American universities, though it may affect who gets tenure and who does not.

What needs to be clear is that the concept of literary value is "not grounded in an 'institution of criticism,' as is sometimes said. Criticism is not an institution but a disciplinary discourse inhabiting a historically specific educational institution" (Guillory 1993: 56). Criticism is an expression of specific currents, codes, demands, and needs within the institution. Educational institutions, therefore, do not depend on any particular literary value or meaning, just on the continuation of concepts of value and meaning in general. In this century, the patterns in the relationship between literary value, the university, and society suggest that as long as smart, innovative, and articulate critics lay claim to finding meaning in Shakespeare's plays, and as long as the institution continues to embrace that meaning as its cultural capital – which it must do because it is its *raison d'être* – then the show will go on, much as it did (of course with small changes) prior to the supposed revolution.

While we are often invited to believe that universities exist foremost to nourish, improve, and reproduce society (the university where I did my graduate work has "In service of the nation" as its motto), we cannot ignore Guillory's potent claim that "[i]nstitutions of reproduction succeed by taking as their first object not the reproduction of social relations but the reproduction of the institution itself" (1993: 57). There is nothing sinister about this: institutions quickly develop an internal logic and defenses to protect their "being" from the outside world and secure their survival. In sum, if (1) "value" is not inherent in works of literature (but is a product of their transmission), if (2) value is not grounded in literary criticism (because "[c]riticism is not an institution but a disciplinary discourse inhabiting a historically specific educational institution" [Guillory 1993: 56]), and if (3) educational institutions are inclined first and foremost to reproduce themselves, then, clearly, Kernan and company are trying to dispose of the wrong corpse when, in a misguided effort to "save" literature and society, they try to bury scholars who are committed to finding a different sort of value in the texts they study.

Literature will continue to have value as long as new generations of critics produce that value. But this is not entirely up to the academic community, or to the editorial boards of journals and university presses who publish criticism. It should be pointed out that if in the future literature is to occupy a privileged space in society, then English professors must be perceived as possessing and safeguarding what society recognizes as cultural capital. In the long run, arguments like Guillory's about the origins of literary value and the constitution of literary capital are not going to hold water if conservative pundits are successful in persuading the politicians and the general public that the leftists, feminists, and poststructuralists are killing literature and destroying the very fabric of our society. This should give us pause. If the demonization of the current recontextualization and politicization of literary classics removes their aura of cultural capital in the minds of parents, students, and politicians – if the consumer comes to believe fearmongers like George Will – then although this may take years, we can all start digging our graves.[12]

Note that the danger lies with the pundits and not with the students. The danger to literary value lies with the pundits because students are not easily swayed from their core beliefs by what goes on in the classroom. I just finished teaching *Paradise Lost* to a class of undergraduate English majors. I did my utmost to emphasize the controversial elements in Milton's theology and the problem, noted by many critics, of Milton's God. I suggested that the poem supports a reading of Milton's God as petty, vindictive, needy, uncaring, undramatic, illogical, violent, cruel, and boring. After the term, many students told me, or wrote in their evaluations, that our discussion of *Paradise Lost* had caused them to question aspects of their own Christian beliefs. But – and this is the point – to a person, they all insisted that our discussions ultimately reaffirmed and strengthened their Christian faith. If, as someone like George Will might think, I had been trying to transform my students into poststructuralist atheists, then it is quite apparent that I failed miserably. If this example is indicative of how students actually respond to atypical interpretations of texts, then this puts Kernan, Bloom, Vickers, Will *et al.* in a very odd position as they aim to save literature from the barbarians. For if most of our students do not see anything wrong with the way literature is taught, then literature continues to play a significant role in the university. But if the neo-conservative assault on new critical methods poisons the "national mind" – if parents and politicians are led to believe that all literature professors talk about is masturbation, homosexuality, imperialism, the death of the author, political oppression, racial oppression, and the oppression of women, and that it is bad or wrong to talk about those things – then they, in an effort to save a conception of literature that made and defined their careers, are well on their way to destroying literature's cultural capital. Rather than accusing a whole generation of critics of being killers, desecraters, and relic mongers who fight over "the right to identify the smells arising from the literary corpse" (Kernan 1990: 5), traditionalists should understand that they themselves are part of a process that was true long before the emergence of Derrida, Foucault, feminism, new historicism, and cultural materialism, and continues to be true: "The struggle for cultural supremacy is a war to the death, a war fought over the dead" (Taylor 1996: 9).

Notes

1 What we should infer from this is unclear; the body may be buried more deeply, at a depth of 17 feet (as tradition has it), or it may have rotted away entirely. Or it may not be exactly under the current gravestone, which replaced the original one that had crumbled by the middle of the eighteenth century (Hamilton 1985: 4). It is also possible that the sexton disregarded the curse on the gravestone and tossed the poet's remains in the "bone house" to make room for a fresh corpse (4).

2 Gary Taylor accurately notes that "[l]iberal intellectuals in the West lost the culture wars of the 1980s in part because they surrendered the mechanisms of cultural selection to their opponents. They made no secret of their contempt for the public. ... [T]he academic establishment has increasingly separated itself from the rest of society. ... At academic conferences, in faculty lounges, a thousand sarcasms bloomed and died, while Allan Bloom's *The Closing of the American Mind*

and Joseph Campbell's *The Power of Myth* rode *The New York Times* best-seller list and conservatives in America, Canada, Great Britain, and Germany won election after election" (1996: 13).

3 It is perhaps unfair to lay this at the feet of Levin *et al.*, because they do not intentionally invite such appropriations, but these appropriations are an inevitable consequence of their labors.

4 I do not mean to suggest that Levin *et al.* should stop criticizing the new critical approaches – on the contrary, I believe that their work is often extremely valuable in fine-tuning Marxist and feminist and other approaches – but we should not kid ourselves into believing that their authorial intentions will surface in public discourse.

5 Less than five years after the publication of *The Death of Literature*, Kernan published a delightful book on Shakespearean performance at the Jacobean court (1995). Harold Bloom appears to share Kernan's mixture of bleakness and optimism. Bloom writes that Shakespeare may be the only canonical writer "that can survive the debasement of our teaching institutions, here and abroad. Every other great writer may fall away, to be replaced by the anti-elitist swamp of Cultural Studies. Shakespeare will abide" (1998b: 17).

6 I borrow the term "cultural capital" from Guillory who, in turn, gets it from French theorist Pierre Bourdieu: "First it is *linguistic* capital, the means by which one attains to a socially credentialed and therefore valued speech, otherwise known as 'Standard English.' And second, it is *symbolic* capital, a kind of knowledge-capital whose possession can be displayed upon request and which thereby entitles its possessor to the cultural and material rewards of the well-educated person" (Guillory 1993: ix). What Guillory is most interested in is who in our society has access to cultural capital and how it is distributed among different classes, or, to put it slightly differently, how "class determines whether and how individuals gain access to the means of literary production" (ix).

7 In his latest book, Bloom asserts that "High Romantic Bardolatry, now so much disdained in our self-defiled academics, is merely the most normative of the faiths that worship" Shakespeare (1998b: 3).

8 See Bristol 1990: 15.

9 My reading of *Lucrece* has been shaped by Kahn's (1995) fine essay on the poem. Likewise my comments on *Much Ado* are influenced by Cook's (1995) work.

10 There are, of course, isolated exceptions to this. See Linda Woodbridge 1991: 295.

11 "Containment" refers to the idea that "subversion" is not a legitimate threat to established power in society but a direct and necessary product of power, designed to underscore the rightness and legitimacy of that power, and is hence contained by it. See Greenblatt 1988: 21–65; also see Dollimore 1985: 2–18.

12 For an astute analysis of how critics use demonization to discredit one another, see Levin 1998.

2
Entry on Q

TERENCE HAWKES

I Et in Arcadia ego

The small crowd of locals was curious. None of them had seen a canoe launched on the river before. However, its two inhabitants seemed intrepid enough. Spurred less by pleasure than by the prospect of discovery, they committed themselves boldly to the stream. A long, meandering journey with much tedious pulling through reed beds lay ahead. But, on the second day, their efforts were rewarded:

> Beyond the barrier we looked to right and left, amazed. We had passed from a sluggish brook, twisting among water-plants and willows, to a pleasant, expanded river, flowing between wide lawns, by slopes of bracken, by the roots of gigantic trees – oaks, Spanish oaks, wych-elms, stately firs, sweet chestnuts, backed by filmy larch coppices.
>
> This was Arden, the Forest of Arden, actually Stoneleigh-in-Arden, and Shakespeare's very Arden.
>
> Actually, as we rested on our paddles, down to a shallow ahead – their accustomed ford no doubt – a herd of deer tripped daintily and charged across, splashing; first the bucks, in single file, then the does in a body. The very bed of Avon changes just here: the river now brawling by a shallow, now deepening, and anon sliding over slabs of sandstone. This (I repeat) is verily and historically

> Arden. We know that Arden – a lovely word in itself – was endeared to Shakespeare by scores of boyish memories; Arden was his mother's maiden name. I think it arguable of the greatest creative artists that, however they learn and improve, they are always trading on the stored memories of childhood. I am sure that, as Shakespeare turned the pages of Lodge's *Rosalynde* – as sure as if my ears heard him – he cried to himself, "Arden? This made to happen in a Forest of Arden, in France? But I have wandered in a Forest of Arden ten times lovelier; and, translated thither, ten times lovelier shall be the tale!" …
>
> … Now, in Stoneleigh Deer Park, in Arden, I saw the whole thing, as though Corin's crook moved above the ferns and Orlando's ballads fluttered on the boles. There was the very oak beneath which Jacques moralised on the deer – a monster oak, thirty-nine feet around (for I measured it) – not far above the ford across which the herd had splashed, its "antique roots" writhing over the red sandstone rock down to the water's brim. And I saw the whole thing for what the four important Acts of it really are – not as a drama, but as a dream, or rather a dreamy delicious fantasy, and especially a fantasy in colour.
>
> (Quiller-Couch 1918: 122–24)

The first casualty of this disturbing encounter is obviously its reporter's style. The sub-romantic fruitiness, those awkward "very's" and "actually's," the gauche suburban pastoralism of "filmy" coppices, "brawling" rivers, and the dire explanatory specters of mothers and childhood speak ominously of a naive, almost provincial sensibility and the impact upon it of a sudden, breathless arrival at the center of things. The "monster" oak, primly measured, the too-pat materialization of the herd of deer, the nudging reference to Jacques, may offer to defend the moralizing as somehow appropriate to such a splashy, orgasmic confrontation with the *fons et origo* of a whole culture. But we could be excused for thinking that the resultant "dreamy delicious fantasy" smacks more of *Rebecca of Sunnybrook Farm* than of *As You Like It*. It is hardly what one might expect from the King Edward VII Professor of English at the University of Cambridge.

II 'A babbled of green fields

Yet Sir Arthur Quiller-Couch (1863–1944), appointed to that position in 1912, was noted as much for his mellifluous style as for his

Liberal politics. Under the sobriquet "Q" he had earned his living as a journalist, popular novelist, and producer of *belles lettres* long before becoming an academic. Perhaps it shows. In the event, he would be only the second holder of the most prestigious – indeed, then, the sole – Chair of English at Cambridge, whose first incumbent, A. W. Verrall, a classicist, had died within months of his election. Modern academics can only peer wistfully at the Arden within whose leafy glades such an appointment was feasible. For, as John Gross points out, in 1912 Q effectively had no learned publications to his credit and no experience of university teaching. In fact, politics seems to have played the largest part in the matter. According to Gross and E. M. W. Tillyard, the Liberal Prime Minister Asquith had originally intended to offer the job to Sir Herbert Grierson, recent editor of the poems of John Donne, but had allowed Lloyd George to persuade him that a post of such eminence ought rather to be a Party appointment (Tillyard 1958: 39; Gross 1973: 205–09).

Q filled that bill, without doubt. He had worked long and hard for the Liberal Party in his native Cornwall for many years, holding most of the major public offices: County Councillor, Alderman, Justice of the Peace and, ultimately, Mayor of Fowey. He was, it might be said, to the manner born. The Liberal Party had always felt itself to embody a kind of essential Englishness: something compounded of, and supported by, elements George Dangerfield nominates as "Free Trade, a majority in Parliament, the ten commandments, and the illusion of Progress" (1961: viii). Successors, in the British political tradition, to the Whigs, groups of politicians began to refer to themselves as Liberals in the 1830s. However, the first truly Liberal administration was not formed until 1868, when Gladstone became Prime Minister. Under Gladstone, Liberalism flourished, combining a commitment to human "freedom" and "progress" – that is, Free Trade, private enterprise, and broad-based political reform – together with a belief in the value of individual personality and social justice, tempered by a mistrust of the powers of the state and the notion that wars should be "fought at a distance and if possible in the name of God" (7). Split in 1886 over Irish Home Rule, the Party nevertheless regrouped as a credible force and finally proved convincingly victorious in the election of 1906 when, under Sir Henry Campbell-Bannerman and Asquith, it proceeded to place even greater emphasis on human rights and social and political reform than Gladstone had done. The Liberal Party remained the major party in opposition to the Conservatives until

1918, when it began effectively to be supplanted by the Labour Party.

Its terminal decline arguably dates from 1910: a year which, marked by the death of King Edward VII and an ominous appearance of Halley's Comet, brought compensatory highlights in the form of the no less bright star of Q's knighthood. Awarded primarily as a recognition of his political activities, the honor virtually confirmed him as one of his country's leading embodiments of Liberalism. On returning to Fowey from the investiture, he was greeted by the town brass band playing "He's A Fine Old English Gentleman." What further qualification, it might be asked, could be required – at least in 1912 – of a Professor of English?

Nevertheless, to quote Dangerfield again, the year 1910 also "stands out against a peculiar background of flame. For it was in 1910 that fires long smouldering in the English spirit suddenly flared up, so that by the end of 1913 Liberal England was reduced to ashes" (1961: viii). However questionable a thesis of general conflagration might be, there can be little doubt that a succession of incendiary outbreaks lit the national sky. Amongst them were the Party's momentous and successful battle to curb the powers of the House of Lords, a victory from which it never recovered; the prospect of a rebellion in Ulster as a result of movements toward Irish Home Rule; increasing militancy of the suffragette movement; and a gathering momentum of strikes marking growing trade union unrest and the prospect of revolutionary working-class alliances. The war which began in 1914 merely postponed the resolution of these developments, heralding a new, harsher world in which inherited Liberal visions and imaginings would be forever swept away. In the England that emerged from its Armageddon, there remained only the ghostly memory of what Dangerfield describes as "that other England, the England where the Grantchester church clock stood at ten to three, where there was Beauty and Certainty and Quiet, and where nothing was real" (1961: 441–42). By then, Q's only son was also dead.

III Other Eden

Confronted, as it were, with things dying, the Liberal professor committed himself to things new-born. The full impact of Quiller-Couch's appointment in Cambridge was to prove momentous. Whether or not his personal contribution should be seen in terms of "complaisance" or "acquiescence," there can be no doubt of his crucial involvement in the machinations, deliberations, and haphazard events which in 1917 resulted in the establishment of "English Literature, Life and Thought" as an academic subject there (Mulhern 1979: 21, 22).[1] Opposition was considerable, and his support and commitment were vital to the project.

He had, after all, been enlisted in a specific cause. Viscount Rothermere, the newspaper proprietor who endowed the King Edward VII Chair, had made clear his requirement that, in promoting the subject of English Literature, the professor should be committed to "treat this subject on literary and critical rather than on philological and linguistic lines" (Tillyard 1958: 38). In the event, Quiller-Couch's – and the country's – anti-German prejudices, fuelled by the war, proved decisive in creating a climate appropriate to the exclusion of "Teutonic" philological studies from its sphere, ending what the crusading J. Churton Collins had already denounced as literature's "degrading vassalage to Philology" (cited in Tillyard 1958: 31). Almost at a stroke, this stratagem gave "English" at Cambridge, and worldwide, some of the characteristic lineaments it retains to this day: its project to function not as a narrow academic specialism, mired in the minutiae of Old and Middle English phonetics, but as the basis of a general humane education, engaging freely with the pressures of the modern world and valuing and promoting the individual human experience of them (31–32).[2] The "fine old English gentleman" turned out to be not only one of the founding fathers of a hugely expanding field of study, but also instrumental in imposing on it a form and purpose which most of its native-language students in the world can still – however dimly – recognize. Faced with the death of Liberalism, Q assisted at the birth of a subject which, certainly in its early Cambridge manifestation, and despite a complex history and the counter-claims of some of the younger firebrands involved, could be said to have embodied many of Liberalism's central, defining principles (81–92).[3]

Within the overall structure of the Tripos (the Cambridge examination for the B.A. honors degree), Q had a particular favorite scheme, one which, when realized, lent the subject an even more distinctive flavor. This was a paper on what he called "the English Moralists." Asked, by objecting colleagues, which authors he intended by this, his usual retort, according to Tillyard, was "a lyrical outburst on the glories of their writings issuing into a roll-call of the great names: 'Hooker – Hobbes – Locke – Berkeley – Hume'; and ending with an exhausted 'my God,' as emotion got the better of him" (1958: 108).[4] The "Englishness" which such texts (perhaps surprisingly, in the case of Hume) could apparently claim to contribute to moral philosophy seems to be the issue. John Gross's judgment that Q's "whole conception of English literary history was bound up with a romantic notion of thatched-and-timbered Englishry" finds a certain confirmation here as well as in the passage quoted above (Gross 1973: 206). In fact, it might even be said that Arden – located in the middle of England by the intrepid expedition of Q and his friend – crystallizes into a sunlit memory of a pre-war Liberal England sadly regretted, damply yearned for.

Shakespeare has long been the fatal Cleopatra of those in thrall to such visions and one of the projects to which Q firmly committed himself at Cambridge was his joint editorship (with John Dover Wilson) of the "New Shakespeare," to be published by the University Press. Superseding the older "Cambridge Shakespeare," this was to be a series of single-volume editions of the plays, based on A.W. Pollard's "new scientific method – critical Shakespearean bibliography," on Percy Simpson's views of "play-house punctuation," and on Sir Edward Maunde Thompson's ideas about Shakespeare's handwriting. Thus armed, the editors hoped at times to be able to "creep into the compositor's skin and catch glimpses of the manuscript through his eyes" and in consequence begin to penetrate to the heart of the "great national Poet." The project began in 1921 with an edition of *The Tempest* (Quiller-Couch and Dover Wilson [eds] 1921: xxix–xxx, xv).

IV No holds bard

The "New Shakespeare" edition of *As You Like It* appeared in 1926.[5] Q's "Introduction" deploys all his characteristic (if by now slightly dated) charm. Despite that, it almost founders on submerged metaphors in which the absence of Quarto editions of the play and the fact that its only text is the First Folio of 1623 seem to link the editing of the New Shakespeare with his early exploratory probes down the river Avon to Stoneleigh. He begins:

> In *As You Like It* – the very title is auspicious – an Editor may take holiday and, after winning through Quarto thicket after thicket obedient to the Folio order, feel that he has earned a right to expatiate, enjoy his while in Arden and fleet the time carelessly.
> (Quiller-Couch and Dover Wilson 1926: vii)

After a perfunctory discussion of sources, he moves rapidly to a consideration of the play's central focus, the very English Forest of Arden. The Englishness of the location, itself the source of Shakespeare's "native wood-magic" (x) ensures that Arden is "entirely different from Lodge's forest of Ardennes" (x) and Q's enraptured account of the place seems to find in that a license for breathtaking forays into biography:

> This Arden, on the north bank of Avon, endeared to him by its very name (name of his mother), had been the haunt where he caught his first "native wood-notes wild," as the path by the stream had been his, known to this day as the Lovers' Walk.
>
> (Quiller-Couch and Dover Wilson 1926: x)

The evocation of local habitation and name seems to incite the now familiar theme-park frothing:

> Time has softened down Stoneleigh-in-Arden to a stately park, with Avon streaming through; but the deer are there yet, and the ford that "Makes sweet music with the enamelled stones" over which the deer splash – bucks leading in single file, does following in a small cohort; and there are the gnarled oaks with antique roots twisting through the bank. ... [W]ith no stretch of imagination, we can still see the crooks of Phebe and Silvius moving, beribboned ...
>
> (x–xi)

The position constructed for the reader is quite clear: "To put it shortly, he who knows Arden has looked into the heart of England and heard the birds sing in the green midmost of a moated island" (xi). Somewhat precariously (England's insular status having always been more metaphorical than geographical) the First Folio text even begins to take on some of the characteristics of the "moated island" itself. Imbued with an essential Englishness, it remains, so far as foreigners are concerned, wholly sequestered: "Herein possibly lies the reason why, of all Shakespeare's plays, *As You Like It* has never crossed the Channel, to be understood by Continent sanctioners, readers, critics" (xi).

Of course, the play readily constructs for us its own Arden of manifest textuality: poems appear on trees, there are books in the running brooks. But Q's metaphor smugly intensifies Shakespeare's, presenting Arden as a kind of hermetic, English page, intelligible only to natives and impenetrable to lesser breeds without the Law.

As a result, "our point is here that continental critics who have not seen the phenomenon or heard the birds singing through it, cannot understand this particular play" (Quiller-Couch and Dover Wilson 1926: xi). Unsurprisingly, the German critics find themselves particularly disabled. In his "General Introduction," Q had spoken scornfully of the "volume of laudation" surrounding Shakespeare, swelling and rising "ever with a German guttural increasing in self-assertion at the back of the uproar" (Quiller-Couch and Dover Wilson 1921: xvi–xvii). In the case of *As You Like It*,

> The Germans especially are like the Wise Men of Gotham, "all at sea in a bowl". They are sailing, in a bowl, on perilous seas of which they possess no chart. Fortunately for the mirth of Shakespeare's countrymen they now and again cancel each other out.
> (Quiller-Couch and Dover Wilson 1926: xi)

Q then pillories passages from "the solemn Ulrici and the solemn Gervinus" (xi) side by side, inviting our derisive recognition that "neither one nor the other has a notion of what he is talking about" (xiii).

Echoes of the war clearly inform such antics, but the pulse of Q's involvement in the construction of "English" as an academic subject, thankfully free from Teutonic distractions, is also palpable. Arden's "English" character thus takes on a slightly alarming double dimension as nationhood and academic subject merge. What need have we of foreign critics when, in this play, or syllabus, Shakespeare "has been at pains to provide us with a couple of his own moralists and philosophisers" much better suited to the task (Quiller-Couch and Dover Wilson 1926: xiii)? The names of these English Moralists are of course Jacques and Touchstone. As an "amused critic" (xiv), Jacques is far more trenchant and incisive than any German pedant or "polite French" poseur might be, and Touchstone's level-headedness and common sense, his "loyalty and complete honesty" (xv) are all the "correctives or sedatives" (xvii) that a sober-minded English student might require. These, it seems, are the veritable Hookers and Hobbes of the play. To "philosophise" it further would be "absurd" (xvii) or (same thing) foreign, for, in the end, its mystery lies beyond the reach of criticism: "its pastoral guise is the guise of a feeling that goes deeper into mortal concern than criticism can easily penetrate" (xvii). This can only be the realm of "common sense" and one can almost hear the exhausted "my God" that would confirm it.

As if in final declaration of intent, the edition's frontispiece offers a portrait, not of Shakespeare, but of Michael Drayton, "whose description of the Forest of Arden in *Polyolbion XIII* has many points of resemblance to Shakespeare's Arden in this play" (Quiller-Couch and Dover Wilson 1926: v). One is left at last with a peculiar sense that, for Q, the Forest of Arden in *As You Like It* finally and mysteriously merges with the vanished England of his youth, and of Liberalism's Victorian heyday. It proved a durable and sustaining conceit. Writing, at the end of his long life, of memories of his home town of Fowey, he recalls a

> run of remarkable summers and the general security of life in and around Queen Victoria's first Jubilee to weave the spell within which we "fleeted the time carelessly, as they did in the golden world": with tennis and cricket, impromptu dances and (best of all) water parties, supper picnics beside the river …
>
> (Quiller-Couch 1944: 90)

V Lore and order

If Q's Arden stands as a kind of immemorial, sunlit Liberal Valhalla, a pre-1914 tennis-strewn, cricket-flecked and picnic-studded paradise, a notion of Free Trade appropriately prevails there whose principles guarantee even the play's rather "huddled up" ending (Quiller-Couch and Dover Wilson 1926: xvii). However, it fails effectively to conceal a large contradiction which this very stance appears to generate in the "New Shakespeare" edition. On the one hand, Q argues, although the concluding nuptials seem "wildly incongruous with the English Arden Shakespeare has evolved for us out of his young memories," nevertheless "Arden, having room for all fancy beneath its oaks, has room for all reconciliations on its fringe, and Hymen, surely, makes a better sealer of vows than, say, Martext, discoverable in that land" (xviii). In short, Arden can absorb any and all such incongruities.

On the other hand, the notes to the text (largely the work of J. Dover Wilson?) prove less generous. Here the moated island seems to require a more vigorous defense, and the entry of Hymen and the subsequent masque (5.4.105–43) is dismissed as rudely intrusive. In fact, the scene's wholesale removal is recommended:

> There is no dramatic necessity for this masque-business; the appearance of Hymen is completely unexpected. … Hymen's

> words, whether spoken or sung, do not seem to us in the least Shakespearian; and they might all be omitted without loss to the context. In a word we regard the masque as a non-Shakespearian interpolation…
>
> (163)

Perhaps this suggests an iron fist within Q's velvet glove. Certainly, the English Arden he constructs for *As You Like It* can brook no foreign elements that would dilute either its Englishness or its quintessential Shakespearean quality. The fact that these are coterminous for Q reinforces the point and justifies his edition's recommended cut. A Liberalism as English as his must be prepared, paradoxically perhaps, to repel potential boarders as part and parcel of its larger stance. And Q was in no doubt as to the extent to which English Liberalism's principles were inextricable from the traditions of an English way of life. Indeed, the American T. S. Eliot's remark about contemporary society being "worm-eaten with liberalism" provoked uncharacteristic outrage and indignation in him: "This 'Liberalism' which Mr. Eliot arraigns as a worm, eating itself into the traditions of our society, reveals itself rather as Tradition itself … " (Gross 1973: 208) – of the very essence of Englishness, that is: something which a mere American could scarcely be expected to grasp. *As You Like It*'s idyllic Forest of Arden is quite clearly cut from the same cloth.

Of course, such idylls demonstrate that meaning is finally made, not found. Cultures characteristically construct sets of polar opposites to this end. Not always overt, or even formally designated, these work most powerfully when unrevealed or unrecognized, even by those whose ways of life they covertly, albeit powerfully, shape. Constructing difference, we construct ourselves: we are what we oppose. However, we may also, for complex historical reasons, slightly misconceive some of the systems of opposition and difference most powerfully at work in earlier societies, by imposing upon them characteristics derived from our own. If the Englishness/Foreignness opposition that Q constructs as the basis of his reading of Arden turns out to be sustainable only at the cost of the excision of a chunk of the otherwise admired Folio text, then a case exists for arguing that it may be generated by its editor's particular stance in the matter.

In fact, to abandon that commitment for the moment is to encourage the emergence of a set of different, no less distinctive oppositions, some of which find a confirming echo in a number of other Shakespearean texts. One evident example – specifically in the matter of marriage – sets the notion of an abstract, computed, and codified "law" against an inherited tradition of specific local custom and practice, which claims equal, if alternative, validity.[6] In short, it pits "law" against what might be termed "lore." In this case, it sets marriage as legally authenticated by a church ceremony against marriage as validated in terms of the traditional "lore" surrounding the ceremony of "troth-plight." Still valid in early modern Britain, "troth-plight" involved a joint declaration of intent before witnesses and took the specific form either of *sponsalia per verba de futuro* (when the parties promise each other that they will at some future time become husband and wife) or of *sponsalia per verba de praesenti* (when they commit themselves to take each other as husband and wife on the spot, at this present moment).[7] The church withheld wholesale approval of the practice and expected its subsequent blessing of the union to be solicited. Nevertheless, it remained firmly established, is referred to elsewhere by Shakespeare (e.g., in *Measure for Measure*) and may indeed have been the initial mode of the Bard's own marriage.

Certainly the issue comes to the fore at the ending of *As You Like It*. The scenes involving Sir Oliver Martext obviously raise the matter, particularly when that peculiar priest's evident readiness to marry Touchstone and Audrey "under this tree" (3.3.59) (despite his concern that the ceremony should be "lawful" [63–64]) is set against Jacques' scornful dismissal:

> And will you, being a man of your breeding, be married under a bush like a beggar? Get you to church, and have a good priest that can tell you what marriage is. This fellow will but join you together as they join wainscot; then one of you will prove a shrunk panel, and like green timber, warp, warp.
>
> (3.3.78–83)

Nonetheless, another troth-plight marriage virtually takes place in 4.1 when Orlando and Rosalind/Ganymede enact a *sponsalia per verba de praesenti* ceremony in the presence of Celia:

> *Orlando*: Pray thee marry us.
> *Celia*: I cannot say the words.
> *Rosalind*: You must begin, "Will you Orlando –"
> *Celia*: Go to. Will you Orlando have to wife this Rosalind?
> *Orlando*: I will.
> *Rosalind*: Ay, but when?

Orlando: Why now, as fast as she can marry us.
Rosalind: Then you must say "I take thee Rosalind for wife."
Orlando: I take thee Rosalind for wife.
Rosalind: I might ask you for your commission; but I do take thee Orlando for my husband. There's a girl goes before the priest, and certainly a woman's thought runs before her actions.

(4.1.120–33)

The extent to which the play may be said, in presenting this opposition, to favor troth-plight marriages to some degree is not entirely clear, but it seems to form part of an overarching recognition of the claims of "lore"over those of law discernible at large in the plays. Certainly, it prepares the ground for the final troth-plight ceremony performed by Hymen with which the play climaxes, and perhaps suggests a dimension, otherwise hidden, in the enigmatic lines with which Hymen seals the contract:

Here's eight that must take hands
To join in Hymen's bands,
If truth holds true contents.

(5.4.127–29)

My argument is a simple one. To accept the play's bias against a codified, reified, and book-based "law" is at least to warm to its commitment – perhaps in the name of Shakespearean drama at large – to "lore," orality, face-to-face communication and its attendant prolific ambiguity and fruitful shiftiness of meaning. This must then have a considerable, expanding effect on that last line. To discern "troth" already at work in "truth," and to allow that the emphasis in "contents" may slide readily from the first to the second syllable, is to confront issues – albeit unresolvable – that may reasonably be thought to lie near to the heart of Arden.[8] After all, *As You Like It* is a play in which all manner of preconceptions about the nature of love and marriage are subjected to close and often withering scrutiny. It would be surprising if the Hymen scene, in which troth-plighting becomes a source of genuine content, were not central to such concerns.

That such a reading "saves" – indeed, makes pivotal – a chunk of the play that the "New Shakespeare" edition of it would excise is of course no knock-down argument in its favor. It merely highlights the partiality inherent in all readings of all texts. But Q's influential version certainly indicates a number of the dangers implicit in the mirage of an uncomplicated, unified, and coherent Forest of Arden that awaits us somewhere beyond the reeds of the river Avon. Like the uncomplicated, unified, and coherent England for which it stands, this is at best a mere phantom, at worst a template of crude, Procrustean rigor. Constructed in the shadow of the events of 1914–18, perhaps more fervently embraced in the light of those signs of social discontent that climaxed in the General Strike of 1926, the year in which this edition of *As You Like It* appeared, it can claim, nevertheless, no higher status. Oddly, the date of its ultimate dispersal – such is the tenacity of dreams – remains a matter for conjecture.

Notes

1 The terms "complaisance" and "acquiescence" are those of Mulhern. His account presents I. A. Richards, E. M. W. Tillyard, and of course F. R. Leavis as much more crucially formative elements in the establishment of Cambridge English. But it remains the case, however much this complicates the issue, that "English" was unlikely to have emerged at Cambridge in the form it took without the influence, approval, and persistent advocacy of the King Edward VII Professor. See, for instance, Quiller-Couch's lecture "On a School of English," delivered in Cambridge in October 1917, in his *On the Art of Reading* (1921: 95–114). The account given by E. M. W. Tillyard in *The Muse Unchained* (1958: 13 and 60–69) is of considerable interest here. Tillyard's conclusion that Q "was essential to the group that founded the tripos, if only for negative reasons" (50) doesn't wholly support the above argument, but the matter is obviously complicated and he is at pains to describe his own account as "one-sided" as well as "personal, hence limited" (Preface). Claiming, later, that Q "did not do much to give English Studies at Cambridge their future shape," he also records his own "delight" at hearing him lecture on *As You Like It*, as well as his belief that the large audiences Q initially commanded were a considerable factor in the subject's early success (65–70). Basil Willey refers with admiration to "the quality of the faith, the conviction, with which Cambridge English, thanks largely to Q's evangelical zeal, began its pilgrimage" (1968: 16). On Q's wide-ranging influence on the subject, particularly on the importance of "background studies," see Willey 1968: 17–18. Willey concludes that "Q was a product of the last phase of England's greatness – the era of Kipling and Elgar and Edward VII; he was intensely, and even sentimentally patriotic; unobtrusively but sincerely Christian; a passionate believer in liberal education, liberal politics, and

the idea of the gentleman. ... I can think of no better way of conveying the ethos of those early years of Cambridge English. At that time Q really was its prophet, propagandist and spokesman; he provided it with a creed, he proclaimed its saving power, and he uttered what was latent in our own minds and thoughts" (20).

2 Tillyard writes: "we thought that if a man entered his subject in this way he could learn to deal with the experience of life better than if he had been trained to accumulate the facts of vowel-changes in Middle English dialects or of literary biography" (1958: 83).

3 See Tillyard (1958: 82–92). Like Basil Willey (above, n. 7), he employs the more general, uncapitalized term "liberalism" to characterize the essential quality of Cambridge English Studies, but makes it clear that, in this matter, and despite his "gossipy" style, Quiller-Couch gave a genuine lead (83–84). See also his analysis of factors later undermining the "grounding principle of liberalism" in the subject (127–28). There are, of course, a number of different accounts of the development of "English" as an academic subject in Britain. For a provocative and persuasive alternative history, see Robert Crawford (ed.) *The Scottish Invention of English Literature* (1998).

4 Tillyard judges the "English Moralists" paper to be "Q's most tangible service to the Cambridge English School." The paper proved "a success from the beginning" (1958: 118). Willey confirms this (1968: 17–18).

5 All references to *As You Like It* are from the New Shakespeare edition (Quiller-Couch and Dover Wilson 1926).

6 On this notion of law, see Eagleton 1986: 35–63.

7 See Schanzer 1960: 81–89.

8 See Evans 1986: 145–90 and Grady 1996: 210.

3
Romancing the Bard

LAURIE E. OSBORNE

Shakespearean references appear frequently in that most vilified of American genres, the romance novel. Jayne Ann Krentz even uses Shakespeare to define one typical romance narrative – "the familiar battle between the sexes, or The Taming of the Shrew story … [where] the man is the one who, for once, is forced to find a way to make the relationship work" (1992b: 139). Shakespeare appears most often in two subgenres, Regencies and historical romances. Both genres are overtly, even aggressively patriarchal in their double standards and policing of female virtue. Both offer dominant men who are subdued and matched by women who effectively subvert masculine control over their lives and marital choices. Since marriage remains the goal and resolution, however, patriarchy remains intact. Shakespearean allusions become pivotal in this paradoxical combination of female agency and patriarchal dynastic demands.

I argue that Shakespeare in contemporary American romance serves the needs of (a) authors, by bolstering their status and offering the private pleasures of erudition; (b) characters, by modeling strategies for creating both emotional distance and cultural connections; and (c) readers, by at once reinforcing and challenging the culturally conservative codes of the romance. On one level, Shakespearean references affirm the literary range of professional novelists well aware of the continuing low status of their genre

(Barlow and Krentz 1992: *passim*). Just as important, however, Shakespeare and his plays facilitate the creation of both character-driven obstacles and romantic enablers, while establishing accessible historical escapism. As a result, these novels often reconstruct the plays, in whole or in part, within a predominantly female genre, predominantly read by women, in ways that challenge both canon and patriarchy.

Shakespeare's noticeable presence in romance originates with British novelist Georgette Heyer, who founded the Regency romance. Heyer's complex, often unmarked, appropriations of Shakespeare set the stage for subsequent, less subtle incorporations. In her *Friday's Child* (1944), Heyer invokes and punctures Shakespeare's authority when Hero Wantage admits that her name comes from Shakespeare. Her companions are doubly horrified, first that Hero might be a bluestocking (her husband of convenience hastily disclaims any intellectual tendencies in his new bride) and second, that they might actually be forced to watch one of his plays. In *Black Sheep* (1967), Heyer initiates Shakespearean gender reversals in romance with Miles Calverleigh's declaration to Abigail Wendower. He offers an entirely appropriate comment from Helena in *All's Well That Ends Well*: "'I was always a poor hand at making flowery speeches.' He smiled at her again a little ruefully. '*That I should love a bright particular star*'" (Heyer 1967: 161; 1.1.81). Whereas Helena laments that her low social class puts the man she loves beyond her reach, Miles, the black sheep in question, acknowledges that he is unsuitable because of his youthful transgressions rather than his social class. More subversively, in *Sprig Muslin* (1956) Heyer invokes *Romeo and Juliet*'s balcony scene, underscoring how far from the star-crossed lovers are the wilful Amanda and her would-be rescuer:

> Perched on a stable-ladder, a modern Romeo and his Juliet discussed ways and means. It did not take them long to discard the trappings of convention. "Oh, I wish you will not call me Miss Smith!" said Juliet. "Amanda!" breathed Mr. Ross reverently. "And my name is Hildebrand."
>
> (Heyer 1956: 165)

As quickly as the pair abandons convention, Heyer moves on from the Shakespearean allusion that mocks rather than supports romantic illusions.

Heyer's *The Unknown Ajax* (1959) invokes Shakespeare in the title and playfully inverts the prejudices against Ajax that abound in

Troilus and Cressida. Vincent Darracott, who has been supplanted as the earl's heir by an unknown cousin, speaks most of these lines. That cousin, Hugh Darracott, is unacceptable to both his grandfather and cousin because of his father's marriage to a weaver's daughter. This complicated background explains both Vincent's assumptions about Hugh – that he is an oversized oaf from the merchant class – and the form his hostility takes – taunting references to Hugh as the intellectually challenged, yet heroically proportioned Ajax in *Troilus*. Vincent's Shakespearean barbs insult Hugh on two levels, by suggesting that he is as dimwitted as Ajax and by flaunting the superior education that Vincent has presumably received. But instead of foolishly using his strength to resolve the major plot crisis, Hugh so cleverly deceives the excise man who tries to arrest the heroine's younger brother that her final accolade completely inverts the "Ajax" slurs: "Noble Ajax, you are as strong, as valiant, as wise, no less noble, much more gentle, and altogether more tractable!" (Heyer 1959: 314; 2.3.140–42). Even though in *Troilus* Agamemnon's words falsely praise Ajax only to provoke Achilles into action, Heyer's heroine uses the lines approvingly to describe Hugh, whose tractability has made him look easily manipulated to his prejudiced relatives. Heyer's revision of Shakespeare's Ajax, valuing rather than deriding him, prefigures other ways in which romances revise Shakespeare, often by inverting his hierarchies – particularly those of gender.

Another strategy of appropriation appears in *Venetia* (1958), where the lovers-to-be quote Shakespeare during their first meeting. When the rakish Damerel steals a kiss and comments, "And beauty's self she is" (Heyer 1958: 27), his quotation's unspoken next line ("When all her robes are gone") offends proprieties, but so does the sequel to Venetia's response that he is "a most pestilent complete knave" (28). Her quotation comes from *Othello*, where Iago claims that Cassio desires Desdemona; the next line reads, "and the woman hath found him already" (2.1. 239–40). Since Iago insists on Desdemona's intimacy with Cassio, Venetia's embarrassment is understandable, though Heyer does not explain it: "Venetia, who had suddenly remembered the rest of the quotation, replied, 'If you don't know, I certainly shan't tell. *That* phrase is apt enough, but the context won't do'" (1958: 28). Heyer does, however, give clues, since Damerel remarks that he had better study his Shakespeare and offers his own more recognizable quotation: "My reputation, Iago, my reputation!" (28; 2.3.246). He quotes Cassio's lament for the reputation he has lost by becoming drunk at Iago's instigation, so both characters obviously know the context for Venetia's earlier comment. Although the *reader* may not get the joke or the subtle suggestion that Damerel, like Cassio, has lost his reputation for an indiscretion provoked by another, this Shakespearean bantering shows that the characters understand one another. As the Regency genre evolves, using Shakespeare as a shared language often signals the intellectual compatibility between hero and heroine.

If Heyer's Shakespearean allusions nestle unobtrusively in her novels, later romance novelists do not hide their Shakespeare. Least interesting are Shakespearean titles, dedications, or chapter headings, since these references often present lines from the plays in isolation. For example, Patricia Veryan's novels often sport Shakespearean titles – *Love Alters Not* (1987), *Men Were Deceivers Ever* (1989), *A Shadow's Bliss* (1994) – but the references do not extend far beyond the title. Surprisingly, many romance novelists allude to the plays or characters in this partial way.

For example, Joan Wolf uses Shakespearean quotations among her chapter headings in several novels (*The Counterfeit Marriage* [1980], *A London Season* [1981], *His Lordship's Mistress* [1982]). For *Fool's Masquerade* (1984), in which Valentine Ardsley, orphaned and escaping the unpleasant plans of her guardians, disguises herself as a groom for Diccon, Earl of Leyburn, Wolf gives only two quotations from *Twelfth Night*, one at the start of each part. The first half of the novel opens with: "My father had a daughter loved a man / As it might be perhaps, were I a woman, / I should your lordship" (Wolf 1984: 5; 2.4.106–8). The allusion not only reveals the narrator's crossdressing to readers who know that Viola disguises herself as a page in *Twelfth Night*, but also anticipates that Valentine, like Viola, will fall in love with her master. The second headnote foreshadows Diccon's belated discovery that he loves her:

> Your master quits you; and for your service done him,
> So much against the mettle of your sex,
> So far beneath your soft and tender breeding,
> And since you called me master for so long,
> Here is my hand: you shall from this time be
> Your master's mistress.
>
> (125; 5.1.310–14)

Although all chapter headings in Wolf's earlier novels apply to their content, the *Twelfth Night* references in *Fool's Masquerade* have more extended influence, since the plot both works through the difficulties of the disguised Valentine's love for Diccon and, perhaps more significantly, details Diccon's protracted discovery that he loves her. His evolving awareness of his feelings proves crucial in romance (as it apparently is *not* in Shakespeare) because the genre depends on the masculine acknowledgment of emotion as much as on active female choice.

When pertinent, such epigrams are typically less involved with the actual narratives than in *Fool's Masquerade* (1984), in some cases functioning as an authorial grace note. Edith Layton notes that her Shakespearean references may elude her readers but gratify her:

> I confess, I like to put Shakespeare in many of my books, not just in hopes that association will give me some polish but because the references please me … I thought it would be especially noticeable in … *Game of Love*, given the quote on the first page, and the main character, "Lion", aka Arden. But alas! No one ever wrote to tell me they noticed that.
>
> (Osborne 1997)

Since Layton opens *Game of Love* (1988) with a quotation from *A Midsummer Night's Dream* and characterizes her hero, Arden Lyons, as the beast courting a fairy princess, her expectations seem reasonable. References to Shakespeare clearly signal that these authors are serious writers. Although A. S. Byatt acknowledges, in her essay on Heyer, "how difficult good escape literature is to write" (1992: 233), romance novelists themselves are well aware that:

> Nothing about the romance genre is more reviled by literary critics and, indeed, the public at large, than the conventional diction of romance. Descriptive passages are regularly culled from romance novels and read aloud with great glee and mockery by everybody from college professors to talk show hosts. You would think that we romance novelists … would have the wit to clean up our act. After all, we are talented professionals.
>
> (Barlow and Krentz 1992: 24)

Krentz and Barlow suggest that these much-derided patterns of language are crucial to relating particular fantasies to their audiences. As a result many affirm their position as "talented professional" writers indirectly – some through the allusions to Shakespeare, whom Deanna James characterizes as the greatest writer of all time and credits with the inspiration for the multi-act structure of her *Acts of Passion* (1992b) and *Acts of Love* (1992a) .[1]

However, Shakespearean references are too pervasive to serve only self-legitimating purposes. These novels often rework Shakespearean language and plots in the service of romance. As in Heyer's work, references fall into several categories beyond epigrams and titles: Shakespeare-quoting characters, incidental Shakespeare, Shakespeare as historical context (especially in the actress-novels), and full-scale reworking of Shakespeare-as-solution or plot resolution. "Uncle Will" even occasionally surfaces as a character, although those novels engage Shakespeare's biography rather than his work.[2] Even when these patterns overlap, the individual novels position Shakespeare differently.

For example, several romance novelists incorporate characters who compulsively quote Shakespeare. These range from the random quoter like Victoria in Julie Garwood's *Prince Charming* (1994) to Lucinda Benedict, who quotes Shakespeare through three novels by Kasey Michaels, to the Shakespeare-obsessed father in Susan Carroll's *The Lady Who Hated Shakespeare* (1986). In these novels, reciting Shakespeare demonstrates the character's self-protectiveness: both Garwood's Victoria and Carroll's Walter Renwick quote the Bard to distance themselves from their emotional problems. Lucinda Benedict of Kasey Michaels' alliterative trio of novels (*The Tenacious Miss Tamerlane* [1982], *The Playful Lady Penelope* [1988], and *The Haunted Miss Hampshire* [1992]) differs from Victoria and Renwick both because she quotes other literary figures and because she speaks *entirely* in quotations – her every utterance appropriates the Bard or another male literary authority. Shakespeare's language both isolates these characters and enables them to speak.

These quotations set Shakespeare's language in an unusual relationship to the understood values of romance:

> Women enjoy telling. We value the exploration of emotion in verbal terms. We are not as interested in action as we are in depth of emotion. And we like emotion to be clear and authoritative, not vague or overly subtle the way it often seems to be in male discourse.
>
> (Barlow and Krentz 1992: 35)

Barlow and Krentz argue that verbal acknowledgment of emotion is crucial; compelling the blocked male figure to articulate his emotions signals the romance heroine's success. Thus, verbal skill and intellectual clarity about emotions can indicate a character's significance. Not surprisingly, the three Shakespeare-quoters I have mentioned are secondary figures as well as characters who have difficulty expressing their feelings.

Paradoxically, these characters also enable romantic union: Shakespearean quotations ultimately both express and distance emotion, making a bridge between the emotionally eloquent female characters and the taciturn males. Although Garwood's Victoria has only slight influence, Lucinda Benedict and Walter Renwick are simultaneously involved in their quoting and implicated in matchmaking. Lucinda encounters an array of increasingly bemused young ladies in Michaels' three novels. Either troublesome or in trouble, Miss Tamerlane, Lady Penelope, and Miss Hampshire each discovers true love thanks to a woman who speaks only the words of dead men. Lucinda's quotations are *bricolage*, overt acknowledgment that all language has been used and overused, especially the characteristic language of the romance novel.

Lucinda demonstrates, however, that "used" language enables romantic union, as she quotes freely from many sources. Indeed, she must quote other writers around the dowager duchess who berates her in the final novel where Lucinda appears as a ghost:

> "Shakespeare! How dare you quote the great Will to me, you vacantly grinning twit ... It's one thing to come back and haunt me, but to quote Shakespeare to me at the same time? No! It is too much for one old woman to bear!"
>
> (Michaels 1992: 87)

Nonetheless, Michaels clearly envisions Shakespeare as central. Not only does Lucinda describe her position, entrapped between life and afterlife, with Hamlet's lines ("Clasping her beringed hands theatrically to her lace-draped breast, she exclaimed, 'Oh God! I could be bounded in a nutshell and count myself a king of infinite space, were it not that I have bad dreams.' Shakespeare"[63–64; citing *Hamlet* 2.2. 248–50]), but Michaels also deliberately invokes Shakespeare at the end of the final book:

> So we have bid a final, fond farewell to Aunt Lucinda, who is off to rejoin her adored Jerome, knowing that she would not wish our regrets, but only quote from the dowager duchess's beloved bard: "If ever thou shalt love, / In the sweet pangs of it remember me ..."
>
> (184; citing *Twelfth Night* 2.4.14–15)

Thus, Lucinda usurps Orsino's hyperbolic claim. Unlike Orsino, who announces himself the pattern of love in his passion for Olivia only to change the object of his affection entirely at the end of *Twelfth Night*, Lucinda, who has patiently awaited a reunion beyond the grave with her husband Jerome, becomes the one who has truly loved, helping several heroines achieve the heightened romantic union Orsino only describes.

In *The Lady Who Hated Shakespeare* (1986), Mr. Renwick's quotations are less extensive, yet his Shakespearean references isolate him more thoroughly. For example, Renwick responds, "The lady doth protest too much, methinks" (Carroll 1986: 16; *Hamlet* 3.2.210) to his daughter's tale that an unknown man (our hero Miles) has insulted her (by quoting a Shakespearean compliment), dropped her in the stream (she ordered him to put her down), and kissed her. Cordelia has indeed overreacted to the compliment; the lady hates Shakespeare because he seems to have alienated her father's love. Having moved them to Stratford-on-Avon and devoted himself to his passion for Shakespeare apparently in response to his wife's death, Renwick reads Shakespeare's plays to her every evening, obsessively but not eloquently:

> She loved her Papa dearly, but his reading voice lacked all expression. He recited the lines in such a dreary monotone that even the impassioned love scenes between the Queen of the Nile and her Roman swain sounded like the grimmest of Sunday sermons.
>
> (42)

Shakespeare, however, is also used to mark Renwick's emergence from emotional isolation: he quotes *Lear* when Cordelia nearly dies while playing Desdemona in the local amateur *Othello*. She is predictably disgusted: "She had nearly been killed … And Papa. He had not said a word except … except Shakespeare!" (172). She scarcely relents after the hero scolds her:

> "Think of how your father reads Shakespeare, so expressionless. Yet the way he spoke those lines from *Lear* tonight! Good God, Delia, he showed his love for you in the only way he knew how."
>
> (177)

Shakespeare's language shifts from being an obstacle between father and daughter to being the expression of his love when she is genuinely endangered. Moreover, Renwick has invited the appropriate prospective bridegroom to meet his daughter. Though based in part on Miles's interest in Shakespeare, his choice for his daughter proves sound.

Shakespeare-quoting characters like Lucinda and Walter Renwick seem, at first glance, caricatures or socially isolated cultural parasites, but their reasons for embracing Shakespeare prove to be complex negotiations with personal shyness (Lucinda's difficulties speaking in society) or trying personal conditions (Renwick's efforts to deal with the death of his spendthrift wife). In the process, Shakespeare serves both the characters' isolation and their social reinstatement.

The most interesting Shakespeare-quoters establish both character and relationships by appropriating his words. In *The Game of Love* (1988), Edith Layton's gigantic hero, Arden Lyons, embodies the sentiment expressed by the opening epigram from *A Midsummer Night's Dream*, that "a lion among ladies is a most dreadful thing" (5; 3.1.28–29). An Earl's bastard, he proves noble despite his illegitimacy in part through his use of Shakespeare, likening his lady to the pearl in the Ethiope's ear from *Romeo and Juliet* (1.5.43) and challenging an army deserter with Falstaff's words about honor from *1 Henry IV* (5.1.127–39). His accurate reading of Falstaff's speech reveals an innate nobility, especially in contrast to the well-born army deserter who mistakenly applauds Falstaff's reading of honor. Arden, as it turns out, is the "true lion" who does not want to touch the "princess," who in turn must convince him of his worth. For Layton's hero and others, Shakespearean language affirms a character's status (despite apparent degradation or illegitimacy) as well as his or her suitability for a comparably literate mate.

Shakespearean quotations also identify a particular kind of heroine, namely the intellectual or bluestocking. These characters – Joan Overfield's Elinor Denning (*The Spirited Bluestocking* [1992]), Brenda Hiatt's Deirdre Wheaton (*The Ugly Ducking* [1992]), Carla Kelly's Ellen Grimsley (*Miss Grimsley's Oxford Career* [1992]) – reveal unusual intellect for Regency heroines, in part through Shakespearean references. The same quotations establish their compatibility with heroes who often either quote Shakespeare first or quote back to their bluestocking beloveds. These references also ally the heroines with their 1990s readers, especially since the heroines often read Mary Wollstonecraft and advocate feminist changes in government, education, or science.

Beyond these effects in characterization, Shakespeare also contributes to structure both in isolated incidents and more globally in broad plot revisions. In many Regencies and historical romances, Shakespeare encodes and potentially revises plot situations in ways that relate to the reader's cultural context. Some such references function as "incidental Shakespeare," non-quoted allusions that are typically tied only to specific incidents. For example, characters often draw on *Hamlet* to persuade someone to action, either romantic or political. In Loretta Chase's *The Vagabond Viscount* (1988), Max (Lord Rand) reinterprets *Hamlet* to persuade his friend to propose:

> "Can't think about those things or you end up thinking and hesitating forever."
>
> "Like Hamlet, you mean."
>
> "Exactly. There he was meditating, waiting, and watching – and where does it get him? His sweetheart kills herself. Don't blame her. The chap wore out her patience."
>
> Mr. Langdon considered this startling theory briefly, then objected to it on grounds that *Hamlet* was not first and foremost a love story. There was, after all, the matter of the father's murder to be avenged.
>
> "On whose say-so?" Max argued. "A ghost. He had no business seeing ghosts. If he'd attended to the girl properly, he wouldn't have had time to see ghosts."
>
> (149–50)

Max relocates the significance of *Hamlet* squarely in the love plot. Thus, Chase simultaneously uses and interrogates Shakespeare as a kind of cultural shorthand. Comparable incidental references appear in: Joan Wolf's *The Counterfeit Marriage* (1980) / *Hamlet*; Elizabeth Mansfield's *Matched Pairs* (1996) / *Romeo and Juliet*; Jo Beverley's *The Stanforth Secrets* (1989) / *Othello*; Rita Boucher's *The Would-Be Witch* (1997) / *The Tempest*; and a host of other romance novels.[3] *Hamlet* invokes paralyzing indecisiveness; *Romeo and Juliet*, reckless or thwarted love; *Othello*, destructive jealousy; *The Tempest*'s Caliban, lust, and so forth. Incidental Shakespeare *relies* on Shakespeare to connote emotional states; however, such references frequently interrogate the plays as well. Once again Shakespeare both articulates the romantic obstacle and enables its resolution, but in these cases is more often tied to actions or situations than to character development.

More widespread appropriations occur in romance novels that take the Regency stage as their context; these actress-novels use

Shakespeare to give readers a sense of historical context that also offers comforting familiarity. Margaret Evans Porter's *Toast of the Town* (1993), Joan Wolf's *His Lordship's Mistress* (1982), and Carla Kelly's *Miss Billings Treads the Boards* (1993) take up the actual life in the Regency theater. Porter's novel refers frequently to *Twelfth Night* in the story of Flora Campion, a professional actress who finds talent insufficient to distinguish her from her less respectable colleagues. Playing Olivia opposite a flirtatious actress who flaunts herself as Viola, Flora, too, attracts an ardent nobleman. His pursuit of her illuminates the perils of a thoroughly researched Regency theater world, part of the knowledge that many romance readers claim to gain from their reading (Radway 1984: 26–45). Both Joan Wolf's *His Lordship's Mistress* (1982) and Carla Kelly's *Miss Billings Treads the Boards* (1993) feature nonprofessional actresses. Wolf's heroine Jessica coolly plans her career to acquire a protector in order to save her family's one remaining property. She performs Shakespeare to considerable acclaim, but retires after a triumph as Lady Macbeth. Kelly's Kate Billings accidentally encounters a touring company undergoing financial problems and plays the widow in *Taming* to help them. All three novels take the theater seriously as historical context and use Shakespeare as the "familiar other," collapsing while invoking historical difference. His texts primarily constitute setting; none of the three novels actually incorporates Shakespearean plots.[4]

Some actress-novels use Shakespeare as more than context. Christina Dodd's *The Greatest Lover in England* (1994), Deanna James's *Acts of Passion* (1992b), and Mary Balogh's *Christmas Belle* (1994) not only use Shakespearean language, but also offer revised Shakespearean narratives. These novels underscore the affinities between Shakespearean drama and romance conventions through active revision and extension of Shakespearean plots, reworking cultural context for their readers.

In *The Greatest Lover in England*, Rosencrantz, a girl disguised as a boy-actress, not only knows "Uncle Will" Shakespeare, but also performs Ophelia in the first performance of *Hamlet*, a role that reflects her own history as a young girl doubly orphaned, losing her father to plague and her foster-father to Queen Elizabeth's displeasure. Rosencrantz's performance coincides with her reunion with both her foster-father and her lover. When the foster-father appears onstage over her "corpse," his presence transforms the tragedy into comic union:

> Someone stood over her. She tried to peek through the tiniest slit in her eyelids, but shadow concealed his face. Then he spoke Hamlet's line in familiar, beloved tones. "What, the fair Ophelia!"
>
> Emotions – amazement, jubilation, exultation – burst forth inside her. She sat up on the bier and reached out. "Dada!"
>
> ... Rosie looked toward the row of chairs and half rose in thankfulness, then realized – the play! But no one seemed to care. The audience was crying, laughing, and clapping, involved in the story unfolding before their eyes and forgetting the fiction that had earlier absorbed them. All sense of tragedy had vanished, and nothing would restore it now.
>
> (Dodd 1994: 362; paraphrasing *Hamlet* 3.1.91)

Dodd's disrupted *Hamlet* explicitly acknowledges how romances use Shakespeare's tragedies. This novel transforms *Hamlet.* The lost birthright, mourning paternal loss, and fears of sexual betrayal are recycled through the female Rosencrantz who, typically for romance, resolves these conflicts by marrying the man whom her resurrection has deprived of land and fortune. Just as important, the tragic plot is abandoned freely – even by "Uncle Will."

Deanna James's *Acts of Passion* (1992b) follows a strikingly similar pattern. Miranda Drummond, appalled that her mother plans to marry the man she thinks murdered her father, stows away with "Sons of Thespis, Royal Shakespearean Company by Appointment to Her Majesty Queen Victoria." When she becomes the lead actress, her roles extend throughout the Shakespearean canon, but *Hamlet* remains the central play. At one point Miranda claims to *be* Hamlet and in fact elicits her stepfather's public confession by restaging with actor-ghosts the battlefield slaughter that he arranged in order to widow and woo her mother.

Like Dodd, James includes Shakespearean quotations as chapter headings. She explains the strategy and openly claims Shakespearean structure in her Afterword:

> By now you have perceived that *Acts of Passion* is constructed like a play by William Shakespeare. In further homage to the master writer of all time, I have begun each chapter with a quotation to foreshadow what will follow. I hope the sources have piqued your interest. If so they have served their purpose well. I further thought to allow you the fun of seeing how well you remembered your Shakespeare. Have you tested yourself thus far?
>
> (James 1992b: 477)

Since the quotations from less popular plays such as *Pericles*, *Cymbeline*, and *King John* surely escape most readers, this transformation of romance into memory quiz seems destined to put her public down. Her claims to Shakespearean structure, as well as the unexpected test on the "master writer of all time," insist on the novel's artistry; Miranda's enactment of a Hamlet-like revenge revises the plot utterly in terms of female revenge and action.

These actress-novels also rework Shakespeare's female characters. Mary Balogh's *Christmas Belle* (1994) takes up *Othello* in recounting actress Isabella Gellée's pursuit of love and respectability. Long after fleeing London's theatrical scene and her lover's unflattering assumptions about its actresses, she returns to England, widowed with two children and famous as an extremely talented actress, only to end up starring in an amateur theatrical hosted, inevitably, by the grandparents of the lover whom she fled. During their early reacquaintance, the amateur Christmas production, which Isabella has agreed to direct and which includes most of the house party, seems focused on Portia from *Merchant of Venice* and Kate from *Taming* in the excerpts that she plans to perform. Soon, however, the emphasis settles decidedly on *Othello*, as Balogh reveals that Jack Frazier, the hero, drove Isabella away with his extreme jealousy. Jack naturally plays the Moor opposite Isabella's Desdemona, provoking the audience to weep "for the world beyond innocence, where love did not always bring happiness, where there could be so many misunderstandings and tragedies because people would not talk openly with each other – even with those they loved" (Balogh 1994: 205).

The novel's narrative of early jealous insecurity and accusations of adultery echoes *Othello*, but the lovers, older and wiser, get another chance largely because Isabella cannot embrace Desdemona's submission:

> She could not understand Desdemona. Although she had played the part several times before, she suddenly felt locked outside the person who was Desdemona. She could not feel with Desdemona's heart or think with her mind or breathe the air she breathed. She wanted to become angry. She wanted to fight back the way she had fought back nine years ago. She wanted to hurt him as he was hurting her. She had done it once, and she thought she had succeeded well enough. ... No, she could not be Desdemona.
>
> (Balogh 1994: 143)

Rather than submitting to her lover's belief in her sexual treachery, as Desdemona seems to do, Isabella had fought back by falsely claiming that she had taken lovers and by fleeing her unreasonably jealous lover. Whereas Desdemona lies about who killed her ("Nobody, I myself" [*Othello* 5.2.133]) in order to protect her husband, Isabella lies to exploit Jack's/Othello's greatest fear – that she has betrayed him. She saves herself by fight and flight. Moreover, their "performance" of *Othello* allows Jack his fantasy of the submissive, betraying woman only to reflect his own excessive jealousy back at him. His recognition that his jealousy, like Othello's, was groundless is crucially mediated through the "amateur" Shakespearean performance.

The Lady Who Hated Shakespeare even foregrounds the nineteenth-century prunings of Shakespeare in its amateur staging of *Othello*, which is radically revised by a character (presented as officious and troublesome) who objects to husbands strangling their wives. When Delia steps in as Desdemona, she inadvertently restores the radically bowdlerized text to the fuller version she recalls from her father's endless reading. Even as she apparently opposes revision of the play, however, Delia gets caught in the murderous plot to strangle the young woman whom she understudies. Carroll's use of *Othello*, like Balogh's, acknowledges the romantic obstacle in that play – jealousy and male aggression – but revises it. When Delia takes the role of Desdemona, she is endangered not because of undeserved sexual jealousy, but because of the mistaken fears of a valet disguised as a nobleman who thinks that she, rather than the original actress, is blackmailing him. In effect, anxiety about preserving class position displaces anxieties about female sexuality.

The most elaborate appropriation and reinterpretation I have discovered so far, Michelle Martin's reworking of *Much Ado About Nothing* in *The Hampshire Hoyden* (1993), not only stages Shakespeare as the common language shared by hero and heroine, but also invokes the slandered maiden tale as an eminently suitable narrative for romance. This novel strategically uses Shakespearean allusions against one another in several contexts.

First Kate Glyn and Theo Blake quote Shakespeare to each other frequently. Although Theo initially identifies himself with Hamlet because he deeply mourns his brother, Kate provokes him out of his melancholy with Shakespeare. Her resistance to matrimony and his melancholy emerge and merge in frequent quotation wars:

Lord Blake's eyes widened ... "And so you will be a barren sister all your life, chanting faint hymns to the cold fruitless moon."

Miss Glyn tsked at Lord Blake. "'Would it not grieve a woman to be overmastered with a piece of valiant dust? To make an account of her life to a clod of wayward marl?'"

Lord Blake sighed and shook his head. "I really must find a chink in your Shakespearean armor, or I'll be all out of charity with myself."

(Martin 1993: 58–59; *Dream* 1.1.72–73; *Much Ado* 2.1.51–53)

Theo rarely gets the last quoted word. In fact he soon finds that he feels "downright cheerful – morning, noon, and night. He had shed Hamlet's mantle without remorse to reveal ... Puck?" (125–26). He registers his own changed perspective with Shakespearean substitution.

The wittiness of their Shakespearean battle so dominates the novel that it is easy to overlook the lovely Georgina, whom Kate is reluctantly chaperoning for the London season and who falls instantly in love with Sir William Atherton, freshly returned from the wars. Their easy mutual affection and prompt, trouble-free courtship seem merely the background to Kate's and Theo's more lively interactions until Kate's former betrothed, who is pursuing Georgina, and Theo's would-be fiancée, in imitation of *Much Ado About Nothing*, decide to stage Georgina's "betrayal" of William before her bedroom window and smash the engagement. While reworking Shakespeare's slandered maiden tale as a breach of Regency proprieties with wide-ranging social consequences, *The Hampshire Hoyden* (1993) also revises the alliance between Kate and Theo, who work together to uncover how William was fooled. Rather than being tricked into love, the pair discover that they are more than compatible verbal sparring partners during the highly emotional collapse of their friends' betrothal. Martin extends the time it takes the two to discover and prove Lord Faulkland's perfidy in order to develop their alliance.

The Hampshire Hoyden (1993) also plays out the reactions of Hero/Georgina and the difficulties and horror of Claudio/William's realization that he has been tricked into ruining his life and that of the woman he loves. As Joan Wolf's *Fool's Masquerade* (1984) extends *Twelfth Night* by exploring Orsino/Diccon's recognition that he loves Viola/Valentine, so Martin elaborates both William's and Georgina's dilemmas, staging their reunion not as the abrupt substitution at the wedding in Shakespeare's play but as a slower healing of serious wounds to trust. Even with Kate's persuasions that "'Despite everything he was told and thought that he heard and witnessed, Sir William still loved you. He still loved the woman he believed had betrayed him, and he hated himself for it'" (Martin 1993: 222), Georgina's forgiveness is hard-won and, ultimately, classic romance fare.

By the end of the novel, Shakespearean quotation duels yield to competing Shakespearean plots: strategies from *Hamlet* help resolve a crisis from *Much Ado*. Rather than wait "till tomorrow ... [to] devise ... brave punishments" (*Much Ado* 5.4.121–22) for the slanderers, the two couples use the play-within-a-play from *Hamlet*. At the Prince's reception, which everyone including Lady Priscilla and Lord Falkland attend, Kate and Theo enact the conspiracy, provoking Falkland to reveal his guilt; both he and Lady Priscilla experience even worse social ostracism than they imposed on Georgina. Martin's novel displays vividly how well Shakespearean narrative structure, with some extensions, can suit the generic requirements of romance: he offers both the obstacles to union and potential mechanisms for alliance.

The paradoxical position that Shakespeare occupies in romance derives from the subgenres in which he appears. Critics and writers who analyze the appeal of romance inevitably argue for the psychological and social significance of different subgenres. For example, in "Mass Market Romance: Pornography for Women Is Different," Ann Barr Snitnow suggests that Harlequins are "too pallid to shape consciousness but they feed certain regressive elements in the female experience," namely the moment of erotic and personal power that (presumably) occurs during courtship (1983: 247). As Kathleen Gilles Seidel puts it, "The first function of the setting of a romance novel is to be Other, to transport the reader somewhere else. The setting often provides the reader with the first and clearest signal that fantasy follows" (1992: 207). Both historical romance (James, Dodd, Garwood) and the more specialized Regencies (Heyer, Carroll, Balogh, etc.) use historical distance as their reproduction of the exotic or the Other. Shakespeare as a participant signals historical Otherness in Elizabethan historicals like Dodd's. His plays and their performances offer a context for the Regencies from Heyer to Martin because of the intense revival of Shakespeare's plays throughout the 1800s. As an indicator of historical difference, Shakespeare proves especially useful since he is both familiar and "Other," sufficiently available in common usage that readers will recognize him, sufficiently "historical" that readers can readily take his works as part of the past.

In their "Otherness," Shakespeare's plays also, paradoxically, normalize the erotics of several of these novels. When Deanna James's Miranda, at sixteen, falls in love with "Shreve Catherwood," her seduction is deeply intertwined with his initial efforts to cast her as Juliet, whose extreme youth masks what amounts to the statutory rape of Miranda. Jack Frazier's destructive jealousy in *Christmas Belle* (1994) is both explained and defused by Isabella's revision of Desdemona. The Hamlet narrative and Ophelia's madness function as the major plot devices repeatedly, as either the impulse to revenge or intimations of madness separate the lovers. The most patriarchal characters – those who chronically quote Shakespeare – become enablers of the romance. Thus Shakespearean obstacles to union are "Other," yet familiar, both tied to historical context and appropriable and revisable.

Shakespearean references also serve an essential anglophilia evident in these subgenres. The attention both readers and authors pay to historical detail underscores how the intricacies of the British aristocracy serve fantasies of hierarchies subverted or used to the heroine's advantage.[5] As a result, Shakespeare often signals challenges posed to the male-dominated social order. Isabella Gellée's revision of Desdemona's passive submission to patriarchal authority ultimately enables the unthinkable marriage between an actress and a peer of the realm. Heyer's Venetia explicitly revises Shakespeare when *she* proposes to Damerel, invoking the very strategies that *Twelfth Night*'s Viola claims she would adopt to woo Olivia: "I warn you, love, that if you cast me out I shall build a willow cabin at your gates – and very likely die of an inflammation of the lungs, for November is not the month for building willow cabins!" (1958: 288; 1.5.237–45). Both Rosencrantz from *The Greatest Lover in England* (1994) and Miranda in *Acts of Passion* (1992b) usurp the central role of Hamlet and work through loss, madness, mourning, and revenge very differently, replacing the icon of Western male subjectivity with a female perspective and revenge with romantic union as the goal. Revising or using Shakespeare becomes a symptom of the feminine challenge to the patriarchal structures of these genres, overt structures that are therefore more readily recognized, if not defeated.

Because patriarchy remains intact and even the most intrepid heroine comes up against that reality, Shakespearean references acquire peculiar resonance. After all, if the plots and characters of Shakespeare's plays can be so readily adapted into romance conventions, how different can the highest of high culture be from the much-scorned, nearly entirely female endeavors of romance? Equally significant, if Shakespeare's texts can be used against each other and invoked to serve temporary female power, then perhaps the male-dominated systems that these historical novels record can be eroded and manipulated from within. Actually, the persistence of patriarchy, which many critics take to be the most pernicious fantasy that the romance offers, seems to me its most realistic component. Certainly romances acknowledge that we are all, male and female, still implicated in patriarchy; Shakespeare both marks that acknowledgment and becomes a means to rework the system.

Notes

1 Susan Baker, in "Comic Material: Shakespeare in the Classical Detective Story" (1994), argues that Shakespeare authorizes detective novelists trying to affirm the quality of their popular fiction.

2 The most blatant Shakespeare appearance in the romance novel is Erica Jong's *Serenissima* (1986), now titled *Shylock's Daughter*. The heroine, Jessica, travels through time and has an affair with Shakespeare.

3 For a brief survey of what I have found, see "Shakespearean Romances by Play": http://www.colby.edu/personal/leosborn/popshak.htm, which lists references by play, often with links to pages that explain or cite the reference.

4 Porter's *Toast of the Town* (1993) may be an exception, since the nobleman's obsessive pursuit of the heroine echoes Orsino's excessive passion for Olivia and revises that passion (since he finally does succeed in wooing the lady).

5 The Romance Readers List (RRA-L) (1998) and the Heyerlist (1998) are only two of several listserv reading groups that discuss historical details, author bibliographies, and other resources. I owe thanks to both groups for responding so generously to my quest for Shakespeare references.

4
Moor or less? The surveillance of *Othello*, Calcutta 1848

SUDIPTO CHATTERJEE and JYOTSNA G. SINGH

All my vulnerabilities, my history, my information and experience, my childhood and my manhood ... had to be hurled into ... the quest for *Othello*. ... We bring private knowledge to a public role. ... I understand the state of exile. I understand a need to belong. ... My father was born in East Africa – the son of Gujerat [*sic*] parents. He spent his childhood in an Islamic community born of the ancient Arab trade routes. My father came to England in 1927 ... and he returned neither to East Africa nor Gujerat (India); to the landscapes that had nourished his pride, his myths, and his morality. ... I think this bred in him a sense of displacement. His beautiful English bride ... was his perfect Desdemona, and I hasten to add no one conspired to destroy them. But I know the chaos that could rise up in his throat when our English landscape became too alien. ... I could see the cry behind his eyes. ... "I want to go home" they used to say; and "I want to go home" went into the crucible to be coined night after night during Othello's disintegration.

(Kingsley 1988: 171)

I

In following historically the representation and appropriation of Shakespeare, one can note how repeatedly the issue of surveillance takes center-stage: namely, how the works of the Bard are used in attempts to set boundaries between elite and popular culture, between colonizer and colonized, between "civilization" and "barbarism," or as in actor Ben Kingsley's reflections above, between "exile" and "home." In this process, however, we can also note how cultural surveillance of and through Shakespeare frequently breaks down. The contingent dynamic of the relation between texts and bodies – between the Shakespearean corpus of works and the performative bodies on stage (and now on film) – is inevitably complicated by the ways in which "Shakespeare," as Michel Foucault's "author-function," performs the cultural work of frequently competing constituencies.

In considering stage and critical interpretations of Shakespeare's *Othello*, it is evident that the play has participated in the complex history of Western/white encounters with non-European races. It is commonplace today to discuss *Othello* in relationship to discourses of race at specific moments in colonial and postcolonial history. For instance, *Othello* may be considered in the context of early Renaissance anxieties about "heathens" and "Moors," or in the context of Victorian celebrations of a civilizing mission premised on the "barbarism" of non-Europeans; more recently, within postcolonial liberationist struggles, the Moor's race has served as a marker for continuing racial oppression and a rallying cry for resistance.[1] Most notably, *Othello* has performed important, though often problematic, cultural work in mediating the codes and conventions that have forbidden or disapproved of miscegenation, or racial mixing – perhaps the most sensitive issue of the play and the basis of all racial surveillance.

When we consider the corporeal, now dead bodies of Othello and Desdemona on stage at the end of the play – the scene of miscegenation that Lodovico feels should "be hid" (*Othello* 5.2.375) from the sight of his Venetian spectators – we cannot extricate the tragic resonance of the moment from *the racialized body of the Shakespearean actor*, black, or white-in-black face, who must confront and play the European stereotypes of the "base Indian" and "malignant" Turk at the moment of his horrific suicide. When one considers how this scene marks the culmination of Othello's and Desdemona's foray into a forbidden domain of interracial sexuality, the cumulative shock experienced by European viewers for several centuries cannot be forgotten.

One has only to recall Coleridge in the nineteenth century, who questioned the tragic stature of the play since, according to him, "it would be something monstrous to conceive this beautiful Venetian girl falling in love with a veritable Negro," or Charles Lamb, who felt "something extremely revolting in the courtship and wedded caresses of Othello and Desdemona."[2] Their horror would no doubt be intensified if the nineteenth-century stage had actually accommodated actors of color. Although today one assumes that only a non-white actor will play the part of Othello, mediating, as in the Market Theatre production in South Africa, in contemporary racial conflicts, most will also feel that the cultural and racial surveillance instigated by *Othello* in earlier, colonial, or racially segregated times is now more muted – so much so, that white actors have started playing the role again, albeit under unusual circumstances. The venerable British actor Patrick Stewart (of *Star Trek: The Next Generation* fame) played the Moor in a 1997 version at the Kennedy Center in Washington D.C., but only in an atypical situation, where the rest of the cast was made up of non-white actors. In 1985, Ben Kingsley (of *Gandhi* and *Schindler's List* fame) played the role in a Royal Shakespeare Company (RSC) production in England. But Kingsley is part-Indian by descent, his real name being Krishna Bhanji, and thus he is "colored" enough to play the Moor. Othello has also been played by Hispanic actors in North America, as in the case of Raul Julia in the Public Theater's 1989 Central Park production in New York. So can one assume, then, that in the late twentieth century we no longer need to recuperate appropriations of *Othello* to do the cultural work of understanding and mediating racial divisions? This premise would imply that we have reached an endpoint in our "progress" toward interracial tolerance.

Such perspectives within and outside the academy typify cultural attitudes about the "end of racism," so much so that race in *Othello* seems to have become a trope: a marker of difference that is safely distanced in time, yet able to encompass all of the long history of racial struggle. To counter this trend, in this essay we want to stress both the discontinuity and persistence of racial struggles and to focus on the nuanced specificity of a seemingly benign instance of nineteenth-century English colonial racial codification, an instance in which the body of an Indian actor both demarcates and destabilizes the racial boundaries intrinsic to colonial power relations at the height of the Victorian empire.

We examine these issues of cultural surveillance and resistance in the context of a theatrical "incident" in colonial Calcutta, 1848, when the racially segregated English theater, the Sans Souci, decided to present Shakespeare's *Othello, the Moor of Venice*, with the part of Othello being played by a "Native Gentleman," a Bengali called Bustomchurn Addy (Baiṣñab Caraṅ Āḍhya). Hitherto, all non-white characters in English plays had been played by white actors on the British stage of Calcutta. Addy's appearance as Othello happened a few years after the African American actor, Ira Aldridge (d. 1867), had played the Moor in Philadelphia. Aldridge then launched a career as an actor spanning four decades in England and Europe, never to return to America. He played not only Othello, but also other Shakespearean roles, including: King Lear, Shylock, Richard III, Macbeth, and Aaron in *Titus Andronicus;* Zanga in *The Revenge* by Edward Young (see below); and Mango in *Padlock*, a comic opera by Isaac Bickerstaff (1735–1812). He owned a home in London and was buried in Lódź, Poland. A statue of Ira Aldridge by Pietro Calvi was erected at the Chicago Public Library in 1954. Aldridge, a great exception to the rule, had crossed the racial divide. But, unlike that of the celebrated African American thespian, Addy's crossing never launched a flourishing career and was fraught with numerous controversies and ambiguities. In fact, the first performance of his *Othello* at the Sans Souci was canceled under instructions from high-ranking army officials of the British East India Company. It was only through the efforts of the civilian theater owner, James Barry, responding to the demands of a curious audience, that the production finally had two short runs.

English reviews of these few performances of Addy's Othello were mixed at best, revealing the rulers' pervasive anxieties about race-mixing, despite their interest in mimetic realism. Doubts were expressed about the Native actor's ability to master the sacrosanct Shakespearean language, and a curious silence was maintained about a Native Indian actor's physical proximity to a white Desdemona, Mrs. Anderson, on the stage. In exploring this incident, we argue that the racial politics implicit in the English responses to this production must be seen in a broader context of other representations of "Moors" on the colonial Calcutta stage. In exploring the representational practices that enabled this unusual event to take place, we also recognize the complex relation between the interest of English theater practitioners in theatrical verisimilitude and the pervasive, pseudo-scientific debates about racial typologies whereby nineteenth-century Europeans often saw Asiatics as being closer to the normative, "superior" European man than the supposedly "inferior" Africans. Yet who should the "Moor" on the stage most closely resemble? Identity and difference, as will be apparent, become vexed issues when it comes to racial demarcation.

II

Nineteenth-century colonial discourse about "race" was hardly monolithic or stable; instead, as the prevailing debates about racial cranium differentiation show, it was fissured by complicated, and sometimes confusing, racial typologies in which we can glimpse the vexed history of European racial stratification. Thus having an Indian, a Bengali youth, play Othello was seen as different and less of a fall from "civilization" than having an African play the part. Yet an Indian Othello was not quite acceptable, either. We can identify in this incident the moment of impossibility of Native participation in British theatrical enterprises, and simultaneously the moment of inevitability of the emergence of the Native's own hybridized Western-style theater, which happened within a few years of this incident. James Barry, the manager of the Sans Souci, along with a Mr. Clinger of the same theater, started training Native amateurs in Shakespearean theatrics and other productions in English in the same year, 1848. By 1857, the first Bengali play in the Western style had been produced. The exclusive space of the Calcutta theaters – one that was to mark the social and cultural boundaries between the rulers and the ruled – also reveals that racial and cultural identity is often theatrical and hybrid, rather than fixed and pure.

From the available historical records, it is apparent that James Barry's production and recruitment of a Bengali actor occurred under the auspices of both an English and Indian patronage. According to *The Calcutta Star*, August 4, 1848, several Indian aristocrats and *bābus*[3] supported the endeavor:[4]

> Under the Patronages of Maharajah Radkaunt Bahadur; Maharajah Buddinauth Roy … Maharajah Prawnkissen Mullick and Brothers; Baboos Greeschunder Dutt and Brothers … Mr. Barry having obtained the above Patronages and also the kind and gratuitous services of a Native Gentleman in conjunction with the

> valuable aid of several English Gentleman Amateurs, will present to his Friends and the public a novel evening's entertainment.
>
> On Thursday Evening, August 10th, 1848, will be acted Shakespeare's Tragedy of "*Othello*" The Moor of Venice … [b]y a Native Gentleman.
>
> (Mitra 1967: 197)

Having a "Native Gentleman" play Othello, the Moor of Venice, was part of a movement in English theaters of Calcutta at the beginning of the nineteenth century toward "ethnic correctness" of representation. In looking for models homewards, the English theaters in Calcutta aimed at verisimilitude and realism, while, of course, adjusting to the climes of the colony, both geographic and cultural. Expectations of English audiences in India were somewhat different from those of their London counterparts, especially when the productions dealt with certain subjects that meant more in the colonies than at home. Prior to Barry's production of the Native *Othello*, several plays on the nineteenth-century stage prominently figured a number of "Moors." A production of *Zanga*, also known as *The Revenge: A Tragedy*, by Edward Young (1683–1765), which originally was performed in London's major theaters, was produced in Calcutta by the locally famous Chowringhee Theatre, described by the *Calcutta Journal* on October 26, 1819 as follows:[5]

> The entrance of Zanga … did not prevent us from being struck with the want of dignity as well as of propriety in the costume. It was neither princely, nor Moorish, and we are satisfied that if a person in such a dress had been seen (not now, but at any past period however near or however remote) in the streets of Tripoly, Tunis, or Algiers, notwithstanding the variety of dresses to be met with in these Moorish cities, he would have been as much regarded as an object of curiosity as an Englishman in the heart of Fez.
>
> The departure from African costume is scarcely pardonable here, surrounded as we are by Mohammedans of Asia, from whom at least our amateurs, whether managers or performers, might have learnt. …
>
> (370)

The reviewer's criticism and commentary focus on ethnic correctness of representation, as the embodiment of the Moors on stage was found wanting in terms of realism. The criticisms suggest that despite the white-faced English actors' best efforts, their costume and demeanor were "contrary to the simple habiliments, the erect attitude, and the graceful walk, not only of the Moors of Africa, but of those by whom we are everyday waited on and surrounded" (370).

The reviewer's concern about correctness of ethnic representation is premised on an implicit surveillance of minute racial distinctions. The author of this review is effectively talking about the performance of colonial authenticity in the colony – the premise that the Native of the colony ought to be represented as the "Native." It is of no concern that the actor performing the character is actually an Englishman. The concern is for the "authenticity" of the representation. The Moor is to carry himself like those "by whom we are everyday waited on and surrounded" and yet have the "erect attitude, and the graceful walk" becoming to the stereotypical Moor. It is also interesting to note the thrust to homogenize by the collapsing of the Moor with the Asiatic Mohammedan, North Africa with India, colony with colony. The question, then, becomes: who is the "real" Moor? Does the colonial idea of the Moor, then, make him real and grant him performative corporeality?

Other "Moors" appeared on the stages of Calcutta's English theaters in the early nineteenth century, evoking similar concerns about racial typologies and distinctions. In 1822, white actors played "Moors" in a production of *The Mountaineers* at the Dum Dum Theatre, which according to the January 18 *Calcutta Journal*, contained "representations of the race that occupied Granada at the period of the history described" (1822: 189). The critic notes positively that the "whole of the Moorish department of the piece, in music, scenery, dress, processions, etc. was well got and well supported, doing equal credit to the liberality and good taste of the managers," but once again, it was the problem of authenticity. The critic describes two characters as follows:

> Zorayda had great bashfulness and timidity, though her complexion prevented our seeing the blushes which usually accompany these in the Fair Sex. Bulcazin Muley, her worthy, was well dressed, and well coloured; the only defect we remarked was the busy ringlets and side whiskers, neither of which were ever worn by the Moors, we believe, as they shave their heads, and either have full beards or mustachios on the upper lip only. (189)

The chance to make a dig at the impossibility of the darker Moorish pigmentation representing the red-cheeked bashfulness of the *fair* sex (who cannot help but be *un-fair* as a Mooress) must have been impossible for the critic to pass up. But the "well coloured" father of un-*fair* Zorayda is marked for the ethnographic inaccuracies of having facial hair on the side only and an unshaven head. Thus, even while generally commending the performances for their representations of the Other, these reviews of both *Zanga* and *The Mountaineers* affirm *the impossibility of accounting fairly for racial Otherness in performance*. But there was no other way. It was unspeakable for the Other to represent himself. Hence, despite the problem of anthropomorphic inaccuracies that this sort of representation contained, the English had to be happy with the black-faced non-Other/Self as the Other.

But the interest in representing the racial Other in the colonial outpost was a very special one. In the discourse emanating from the staging of these Moorish characters, one can note both an affirmation and an elision of racial difference categorized through taxonomies and typologies. The eighteenth-century Dutch scientist Petrius Camper (1722–89) had done some comparative work on racial anatomy. The subtitle of the English translation of Camper's *Works* claims that he based his work on "the natural difference of features of different persons of different countries and periods of life, and on beauty as exhibited in ancient sculpture; with a new method of sketching heads, natural features and portraits of individuals, with accuracy."[6] The first translation of Camper's work had appeared in 1784, and a new edition was published in London in 1821. The pseudo-scientific field of craniology was also of interest in the colonies, and in 1821, the *Calcutta Journal* reproduced a report and a diagram that had been published by the *Liverpool Mercury*. This report presented a study of the shape of human skulls among various races of the world that was based on the *Works* of Camper. Structured as a hierarchy (Figure 1) moving from the primate to Homo sapiens, the diagram consists of a series of engravings showing the development of the human skull away from the apes. The order observed the following progres-

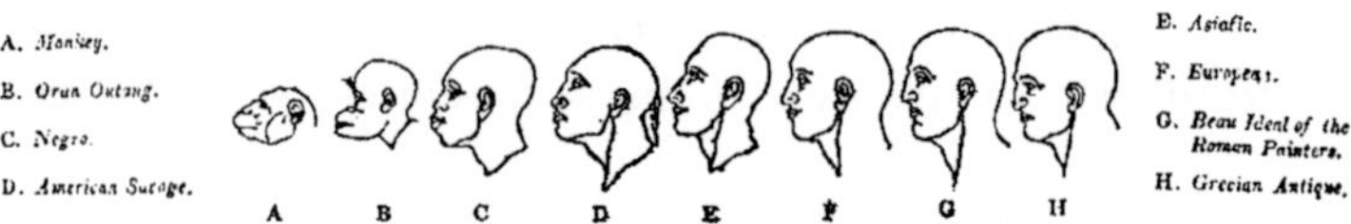

Figure 1 Physiognomy and the facial line, *Calcutta Journal* 1821.

sion: (a) Monkey, (b) Orang Outang, (c) Negro, (d) American Savage, (e) Asiatic, (f) European, (g) Beau Ideal of the Roman painters, and (h) Grecian Antique. The following note appeared with the diagram in the *Calcutta Journal*:

> According to Professor Camper, the facial line of the monkey makes an angle of 42 degrees with the horizontal line; that of the Orang-outang [*sic*], 58; the Negro, 70; the Chinese, 75; European, 80, or 90; the Grecian Antique, 100. If above 100 it begins to grow monstrous.
>
> (1821: 272)

The degree ascribed to the Asiatic places him sufficiently far away from the Negro, the American Savage, and the monkey. At the same time, he is at a safe neighboring distance from the European, allowing the latter a superior remove. The European's 10–15 degree remove from the classical Greco-Roman "perfection" also makes the European category "safe." While the European is some distance away from the "perfection" of the Greco-Roman, the same distance also grants him acceptable "normalcy." While these typologies do not collapse the African and Asiatic as racial categories, this overanxious surveillance of racial distinctions offers telling insights into the colonial production of the Native/Other within the power hierarchy of imperialism and on the colonial stage.

It would be wrong to assume that this theory was accepted monolithically by all Englishmen in India. Even the suggestion, however cautious and double-edged, that the Asiatic was actually not too far in "facial lines" from the English was absurd and abhorrent to many Englishmen in India. A letter written to the *Calcutta Journal* on February 16, 1822, presumably by an Englishman, insists that it would be wrong to conclude from craniological evidence that the English and "Hindoo" are racial relatives:

> I have been much amused and edified by that part of the Asiatic Society lucubrations which regards Hindoo craniology.
>
> We shall get on now: Happy Hindoo! No more shall thy skull bleach useless on the banks of thy Ganges, a play thing for Jackalls and Tiger cubs.
>
> (1822: 416)

The epistler, furthermore, could not accept the notion that the "Hindoos" who are now servants of the Englishmen could ever have been industrious "castle-builders":

> These things seem quite well beyond the range of an untutored mind and there is a well known fact which militates strongly against the supposition. The Hindoos are invariably most excellent SLEEPERS; now the castle-building man is never a good Sleeper.
>
> (416)

This letter reflects the contemporary findings of both craniologists and Orientalists who were proclaiming the supposed racial relation of the Asiatic to the European. However, it was impossible within the scope of the colonial imaginary to see them as equals at any level. While the pseudo-scientific discourse seems anxious to offer neat gradations of difference between Asiatics and Africans, just as Orientalists stressed the original, ancient proximity between Asians and Europeans, these distinctions were blurred on the Calcutta stage, where the categories of "Moors," "Mohammedans," and "Asiatics" often overlapped.

The colonial stage seemed to draw more on prevailing racist fantasies than on academic empiricism. The collapsing of racial categories on the stage was symptomatically related to the ideological rift between projects such as Orientalism and craniology and the pragmatic business of ruling and expanding the Indian empire. The empire had to have its dominant and dominated, the mighty master and the servile servant. The "Moor" of the theater therefore had to be mimetically recreated with an astute eye for anthropological detail that expressed his "Otherness." What was possible and feasible in the pseudo-scientific narrative of race – the linking of Asian and European racial categories – was impossible to realize in the corporeality of the staged body. The staged "Moor" had to be less exact(ing) than the real "Moor," "whiteness" being the stable and all-encompassing category that conferred on Europeans the privilege to build and rule the empire.

III

These impulses, on the one hand to categorize gradations of racial distinctions and, on the other hand, to shade together the very same gradations when confronted with "whiteness," form the background against which James Barry's 1848 production of *Othello* in Calcutta can be understood. In the colonial responses to this production, we can see the ways in which "Shakespeare" performs the cultural and political work of competing, though uneven, constituencies. By the 1840s, the impulse to situate the real "Moor" had moved toward a more genuine concern for replicating observed social realities. The whole issue of representation and power in colonial cultural formations had clearly come to a head. If "Moors" were popular on the English stage, then inevitably a production of *Othello* would, once again, raise the question: Can the "Moor" now represent the "Moor"? Can the Native be made to stage himself?

In 1848, something as yet unheard-of happened. On August 4, James Barry, as the umpteenth owner of the Sans Souci Theatre in white Calcutta and desperate to keep his theater going, ventured to cast a Native gentleman in the title role – "Baboo Bustomchurn Addy." The Moor and the Bengali had collapsed into one for Shakespeare's sake, for novelty's sake, for the colony's sake, and – in Barry's case – for profit's sake. Addy as Othello was not comparable to a black-faced white actor at the Chowringhee Theatre dressed as Zanga, the Moor. He was the "real" Othello. The opening performance of Barry's *Othello* was, however, abruptly aborted due to the opposition of a local military commanding officer, who refused permission for his men to play extras in the production. A letter published in the *Calcutta Star* on August 12 describes the crowd that had gathered before the Sans Souci (Figure 2) that evening on Park Street in

Figure 2 The Chowringhee Theatre, Calcutta, destroyed by fire in 1839. The Sans Souci, where Addy performed in 1848, stood on the same site on Park Street.

white Calcutta: "At last we crept on inch by inch and people began to wonder if their seats were kept for them. How full it must be – By Jove, Barry and the Nigger will make a fortune" (Mitra 1967: 199). The same letter records the reaction of the audience when they discovered that the performances had been canceled that night. The epistler sets up a conversation between members of the excitable crowd:

> No play, said the stout gentleman – What? said the multitude. Othello sick!! No – he ain't painted! [...] Desdemona inebriated! Barry drunk! Iago not come – one gentleman in a white choker roared out, how could you expect him when his very name tells you Aye a go?
>
> (200)

Despite the banter of this letter, historical evidence suggests that the event had more serious political implications. Not only did the military commander pull the soldiers from the cast, but the police were also sent, "having received military notice to arrest the well known amateurs should they have attempted to make their appearance" (203). While no evidence exists to suggest a direct link between the presence of a Native Othello on the English stage and the military-police action, the reviews reveal a different kind of surveillance at work.

IV

The lights at the Sans Souci were lit again on August 17, 1848 and the *Bengal Hurkaru* offered a lengthy review of the performance two days later, on August 19:

> **Sans Souci: The Hindoo Othello**
>
> *Othello*, of Shakespeare's plays, the latest and the best, was the great attraction Thursday night – the player, however, but not the play. Performed by Baboo Bustomchurn Addy ... all expectations were, of course, centred in the young aspirant for dramatic fame, who has gallantly flung down the gauntlet to the rest of the members of the Native community. For in England, it is well known, the poetry of the mind has long given way to the poetry of motion, and Shakespeare, exiled from the country he honours so much, seeks an asylum on the Calcutta boards. ... Pleasanter still it is to record the attendance of the most

> influential members of the Civil Service, impelled, no doubt, some by curiosity, others, we trust, by a worthier motive. … Othello's entry was greeted with a hearty welcome, and the first speech … evidenced considerable study and an absence of that timidity so constantly the concomitant of a first appearance. Slim, but symmetrical in person, his delivery was somewhat cramped, but, under all circumstances, his pronunciation of English was for a Native remarkably good.
>
> (Mitra 1967: 205–6)

While the reviewer evokes a curious nostalgia for the "exiled" Shakespeare seeking "an asylum on the Calcutta boards," he quickly reasserts the divide between England, the home of Shakespearean drama, and the colonial backdrop for this Native performance. The reviewer's praise of the young "aspirant to dramatic fame" is seldom unqualified. His tongue-in-cheek praise of Addy for flinging "down the gauntlet to the rest of the members of the Native community" is accompanied by a reminder of Addy's inescapable Native limitations: "his delivery" was "cramped," but "his pronunciation of English was for a Native remarkably good" (206–7). The *Hurkaru* reviewer also states: "As might have been expected, [Addy] was far from being proficient in the art of bye-play, which was painfully remarked throughout the piece. … [A] better knowledge of stage-business would be a great desideratum" (207). Overall, the reviewer seems pulled apart by conflicting responses, regretting Addy's incompetence in the third act, which "was very poor"; on the other hand, although Addy's "utterance of the finest passage: 'Farewell the neighing steed and the shrill trumpet' etc. was a dead failure" (210; *Othello* 3.3.356), the reviewer nonetheless praises the Native actor for his passion: "The act was more or less relieved by the vitality infused into the part where Othello seizes Iago by the throat, and shortly afterwards by the energetic full-toned declaration of: 'Arise black vengeance … !'" (207; referring to *Othello* 3.3.451).

So continues the rest of the review, with a mixture of praise and condescension; the reviewer laments the "inexperience" of the Native actor and his consequent inability to "depict the ravages of the whirlwind of jealousy which overpowers the soul of the Moor," yet lauds Addy's "success" when, "racked with the tortures of an agonized heart he gave full vent to his suspicions, [saying to Desdemona] 'Come, swear it, damn thyself'" (208; referring to *Othello* 4.2.37).

The reviewer's rhetorical weaving and bobbing leads one to ask: how could an actor with such scant knowledge of "bye-play" and "stage-business" infuse himself with sufficient "vitality" to seize Iago "by the throat" and then give "energetic full toned" justice to the heaving pentameter iambs of Shakespeare's blank verse, despite a "delivery ... somewhat cramped"?

The *Hurkaru* reviewer crowns the ambivalence of his response with this comment on the final act: "In the beautiful soliloquy 'It is the cause, my soul,' the actor was scarcely audible, and that vile lack of turning his back upon the audience told greatly to his disadvantage" (Mitra 1967: 208; referring to *Othello* 5.2.1 ff.). Why was Addy's back turned to the audience in these final moments of the tragedy? Could the Native Addy, despite the license of drama, be seen by the public to kiss and hold Desdemona, played by the English actress, Mrs. Anderson, and breathe her "balmy breath"? (*Othello* 5.2.16). Reviewers in the colonial English press curiously ignore the enactment of potential miscegenation on the stage, a subject that was confronted by Coleridge and Lamb in the metropolis but that perhaps was unspeakable and taboo in the colonial setting. While their silence on the subject speaks volumes, we will never know the reasons for it.

Other English reviewers of Addy's performance also veered between complimenting the Native actor's occasional "good" delivery and physical acting, on the one hand, and castigating him for the lack of the same merits, on the other. *The Englishman*, another English language daily, describes the Native actor as follows:

> Scarcely a line was intelligible, and this did not arise from the low tone of voice; Othello spoke quite loud enough, but he "mouthed" too much. ... Taking it as a whole, we consider the performance wonderful for a Native.
>
> (Mitra 1967: 210)

Despite their criticisms, however, these accounts also testify to the "thunderous applause" of the audiences at the end of the show.

So how did the saga of the Native *Othello* end? Barry's success with the venture led him to attempt a reprise on September 12, 1848, but this second performance was shot down by the English reviewers. The same *Englishman* that had less than a month ago placed "great credit on [Addy's] industry and performance," wrote on September 14:

> We went reluctantly and came back sad. ... Whether our Native friend juggled wisely or well in selecting so difficult a task we will not venture to discuss, but that he failed, in every sense of the word, both in conception and execution, we think everyone must admit. It is not our intention to expatiate with hair drawn minuteness on the demerits of this gentleman as an actor; let it suffice for us to observe that the performance was tame, languid, affected, tedious, and imperfect ... undeservedly imposed upon a kind-hearted and indulgent public.
>
> (Mitra 1967: 211–12)

The anxious ambivalence that characterized reviews of the first performance has disappeared. The project is now "imperfect," an infliction upon an "indulgent" public. As a subject interpellated within a colonialist ideology, Addy was always already doomed to failure. The Native could not speak, even through the garb of theatrical verisimilitude that "made" him the Moor.

Writing about the Hindu Theatre, a theatrical outfit established by a Bengali *bābu* in 1831, a writer for the *Asiatic Journal* notes that Natives ought to "perceive the propriety of confining themselves to the representation of dramas to which their complexion would be appropriate" (Sānyāl 1997: 45). Thus, the Native is cautioned not to speak for the white Shakespeare. Despite James Barry's courageous casting, Addy's Othello could not bridge the racial divide. Addy might well have mouthed the lines of the Bard's Moor to speak his own burdened Native mind:

> Then must you speak
> Of one that loved not wisely but too well,
> Of one not easily jealous, but being wrought,
> Perplexed in the extreme; of one whose hand
> (Like the base Indian) threw a pearl away
> Richer than all his tribe; of one whose subdued eyes,
> Albeit unusèd to the melting mood,
> Drops tears as fast as the Arabian trees
> Their medicinable gum. Set you down this. ...
>
> (*Othello* 5.2.352–60)

Shakespeare's reference to the "base Indian" turns ironic in the face of Addy's "failure." The Native actor had indeed thrown a "pearl ... / Richer than all his tribe" – his identity – into question, "as fast as the Arabian trees" drop "[t]heir medicinable gum."

Despite the daring nature of the undertaking, its "medicinable" potential to bridge the gulf of racial difference, the colonial situation had rendered it quixotic. The Shakespearean Moor, despite his complexion, was not dark enough for the Bengali Native to play. This was Shakespeare, after all, and none but the white English could represent Othello in the best possible way. The (Indian) Other therefore could only be produced by the (English) Self.

Addy's performance, while considered a failure by the English reviewers, nonetheless was an important event on the stage of England's empire. His "brown" Othello stood in for mimetic excess, overbearing in the exactness of its verisimilitude, but pointing to a realm of hybridity – the domain of mimetic alterity – both in the colonial society of India and on its ostensibly exclusive stage. The Native had run out of options. Despite the strictures of racial difference and conservation, the imperial nature of the relationship of the ruler and the ruled had turned the borderland between them liminal, a gray area where the colonial identity of the Native danced with imperial surveillance in a tenuous accord. About ten years after Addy's performance at the Sans Souci, the Bengali intelligentsia would have its own theater as a playground of hybrid constructions.

V

The central theme informing this essay remains surveillance. Has the Shakespearean Moor – be it in Aldridge's, or Addy's, or even Kingsley's performance – meant more than the sum of its players' personal experiences? How has surveillance of racialized spaces through *Othello* transmuted and transmitted itself from the colonial to the postcolonial? To make a final jab at the disciplining gaze of surveillance that *Othello* has accorded imperialism, without discounting the postcolonial liberation agendas it has also vindicated in many radical stage interpretations, let us (re)turn to the essay's opening, Ben Kingsley's personal statement on what impelled and moved him as he performed Othello's nightly "disintegration" on the stage – his metaphoric search for ancestry. Remembering the idea of race as a trope that we mentioned earlier, in an odd way Kingsley is indeed a descendant of Addy. He is, willy nilly, the Indian Moor on the English stage, warping through 150 years of coloniality. A reading of his statement could well lead us to believe that Kingsley's father is Othello and that *Kingsley is playing his father*.

In the personal statement, Kingsley elegantly sentimentalizes his own ethnicity, usefully pointing at the racial reverberations the play produces in his personal odyssey; but at the same time, he evinces little awareness of or interest in the politics of race in contemporary Britain and the place of (his) race in the RSC production. While this is not an attempt to second-guess Kingsley, one could still pose a conjecture: does Kingsley think he is accounting for race and ethnicity by sentimentalizing Othello via his father? He may well be doing the very thing we are attempting to interrogate here: account personally and reductively for a question (signified by the text of play itself) that relates to much larger racial and political constituencies of imperial history. Curiously, in a sampling of reviews and interviews about the production, there were no explicit references to be found about the politics of race or the place of Ben Kingsley's ethnicity in the RSC version of *Othello*. Ira Aldridge had left America and transcended race by physically embodying the Other for the imperial continent, while Addy disappeared after the crash of his second run at the Sans Souci. But what does Ben Kingsley's implicit refusal to place race at the heart of *Othello* tell us? By displacing racial divisions and inequities with *personal* history and thereby denying it political significance, this refusal to confront racial histories de-politicizes *Othello* in the postcolonial landscape. Is imperial surveillance thus perpetuated with the hapless knowledge that we have perhaps only relocated from colonial to neo-colonial, that postcolonial is still a shimmering frontier? But, then, perhaps there are other *Othello*s taking center-stage around the world, producing a more viable postcolonial subject.

Notes

1 For a full account of these appropriations of *Othello*, see Neill 1989, Newman 1987, and Singh 1994.

2 Quotes from Coleridge and Lamb are from Sylvan Barnet's "*Othello* on the Stage and Screen" (1986: 273).

3 The word *bābu* is used in all languages in the Indian subcontinent. The etymology of the word is shrouded in obscurity. It is suspected that the word *bābu* became a signifier of social status only in the eighteenth century. Initially signifying that the person addressed was a landowner, by the end of the century it denoted the economically privileged and with time, softened even further to denote educated men even from the middle class. Some historians have conjectured that the word is actually a Bengali corruption of the English "baboon," which

the colonizers used to identify their subjects and to whose pejorative signification the Natives had no access. But this last theory is yet to be substantiated with concrete evidence.

4 All subsequent citations from *The Calcutta Star* and other contemporary English language newspapers of Calcutta, such as *The Englishman* and *The Bengal Hurkaru*, are from Amal Mitra's *Kalkātāy Bideśī Raṅgālay* [Foreign Theaters in Calcutta].

5 All citations from the *Calcutta Journal* are from New York University's microfilm holdings. Page numbers refer to the volume of the particular year from which the quote is taken.

6 The edition of Camper's book came with the following publishing information: London, Sold by J. Hearne, Priestley, Weale, E. Butler, W. Mason, 1821.

Part 2
Appropriation in practice

5
Remembering *King Lear* in Jane Smiley's *A Thousand Acres*

CAROLINE CAKEBREAD

I *A Thousand Acres* as Shakespearean re-vision

At the 1996 World Shakespeare Congress in Los Angeles, American author Jane Smiley described her 1991 novel, *A Thousand Acres*, as a contemporary rewriting of *King Lear* that attempts "to communicate the ways in which I found conventional readings of *King Lear* frustrating and wrong" (Smiley 1998: 42).[1] In Los Angeles, Smiley talked about her experiences as a student learning about Shakespeare's tragedy for the first time:

> Beginning with my first readings of the play in high school and continuing through college and graduate school, I had been cool to both Cordelia and Lear. While I understood and accepted how I should feel about them, he struck me as the sort of person, from beginning to end, that you would want to stay away from – selfish, demanding, humorless, self-pitying. … My acceptance of his tragedy was pro-forma, the response of a good girl and a good student. I didn't like Cordelia either. She seemed ungenerous and cold, a stickler for truth at the beginning, a stickler for form at the end.
>
> (42–43)

A reaction against traditional readings of *King Lear*, Smiley's novel seems to have been rooted from its inception in the process of "re-vision." Adrienne Rich explains that:

> Re-vision – the act of looking back, of seeing with fresh eyes, of entering an old text from a new critical direction – is for women more than a chapter in cultural history: it is an act of survival. Until we can understand the assumptions in which we are drenched we cannot know ourselves.
>
> (1979: 35)

Smiley situates herself in the midst of this process; she completely refigures "pro-forma" critical responses to *King Lear* by retelling that story through the eyes of Goneril, Lear's oldest, traditionally vilified daughter. She becomes Ginny Cook, the first-person narrator of Smiley's novel.

Living in the fictional farming community of Zebulon County, Iowa in 1979, Ginny learns to cope with her father Larry's legacy, as he suddenly and inexplicably decides to divide up his thousand-acre farm among his three daughters: Ginny (Goneril), Rose (Regan), and Caroline (Cordelia). Ginny and Rose are married to farmers, Ty and Pete (Albany and Cornwall), while Caroline escapes farming life by becoming a lawyer and working in the city. The year 1979 is important, marking as it does the end of Jimmy Carter's presidency, when farmers were being encouraged to take out large loans and disastrous mortgages on their land. While *Lear* operates in a large political and moral sphere, Smiley shows a different sort of tragedy, the near-erasure of the family farm in the American Midwest in the mid-1980s. As in *King Lear*, the novel begins with a public gathering. Smiley's Gloucester figure, Harold Clark, is holding a welcome-home barbecue for his son, Jess (Edmund), who has returned to Zebulon County after having spent years in Canada as a draft-dodger. It is here that Larry announces his plans to divide up his farm amongst his daughters and retire. Ginny and Rose nod their agreement to his plan, while Caroline expresses her doubt and is subsequently disinherited. The novel traces the widening rifts within the Cook family as the land is transferred from father to daughter, with Larry's behavior growing increasingly erratic and the excluded Caroline growing more and more suspicious of Ginny's and Rose's newly inherited control over the farm. The family struggles culminate in a courtroom drama rather than on a battlefield – as in Shakespeare's tragedy – with Larry and Caroline teamed up against Ginny, Rose, and their husbands.

In Smiley's version of Shakespeare's tragedy, the battle for land that pits Larry and "stickler for truth" Caroline against Rose and Ginny is finally subsumed into the larger framework of the novel, in which Ginny learns to connect herself to aspects of her past that are buried in the soil rather than in the farming structures that have been placed upon it. Smiley completely redraws the boundaries of Lear's kingdom, using Ginny's perspective to reassess the "champains riched" and "wide-skirted meads" of Goneril's legacy (1.1.62, 63).[2] In doing so, she examines Lear's monumental decision to divide up his kingdom among his daughters in order to focus upon the "darker" nature of the physical and emotional territory that Ginny and her sister inherit from their father. While Larry ostensibly signs the farm over to his daughters, their ultimate inheritance rests, not on the surface of the land, but in the lies and secrets that it covers up. Smiley creates a landscape that is filled with poisons, with the fertilizers, destructive herbicides, and pesticides that are harbored underneath the seemingly abundant surface of the farm. Decades of chemical use have poisoned the well-water that Ginny and her family drink. Those poisons have been inscribed upon the bodies of women in the Cook family in different ways. Rose and, before her, her mother, are both victims of breast cancer; Ginny is unable to have children and has suffered several miscarriages. Larry's land physically embodies the very "terrors of the earth" (2.4.277) that Lear attempts to conjure up for his daughters. But Smiley also works to undermine the basis of the Cook family itself. At the crux of the novel lies Smiley's most potent addition to the Lear plot: the fact that both Ginny and Rose have been sexually abused by their father. In rewriting the *Lear* story, Smiley offers readers not just a feminized view of Shakespeare's tragedy, but also a depressing and often harrowing portrait of American family life.

In this essay, I shall look at *A Thousand Acres* as the product of Smiley's struggle to map out her relationship to Shakespeare. In working to gain a foothold in her own past – to recover memory from silence – Smiley's protagonist Ginny reflects Smiley's own confrontation with an author whose presence at the hub of the Western literary canon represents a powerful and often overwhelming legacy. The Oedipal model of literary regeneration posited by Harold Bloom in *The Anxiety of Influence* (1973) rests on the assumption that an implicitly male sparring match dominates the experience of writing. Bloom asserts that great literature is the product of "major figures with the persistence to wrestle with their strong precursors, even to the death. Weaker talents idealize; figures of capable imagination appropriate for themselves" (5). Smiley reconfigures the father–son Oedipal paradigm for authorship in light of the monumental father–daughter struggle that is the subject of her novel. In the keynote address at the World Shakespeare Congress, Smiley explained what she gradually had begun to perceive as her own "wrestling match with Mr. Shakespeare" (1998: 55):

> [Shakespeare's] plot was always the test, a puzzle I had to work out. The challenge was sticking to the plot but substituting what many would say was simply a more congenial view of human nature. As I followed him into the story, the Shakespeare that I thought I knew rapidly metamorphosed into a harsher, more alien, more distant male figure. I felt very strongly our differences as a modern woman and a Renaissance man.
>
> (54)

Through his play, Shakespeare begins to reveal himself as a harsh, distant, and importantly, male figure, against whom Smiley struggles to guard her own difference as a "modern woman." Smiley writes herself into Shakespeare's tragedy by feminizing it and transferring it to the American heartland. The novel's epigraph, taken from Meridel Le Sueur's "The Ancient People and the Newly Come," becomes crucial to Smiley's placement of herself in relation to Shakespeare:

> The body repeats the landscape. They are the source of each other and create each other. We are marked by the seasonal body of earth, by the terrible migrations of people, by the swift turn of a century, verging on change never before experienced on this greening planet.
>
> (Le Sueur 1982: 39)

Born in Murray, Iowa, Le Sueur was inducted into the Iowa Women's Hall of Fame on December 12, 1996. Author, poet, and lecturer, Le Sueur was blacklisted during the 1940s and 1950s because of her left-wing beliefs and, throughout her lifetime, remained active in human rights, feminist, and environmental movements.[3] Le Sueur's presence in *A Thousand Acres* indicates Smiley's concern with the literary tradition in which she is writing, apart from her Shakespearean source. While Smiley seeks to "re-enter" Shakespeare's text from a female perspective – in this case, Goneril's – she defines her point of entry in American terms and through another woman writer. If, as Le Sueur asserts, "the body repeats the landscape," that landscape is integral to Ginny Cook's attempts to remember the horrific aspects of her past and to Smiley's overall efforts to re-vision *King Lear*. The Iowan landscape also links Le Sueur and Smiley as writers.

Offering us an alternative to Lear's map of his kingdom at the beginning of her novel, Smiley bodies forth the landscape through Ginny's eyes. Looking from the top of a small mound located at the "intersection of CR #686," Ginny can survey her father's land:

> No globe or map fully convinced me that Zebulon County was not the center of the universe. Certainly, Zebulon County, where the earth *was* flat, was one spot where a sphere (a seed, a rubber ball, a ballbearing) must come down to perfect rest and once at rest must send a taproot downward into the ten-foot-thick topsoil.
> (Smiley 1991: 3)

Ginny's perspective allows the reader an alternative view of the land that she will one day inherit: a narrow map of a flat world, with Zebulon County at its center. But that point of view is contingent upon the place where she is standing, the view afforded to her from the vantage point of intersecting roads. Looking down into the poisoned waters beneath the surface structure of the farms, Ginny finds a new and empowering knowledge of the curses that have plagued her body and her mind. In the converging roads, we can also see the nucleus of Smiley's relationship to Shakespeare, whose text she rewrites from a contemporary, feminine vantage point, filtered through two lenses: her own perspective and that of Meridel Le Sueur. Placing Meridel Le Sueur into the Shakespeare–Smiley equation, we can open up Bloom's linear model of influence and appropriation and look at the novel as a true act of re-vision, a merging together of several different perspectives. We can see in *A Thousand Acres* a new territory taking shape, one that merges the strict, patriarchal family dynamics inherent in Smiley's Shakespearean source with the more localized presence of Le Sueur and so challenges what Smiley refers to in her keynote address as "Mr. Shakespeare's alleged universality" (1998: 56).

II Family histories in Shakespeare and Smiley

Asserting her role in a literary family that includes both Shakespeare and Le Sueur – a father and a mother – Smiley confronts the motherless world of *King Lear* to challenge traditional female roles not only in the Shakespearean, but also in the American family. In this way, Smiley's novel draws upon and furthers other feminist readings of *King Lear*. Marianne Novy, for instance, writes that Shakespeare does not permit Goneril and Regan "to point out wrongs done to them in the past. ... If their attack on Lear can be seen as, in part, the consequence of his tyrannical patriarchy, they never try to explain it as an attack on an oppressor" (1984: 153). Taking the part of Lear's unloved daughters, Smiley rethinks the oppressively patriarchal family of Elizabethan society that Shakespeare represents in *King Lear*. Smiley told her Los Angeles audience that, while traditional interpretations portray Regan and Goneril as "figures of pure evil" (1998: 43), they seemed both sympathetic and familiar to her as women,

> especially in the scene where they talk between themselves about Lear's actions, and later, when they have to deal with his unruly knights. They were women, and the play seemed to be condemning them morally for the exact ways in which they expressed womanhood that I recognized. I was offended.
>
> (43)

Smiley portrays Ginny and Rose as women caught in traditional care-giving roles: working to please their father, cleaning his house, and preparing the meals that he insists upon having at the same time every day. In turn, their efforts are met by Larry's stony silences. While their sister, Caroline, escapes farming life to work in Des Moines, the older sisters are constantly being given a different sort of love-test, the terms of which are defined by their father. In Shakespeare's play, Lear demands of his daughters:

> Which of you shall we say doth love us most?
> That we our largest bounty may extend
> Where nature doth with merit challenge.
>
> (1.1.49–51)

Smiley draws upon Cordelia's response to Lear – "Sure I shall never marry like my sisters / To love my father all" (1.1.102–3) – to measure Ginny's and Rose's interactions with their father, ranging from his domination of their daily routine to the warped sexual relationship that he had forced upon them in adolescence. As Ginny tells us, "My earliest memories of him are of being afraid to look him in the eye, to look at him at all" (Smiley 1991: 19). Like Goneril and Regan in Shakespeare's play, Ginny and Rose seek safety by giving their father the right answers, telling him what he wants to hear. "My father was easily offended," Ginny tells us. "But normally he was easily mollified, too, if you spoke your prescribed part with the proper appearance of remorse" (33). Smiley not only expresses sympathy for Regan's and Goneril's efforts to appease their father by making the reactions of the older daughters comprehensible, but she also translates Cordelia's resonant response to Lear's demand to be mollified – "nothing" (1.1.88) – into Caroline's meticulous but icy allegiance to legalities: "She was always looking for the rights and wrongs of every argument, trying to figure out who should apologize for what, who should go first, what the exact wording should be" (Smiley 1991: 33). Smiley rewrites Shakespeare's play to declare her allegiance to Lear's older daughters and to offer an alternative reading of *King Lear*'s patriarchal family.

For Ginny and Rose, escape from the roles assigned to them by their father entails not the silence of Cordelia, but a full-voiced articulation of their side of the story, a vocal challenge to the version of the past handed down to them by their father. Ginny escapes the farm at the end of the novel, taking a job at a roadside café and leaving behind once and for all her husband and the farm. When Ty comes years later to ask Ginny for a divorce, the two realize how very different their views of the past – of her family's "history" – are. While Ty mourns the loss of the farm and the Cook family history that it represents, Ginny sees the double-sided nature of that legacy. As she explains to him:

> It's good to remember and repeat. You feel good to be a part of that. But then I saw what my part really was. Rose showed me. … She showed me, but I knew what she showed me was true even before she finished showing me. You see this grand history, but I see blows. I see taking what you want because you want it, then making something up that justifies what you did. I see getting others to pay the price, then covering up and forgetting what the price was. Do I think Daddy came up with beating and fucking us on his own? … No. I think he had lessons, and those lessons were part of the package, along with the land and the lust to run things exactly the way he wanted to no matter what.
>
> (Smiley 1991: 342–43)

In recovering her own memories of abuse, Ginny revises the received story of the Cook family legacy, as passed down to her by her father, by reassessing her own role in that history. When preparing poisoned sausages for her sister in a jealous rage over Jess, Ginny nearly succumbs to the tragic fate of her Shakespearean counterpart, who poisons Regan out of love for Edmund. But in the end, Ginny learns to come to terms with her past and, finally, to leave the farm behind. Ginny saves herself and survives, while Goneril is subsumed by the Shakespearean family tragedy, taking her own life.

Ultimately, Smiley's feminized version of Shakespeare's play destabilizes his fixed position at the center of the Western literary canon as her novel becomes a testing-ground for new perspectives on "history," in which fathers and daughters – both literary and familial – are pitted against one another. While Smiley draws on Bloom's agonistic model of influence when she views herself as a writer "wrestling" with Shakespeare, her protagonist recognizes the difficulty of extricating herself from the coded, patriarchal world of the father. As Ginny wonders:

> Perhaps there is a distance that is the optimum distance for seeing one's father, farther than across the supper table or across the room, somewhere in the middle distance: he is dwarfed by trees or the sweep of a hill, but his features are still visible, his body language still distinct. Well, that is a distance I never found. He was never dwarfed by the landscape – the fields, the buildings, the white pine windbreak were as much my father as if he had grown them and shed them like a husk.
>
> (Smiley 1991: 20)

Rejecting a Bloomian, "idealized" image of her father – in which he dwarfs the landscape around him – Ginny reconfigures her relationship with Larry through her own struggle for autonomy, coming to terms with a powerful memory of violation and abuse. Ginny and, indeed, Smiley herself, achieve that vantage point through an awareness of the soil underneath the structures of the farm: Ginny's knowledge of what her father's chemicals have done to her body empowers her, while Smiley draws on her knowledge of the Iowan landscape to achieve an "optimum distance" from Shakespeare and *King Lear.*

III "The body repeats the landscape"

As the epigraph from Le Sueur suggests, Smiley's landscape provides a powerful metaphor not only for Ginny's recovery of repressed memories of abuse, but also for the process of re-vision itself. While Lear attempts to draw borders across his kingdom, Smiley makes the reader aware of the divisions that her narrator perceives within the landscape: a vertical demarcation that extends down beneath the horizontal, flat surfaces of her father's farm and into a dark and uncertain world located beneath it. Ginny's description of Zebulon County as the "center of the universe" at the beginning of the novel gradually gives way to her imaginative descriptions of an alternative landscape underneath the soil. Once a swamp-like sea of reeds and small animals, Larry's farm rests on a network of drainage tiles, a system used by farmers to transform the land from swamp to arable soil. These tiles were laid down by Larry's parents, Sam and Arabella Davis; and although the landscape has been reworked to meet the needs of their descendants, Ginny is perpetually aware of the "sea beneath the soil," the repressed and swampy spaces that once made up the face of the land and now lie hidden underneath the tiles:

> One of my earliest memories, in fact, is of myself in a red and green plaid pinafore, which must mean I was about three, and Ruthie in a pink shirt, probably not yet three, squatting on one of those drainage-well covers, dropping pebbles and bits of sticks through the grate. The sound of water trickling in the blackness must have drawn us, and even now the memory gives me an eerie feeling, and not because of the danger to our infant selves. What I think of is our babyhoods perched thoughtlessly on the filmiest net of the modern world, over layers of rock, Wisconsin till, Mississippian carbonate, Devonian limestone, layers of dark epochs, and we seem not so much in danger (my father checked the grates often) as fleeting, as if our lives simply passed then, and this memory is the only photograph of some nameless and unknown children who may have lived and may have died, but at any rate have vanished into the black well of time.
>
> (Smiley 1991: 46–47)

The seemingly secure world of Chapter 1, with the farmers at its center, gives way to an evocative image of the unknown abyss above which life functions – a dark hole underneath the carefully tilled and controlled landscape. Throughout the novel, the contrast between these two powerful spaces – the "filmiest net" of the farmland and the "dark well of time" on the underside – comes to characterize Smiley's re-vision of *King Lear*. In trying to extricate herself from the continuous present-tense of her father's world, where past sins disappear beneath the "unbroken surface of the unsaid" (94), Ginny must learn to reconcile two very different spaces, the present and the past, in her mind. By contrasting the flat, engineered surface of the farms with the repressed and swampy land that it covers up, Smiley maps out an imaginative landscape that acts as a metaphor for the process of re-vision as her protagonist learns to reconcile herself with her father's curse. In the struggle between Ginny and her father and, in turn, between Smiley and Shakespeare, we can see a new sort of territory taking shape, the lines of which are defined by Shakespeare's play. Smiley's choice to import the structure of *King Lear* – a play in which mothers are conspicuously absent – into *A Thousand Acres* fits into Bloom's idea of the struggle with a father. But Smiley's novel also opens up that paradigm in a different way, achieving an "optimum distance" from her Shakespearean source by adding Meridel Le Sueur's voice to the mixture.

In contrast to those of the Shakespeare-driven figure of Ginny Cook, Le Sueur's experiences as a young girl growing up in the prairies are defined by the presence of women: her mother, her grandmother, and a native American woman named Zona, from whom she learned to see the land from a completely different perspective. As Le Sueur writes in "The Ancient People and the Newly Come":

> There was always this mothering in the night, the great female meadows, sacred and sustaining. I look out now along the bluffs of the Mississippi, where Zona's prophecies of pollution have been fulfilled in ways worse than she could dream. Be aware, she had cried once. Be afraid. Be careful. Be fierce. She had seen the female power of the earth, immense and angry, that could strike back at its polluters and conquerors.
>
> (1982: 48)

Le Sueur's portrayal of the landscape as an oppressed yet powerful female provides an image of the maternal not readily available in Smiley's Shakespearean source. Importantly, both Le Sueur and Smiley locate female power in the natural world. On one level, Smiley evokes a relationship between Ginny and the landscape that is similar to Lear's experience on the heath, a space in which he is able to challenge the order of the world in which he is living, the gods, and the elements. But as Smiley imports Lear's heath to the space of twentieth-century Iowa, she could also be seen as redrawing the dimensions of that space in terms of a more localized, Midwestern tradition of writing that is also feminized.

In *A Thousand Acres*, as in "The Ancient People and the Newly Come," the natural world becomes a site of resistance against the controlled world of Ginny's father and the other farmers. Much of Ginny's self-awakening comes through her growing awareness of her sexuality, primarily in her encounters with Jess Clark, which is figured through Ginny's understanding of the Iowan landscape. The dump in which Ginny and Jess meet is, significantly, the place where the nearly extinct prairie grasses and small animals make their last stand. Ginny can still recall some of the names of the plants that grow there: "I know shooting stars and wild carrots, and of course, bindweed and Johnson grass and shatter cane and all that other noxious vegetation that farmers have to kill kill kill" (Smiley 1991: 124). While Ginny herself paraphrases Lear's desire to "kill, kill, kill" his sons-in-law (4.6.182), Le Sueur's image of the land as a woman oppressed and enslaved by industry underlies Smiley's construction of the natural world in *A Thousand Acres* and is crucial to Ginny's perception of her body. Ginny sees herself taking on the characteristics of different farm animals; she is caged up and commodified like a sow, at one point and, later on, compares herself to a horse "haltered in a tight stall, throwing its head and beating its feet against the floor, but the beams and the bars and the halter rope hold firm, and the horse wears itself out, and accepts the restraint that moments before had been an unendurable goad" (Smiley 1991: 198). Moving between images of freedom and claustrophobic images of entrapment, Ginny's sense of her body is defined as a struggle between the natural world and the structures that her father has placed there. Like the land itself, her body is commodified, divided, and used, while her inner self is pushed further and further underground. The animalistic way in which Ginny perceives herself ironically echoes Lear's misogynistic vision of female sexuality:

> Down from the waist they are Centaurs,
> Though women all above.
> But to the girdle do the gods inherit.
> Beneath is all the fiends'; there's hell, there's darkness,
> There's the sulphurous pit. …
>
> (4.6.121–25)

Ginny internalizes Lear's mistrust of women as she learns to deny her sexuality and her body. "I didn't want to see my body," she tells us. "I assumed that all of this was normal, the way it was for everyone. It went without saying that bodies fell permanently into the category of the unmentionable" (Smiley 1991: 279). Smiley makes the female body a symbolic site of oppression, drawing on Lear's own fears of female sexuality and, in particular, on Lear's correlation between madness, the "mother," and female hysteria: "O, how this mother swells up toward my heart! / *Hysterica passio*, down, thou climbing sorrow, / Thy element's below!" (2.4.54–56). Lear's rebellion against the "rising mother" is an image that also characterizes Smiley's landscape, marked as it is by this vertical struggle between masculine and feminine presences, between fathers and mothers. If, as Le Sueur asserts, the body repeats the landscape, then the body of *A Thousand Acres* provides a point of contact between two alternating parents. In this sense, Smiley's novel both fits into and furthers Coppélia Kahn's vision of the "maternal subtext" underpinning Shakespeare's tragedy, in which Lear's madness enacts an essential conflict between the patriarchal structures that loom on the surface of the text and "the psychological presence of the mother whether or not mothers are literally represented as characters" (Kahn 1986: 35).

Smiley's novel juxtaposes two views of the mother. On the one hand, *A Thousand Acres* creates a *Lear*-like world in which the mother is present only in the Iowan soil – not in the home, but in the cemetery. Victims of breast cancer, the women's bodies pay the price for the chemicals and fertilizers used to control the surface of the land. The mothers who do appear in the novel are not exactly warm and maternal presences. Rose is undemonstrative and cool to her children while, according to Ginny's memories, her own mother was just as no-nonsense a maternal presence as her sister. She did not breast-feed her children and never showed them much affection. As Ginny tells us, "there was no melding with the child into symbiotic and fleshy warmth" (Smiley 1991: 93). In the end, Ginny's mother was powerless – unwilling, even – to protect her daughters from their father's rages. While Ginny does not have an intimate connection to her own mother, she does try to pursue motherhood for herself, through secret and futile attempts to have children. These attempts to become a mother end, tragically, in the fetuses that she buries underneath the barn. Molested by her father, acting as a substitute wife for him and a surrogate mother for her sisters, Ginny's life has been defined by negative encounters with maternal roles.

In her re-vision of *King Lear*, then, Smiley does not merely act as the daughters' advocate. She both challenges the vision of *King Lear* and rewrites the history of the American family, showing that both mothers and fathers are complicit in creating and perpetuating the disasters that befall their children. "Do we know what we are?" Ginny asks Rose at one point (216). Echoing Lear's question, "Who is it that can tell me who I am?" (1.4.205), Ginny speaks of herself in terms of "what" rather than "who," positing the materiality of her existence, her substance. Replete with her father's poisons, containing the remains of her mother and her lost children, the land itself memorializes Ginny's struggle with the past and her relationship to the future, both defining who she is and cursing her, as well. This is the legacy of both parents in *A Thousand Acres*.

The attempt to remember the mother, however, also becomes the key to Ginny's recovery of the past and her ability to forge a new life. Entering the house after her father has left, Ginny searches for and tries to imagine her mother:

> As I neared the house, it seemed like Daddy's departure had opened up the possibility of finding my mother. ... [N]ow that he was gone, I could look more closely. I could study the closets or the attic, lift things and peer under them, get back into cabinets and the corners of shelves. ... Might there not be a single overlooked drawer, unopened for twenty-two years, that would breathe forth a single, fleeting exhalation? She had known him – what would she have said about him? How would she have interceded? Wasn't there something to know about him that she had known that would come to me if I found something of her in his house?
>
> (Smiley 1991: 225)

While Ginny's quest for objects left behind by her mother goes unrealized, she does come face to face with a more tangible and real truth – the truth about her father, the memories of his nighttime visits that come welling to the surface when she enters her old room. The search for her dead mother ultimately brings Ginny to an empowering new knowledge of her father, a memory that rises up to the surface of her consciousness out of her mother's silence. The recovered memories of her father's abuse of her body give Ginny a new sense of herself, a new life that is revealed like a newly exposed skin: "My new life, yet another new life, had begun" (229). Tearing at the walls of her family home, she disassembles that structure in order to find some semblance of her own body trapped within. And, in her efforts to recover her mother, Ginny is able to confront her memory of the father:

> The dressing table was beside the window; the closet door was ajar; the yellow paint on the empty chest was peeling; some bronze circles floated in the mirror; a water spot had formed on the ceiling. Lying here, I knew that he had been in there to me, that my father had lain with me on that bed, that I had looked at the top of his head, at his balding spot in the brown grizzled hair, while feeling him suck my breasts. That was the only memory I could endure before I jumped out of the bed with a cry.
>
> (228)

Ginny's search for her mother allows her to see her father differently and to transform her relationship to him. Watching him violate her body through this memory, she is abruptly forced to confront the dark corners of her own past, a Hades that contains a terrifying vision of her father attacking her while her mother's back is turned. As she tells us,

> One thing Daddy took from me when he came to me in my room at night was the memory of my body. I never remembered penetration or pain, or even his hands on my body, and I never sorted out how many times there were. I remembered my strategy, which had been a desperate limp inertia.
>
> (280)

Opening up the landscape and seeing herself within it, Ginny becomes a Persephone figure, moving back and forth between surface and subtext, between father and mother. She belongs to both, and to neither completely.

IV Re-visioning the anxiety of influence

In her book, *Sister's Choice: Tradition and Change in American Women's Writing*, Elaine Showalter writes about the nature of women's revisions of male-authored, canonical texts:

> The validity of American women's writing doesn't depend on Shakespeare's sister, and it can tolerate no more Dark Ladies. Our brave new world has many women in it, and we must make its myths together or not at all.
>
> (1991: 41)

Showalter's point is an important one, especially in view of the long period of silence that surrounded Le Sueur because her work was neglected, forgotten, and inaccessible to many for decades after she was blacklisted. But in Smiley's novel, the tension resulting from the opposed voices is the strongest testimony of the novel's function as re-vision. Just as Ginny finds a point of re-entry into her body by remembering the ways in which her father violated it, so too does Smiley use Shakespeare's text as a point of entry into the problems inherent in modern American family life: she sees "with fresh eyes," to echo the words of Adrienne Rich.

In *A Thousand Acres*, the tension between the catalogue-ordered house of Ginny's childhood and the land on which it is built is repeated in the interaction between the imported structure of Shakespeare's *King Lear* and the indigenous, Midwestern experiences of Le Sueur, between male and female, father and mother. In Smiley's figurations of the American Midwest, the nightmare vision of American expansion that is the subject of Le Sueur's essay becomes the occasion for Smiley's intensive examination of literary generations in the Western canon, in which certain voices are paved over by others. Le Sueur writes of life in her grandmother's house: "We crouched in an alien land under the weathers, tossing at night on this ancient sea, captained by women, minute against the great white whale" (1982: 53). In this anthropomorphized landscape, the women are melded together in order to survive against the "white whale" of the storms raging outside. Sheltered inside the white-frame house, they are able to survive, three generations of women from different backgrounds. In a similar way, *A Thousand Acres* itself stands as an act of survival.

By delving into the issue of legacy and inheritance from many angles, Smiley makes a statement about the uses of the past and the phenomenon of memory. From the shelter of the front porch, Rose screams at her father:

> We never asked for what you gave us, but maybe it was high time we got some reward for what we gave you! ... This is what we've got to offer, this same life, nothing more nothing less. If you don't want it, go elsewhere. Get someone else to take you in, because I for one have had it.
>
> (Smiley 1991: 182)

The cold way in which Rose assesses her father's gift, reducing their dialogue to a system of punishments and rewards for past deeds, is a comment upon Smiley's use of *King Lear* within her own writing. "We didn't ask for what you gave us," Rose asserts (182). Finally consumed by her father's poisons, she is unable to see beyond her role in his life. But Smiley, in opening up her narrative to what she comes to view as Shakespeare's rather warped take on family life in *King Lear*, voluntarily takes on his perspective. By analogy, Ginny's ability to penetrate her father's exterior and to open herself up to what he must have been feeling at his lowest point as a human being – the point at which he hurt her the most – goes beyond the economics of forgiveness:

> I can imagine what he probably chose never to remember – the goad of an unthinkable urge, pricking him, pressing him, wrapping him in an impenetrable fog of self that must have seemed, when he wandered around the house late at night after working and drinking, like the very darkness. This is the gleaming obsidian shard I safeguard above all others.
>
> (371)

By re-imagining her father's experiences, Ginny moves beyond the "impenetrable fog of self" that characterizes his world view and, in many ways, those of her sisters. She is able to reevaluate her legacy, to go beyond the old codes of debts and pay-backs.

"No more; the text is foolish," asserts Ginny's Shakespearean counterpart (4.2.38). And yet, although the text of our past might seem foolish, it is still a part of who we are. As Ginny tells us at the end of *A Thousand Acres*:

> [A]lthough the farm and all its burdens and gifts are scattered, my inheritance is with me, sitting in my chair. Lodged in my every cell, along with the DNA are molecules of topsoil and atrazine and paraquat and anhydrous ammonia and diesel fuel and plant dust. … All of it is present now, here; each particle weighs some fraction of the hundred and thirty-six pounds that attaches me to the earth, perhaps as much as the print weighs in other sorts of histories.
>
> (Smiley 1991: 369)

Ostensibly, the farm is Ginny's legacy, but beyond this is a final merging of body, landscape, and history. And while Smiley seems to balk at the circumstances of Shakespeare's play, its cruel twists and violent endings, the resulting tension in *A Thousand Acres* is brilliant. While Shakespeare, the imported structure of plot and high cultural capital, seems undermined at every turn by the deep indigenous substance present in Smiley's own powerful writing and in non-Shakespearean sources like Le Sueur, the multiple perspectives are all crucial to the final vision she achieves. "I pondered my new image of Shakespeare," Smiley told her audience in Los Angeles:

> and I thought of him doing just what I had done – wrestling with old material, given material, that is in some ways malleable and in other ways resistant. I thought about how all material, whether inherited or observed, has integrity. The author doesn't just do something with it, he or she also learns from it. The author's presuppositions and predispositions work on the material and are simultaneously transformed by it. I imagined Shakespeare wrestling with the "Leir" story and coming away a little dissatisfied, a little defeated, but hugely stimulated, just as I was. As I imagined that, then I felt that I received a gift, an image of literary history, two mirrors facing each other in the present moment, reflecting infinitely backward into the past and infinitely forward into the future.
>
> (1998: 56)

This image of two mirrors facing one another, with male and female faces reflecting infinitely upon one another, seems to me characteristic of *A Thousand Acres*, a novel that draws attention to the many voices it contains, some louder than others, most of them conflicting. In the end, Ginny's movement from the silence of her past to her not-so-perfect future as a waitress at Denny's restaurant contains hope for the future. Raising Rose's children, providing guidance as an aunt instead of a mother or father, she is part of a new sort of family. Part of that future, however, lies in her ability to address the past, that "gleaming obsidian shard," and to integrate it into a new sense of herself. Smiley's novel involves both a clashing and a merging of perspectives, each challenging the other, and yet facing one another as a means toward an ultimate understanding and cohesion of past, present, and future.

Notes

1 I am grateful for the efforts of a number of people who helped me while I was writing this essay: Jill Levenson, the students and fellows of The Shakespeare Institute, and especially, Tom Matheson and Stanley Wells.

2 All references to *King Lear* correspond to the conflated *Lear* in the *Norton Shakespeare.*

3 For an account of Le Sueur's life and writing, see Elaine Hedges's "Introduction" to Le Sueur's *Ripening* (1982: 1–28).

6

Signifyin' on *The Tempest* in Gloria Naylor's *Mama Day*

JAMES R. ANDREAS, SR.

In *Playing in the Dark: Whiteness and the Literary Imagination*, Toni Morrison examines "how inextricable Africanism is or ought to be from the deliberations of literary criticism and the wanton, elaborate strategies undertaken to erase its presence from view" (1992: 9). Nowhere has the struggle to eradicate the presence in and influence of Africa and Africans on European literature been fought so violently as in the canonical battle over the body of the Bard. Yet Shakespeare wrote no fewer than five plays that feature Africans in prominent, often titular roles, and African American writers and actors have been reacting to, redacting, and "re-visioning" – to borrow a term from Adrienne Rich (1979) – those plays for more than a hundred years. Michael Bristol (1990) has made it abundantly clear that the Bard was fully *Americanized* by the early years of the Republic. Less understood and appreciated is that Shakespeare has been persistently *African* Americanized over the last century as well. The most illustrious of African American writers – Richard Wright, Ralph Ellison, Amiri Baraka, Maya Angelou, Toni Morrison, John Wideman, Ishmael Reed, and, as the present essay is intent on demonstrating, Gloria Naylor – have been busily interpreting, emulating, appropriating, and adapting Shakespeare's African plays and characters throughout the twentieth century.

Mama Day, Gloria Naylor's third novel, first published in 1988 to generally laudatory reviews, is set on a barrier island named Willow

Springs off the coast of the southeastern United States, midway between Georgia and South Carolina. It is inhabited by former slaves, descendants of one Sapphira Wade, a slave mistress of the island's original owner, Bascomb Wade, who deeded the property to Sapphira's African American progeny. The island is presided over by an old woman named Miranda. Naylor's Miranda is a conjure woman, a witch with magical insights, if not powers over natural and reproductive phenomena. She is nearly one hundred years old, knows herbal remedies, and can summon lightning with her walking stick. She also knows the true story of "the great, grand Mother" Sapphira Wade, who in 1823 persuaded her master to deed the island to his slaves and killed him before she vanished in a burst of flame. Miranda wants to pass on the island's history and her knowledge to her grand-niece, Ophelia, whose nickname is Cocoa, a woman as feisty and determined as her formidable female ancestors.

Cocoa is married to George, a successful self-made businessman who has grown up and flourished in New York. When George accompanies his wife on a fateful visit to meet the country relatives in Willow Springs, Naylor's two worlds – island and city – and the opposing realities they represent collide. The island is Black, exempt from the laws that obtain on the mainland, and free from racism; the city is multi-racial, racist, and governed by strict and inflexible codes of ambition and survival. When Cocoa falls victim to a spell cast on her by a rival witch, Ruby, George can save her only by renouncing the reason and self-reliance he has come to depend on and submitting to the folk wisdom of Mama Day, a woman he considers insane. George, however, is ultimately sacrificed for Cocoa. Diagnosed with a weak heart, he suffers a coronary in the aftermath of the great storm Miranda evokes on the island. After George's death, Cocoa seems prepared to accept the responsibilities women like Sapphira and Miranda and her great-grandmother Abigail have voluntarily assumed for generations on the island of Willow Springs.

Even from this simple plot synopsis, Shakespeare's influence on the novel should be readily apparent. *Mama Day* may be structurally modeled after – and undeniably inspired by – *The Tempest*,[1] but in lectures and interviews Gloria Naylor is quick to deny that the play exerted conscious influence on the composition of her novel. Acknowledging William Faulkner's *As I Lay Dying* (1930) and Zora Neale Hurston's *Their Eyes Were Watching God* (1937) as primary influences, Naylor overlooks an obvious source for her story, just as a jazz musician never directly acknowledges his or her debt to tradition, or to a specific song or riff, but proceeds to appropriate given musical materials and refashion them as he or she sees fit.

Gloria Naylor is neither the first Black author to fall under the spell of the Bard nor the first to interrogate the racist implications of his plays. In an early allusion to Shakespeare well before the turn of the century, the Black novelist and poet Charles Chesnutt dubbed Shakespeare "The Homer of the Saxon race." To early African American writers, Shakespeare is an icon of Nordic peoples whose pen not only "paints the minds and hearts of men" – White, no doubt – but whose "lines shall future ages trace" (Chesnutt 1993: 163). "Race" and "trace" are auspicious rhymes for Chesnutt, whose own literary progeny were often interested in erasing the trace of race, or of inverting its influence, in their appropriations and adaptations of the plays. Shakespeare has been conceived of by African American writers as both progenitor and propagator of British canons of taste, culture, class, caste, and foremost, race, a voice of White authority to be reckoned with in a uniquely African way – through the tradition of literary re-creation that Henry Louis Gates, Jr. has identified as "signifying," particularly in reaction to those plays that are hostile to African or Native characters.

Since that anxious celebration of Shakespeare was first recorded in Chesnutt's journals, the relationship between the Bard and African American writers has remained seminal but testy, and can best be characterized as a love–hate affair, with control over literary "progeny" as the driving concern. Of the five "African" plays of Shakespeare, those that feature Africans or Moors in prominent roles – *The Merchant of Venice* (Morocco), *Titus Andronicus* (Aaron), *Othello: The Moor of Venice*, *Antony and Cleopatra*, and *The Tempest* (Caliban, whose mother, Sycorax, is from "Argiers") – *Othello* has inspired re-visions chiefly by African American male writers, while *The Tempest* has generally inspired adaptations by women.

Othello ritualizes the racist's nightmare of the biracial sexual relationship between a White woman and a Black male, which according to Gunnar Myrdal, has suffered "the full fury of anti-amalgamation sanctions" in American history (1944: 56). Early African American writers might well have been incensed by the characterization of *Othello* articulated by one of the Republic's earliest and most respected presidents, indeed a politician liberal on racial matters, if Stephen Spielberg's *Amistad* is correct. Even as he advocated the abolition of slavery in the House of

Representatives in 1836, John Quincy Adams characterized the moral of *Othello* as follows: "the intermarriage of black and white blood is a violation of the law of nature. *That* is the lesson to be learned from the play" (cited in Levine 1988: 39). The explosive paradigm of miscegenation delineated in *Othello* becomes the target for three great male African American re-visions of the biracial sexual myth: *Native Son* by Richard Wright (1940), *Invisible Man* by Ralph Ellison (1952), and *Dutchman* by Amiri Baraka (1964). Wright restages and reinterprets the problematic relationship of Othello and Desdemona in his novel about the murderous encounter between Bigger Thomas and Mary Dalton; Ellison represents that relationship comically in the farcical date of the hero of *Invisible Man* and the White woman named Sibyl; and Baraka reverses or inverts the play's outcome in the murder of the Black man named Clay by a White woman, Lula, in *Dutchman* (Andreas 1992).

With its frequent references to Africa and Africans (Caliban, Sycorax, Setebos, Tunis) and its interrogation of the notions of forced servitude and chattel slavery, *The Tempest* has provoked its share of recent African European and African American responses, including Aimé Césaire's *Une Tempête* (1974; English trans. 1985) and John Edgar Wideman's *Philadelphia Fire* (1990). But we must turn to African American women writers to find the most thoroughgoing interrogations of Shakespeare's highly patriarchal text, which sets his Western magus squarely at the center of the familial, political, dramatic, geographical, and even the metaphysical universe. One of the more creative re-visionings of *The Tempest* is Toni Morrison's *Tar Baby* (1981), which places Shakespeare alongside the African American folk tales of Uncle Remus. The most celebrated recent appropriation of *The Tempest*, however, is Gloria Naylor's *Mama Day*. Without running the risk of satire, parody, or comedy, *Mama Day* systematically turns *The Tempest* upside down, putting women on top and immigrant Natives fully in charge of the island. It displaces Prospero with the character of Miranda, a Black "witch" who converts patriarchy to matriarchy in the domination of a South Carolina sea island not so far from Bermuda, one of the presumed locales for Prospero's island. The novel both feminizes and "negrifies" the patriarchal story line of the play, replacing European characters with an entirely African American cast and restoring the power over reproduction usurped by Prospero to its proper source, women. Miranda oversees pregnancies on the island and manipulates the marriage of Ophelia and George, just as Prospero arranges the union of Miranda and Ferdinand to heal the political rift between

Milan and Naples. The novel also redefines the magic of the wizard in Shakespeare's play as sympathetic and empathetic, rather than autocratic.

One of the basic considerations of this essay is how a Shakespearean text like *The Tempest* is appropriated and transformed by Black writers for their own uses. In *The Signifying Monkey: A Theory of Afro-American Literary Criticism* (1988), Henry Louis Gates, Jr. suggests that African American literature grows out of the tradition of the "talking book." Gates explains that illiterate Africans sold into slavery naturally supposed that books "talked," since that is how the parent language – oral speech – communicated meaning. He notes that as an orally generated and transmitted literature, African American texts exemplify Mikhail Bakhtin's dialogic notion of literary tradition, as well as the liturgical convention of call-and-response in the Black church. A given text operates as an utterance demanding objection, clarification, or revision as a response. If Aristotle considered metaphor the major trope for European poetry, Gates celebrates what he calls "signifying" as the master trope of African and its derivative literatures around the world. To signify in African and African American cultures is to improvise on a given *topos*, narrative, or joke the way a jazz musician improvises on a progression of chords, melodic structure, or spontaneous riff in the previous musician's solo. As Gates explains: "In the jazz tradition, compositions by Count Basie ('Signify') and Oscar Peterson ('Signifying') are structured around the idea of formal revision and implication" (1988: 123). Ralph Ellison explains as well that a vernacular literature like African American writing initiates "a dynamic process in which the most refined styles from the past are continually merged with the play-it-by-eye-and-by-ear improvisations which we invent in our efforts to control our environment and entertain ourselves" (1995: xxi). Playful but willful manipulation of the signifier alters perception of the signified as it appropriates the traditional paradigm. Metamorphosis, rather than metaphor, is therefore at the heart of African and African American narrative style.

The function of signifying, like jazz improvisation, is never to replicate or even simulate, but to complicate, explicate, and recreate. In this sense the plays and plots, or what Aristotle calls the *mythoi*, of Shakespeare have represented aesthetic challenges to African American writers, particularly when the *topos* in a play such as *Othello* or *The Tempest* involves that evanescent bugaboo of European American culture, race. The European text that trumps or trumpets race is the text that the African American writer is going to twist and turn every which way but loose. Finally, if Terence Hawkes is to be believed, such a view of literary call and response or challenge and reciprocation may well be applicable to the study of a Shakespearean play, a text composed, as music is, for performance: "[L]anguage [like Shakespeare's] never occurs in the abstract. It always represents an intervention into a continuing dialogue, and its meanings constitute and are constituted by a response to that context of utterance" (Hawkes 1986: 79). In other words, Shakespeare himself, in his tapestry of folk, literary, and dramatic snippets that constitute *The Tempest*, may be signifying on the texts of Montaigne, accounts of recent exploratory ventures in the New World, and emerging views of Native and African "others."

What cues are contained in *The Tempest* that might have inspired – or goaded – Gloria Naylor and other African American writers to "signify" on Shakespeare? An Africanist reading of *The Tempest* is not as far-fetched as it might appear, even after centuries of excluding racial considerations from discussion of Shakespearean theater. It is, first of all, noteworthy that in 1611, within ten years of the sale of the first slave in South Carolina (1619), Shakespeare provides us with one of literature's first depictions of a Native laboring and suffering on an island plantation. *The Tempest* also deals systematically with the full agenda of colonial and racist doctrines and objectives. Early modern rivalries between Europe and Africa are recorded in the racial slurs of Sebastian and Antonio against Tunis, and Caliban as African is routinely demonized and excoriated. Prospero reminds Caliban repeatedly that he is a "poisonous slave, got by the devil himself / Upon thy wicked dam" (1.2.323–24). Native lands are expropriated, as Caliban emphatically declares: "This island's mine, by Sycorax my mother, / Which thou tak'st from me" (1.2.334–35). Natives are also enslaved, either as indentured servants or chattel slaves. Ariel is an indentured servant, and continually pesters Prospero about his promised emancipation: "Remember I have done thee worthy service, / … / … Thou did promise / To bate me a full year" (1.2.248, 250–51). Caliban is the chattel slave, imprisoned and exploited by the European intruder. As Prospero reminds Caliban: "Therefore wast thou / Deservedly confined into this rock / Who hadst deserved more than a prison" (1.2.348–51). Anxiety about miscegenation resonates in the marriage of the African king, Tunis, to Alonso's daughter Claribel and in Caliban's presumed attack on Miranda which, according to Prospero, initiated the hostilities between them:

> I have used thee
> Filth as thou art with human care, and lodged thee
> In mine own cell, till thou didst seek to violate
> The honour of my child.
>
> (1.2.348–51)

Illicit African gods such as Setebos are worshiped by Caliban, and African religions are associated, through Sycorax, with demonism, witchcraft, and the feminine. European patriarchy is then celebrated as the necessary moral development beyond matriarchy in Prospero's "beneficent" acculturation of the slave. As Prospero claims,

> When thou didst not, savage,
> Know thine own meaning, but wouldst gabble like
> A thing most brutish, I endowed thy purposes
> With words that made them known.
>
> (1.2.358–61)

The comic subplot involving Stephano, Trinculo, and Caliban can be read as a farcical, abortive slave insurrection; alternatively, Caliban can be seen as representative of the Native population, subdued and demoralized by the Western drug, alcohol. He is also repeatedly bargained for by both Antonio and Stephano as a New World exotic with financial potential back in England (see *The Tempest* 2.2.26 ff.).

In short, *The Tempest* articulates a full roster of early modern racial stereotypes as it reaffirms a system of colonial dominion designed to control the Native populations onto which those stereotypes are projected. There is, in other words, rich Africanist "new corn" to be extracted from "old" European, colonial "fields" in *The Tempest* via Gates's clever elucidation of literary signifying. In a recent anthology of critical essays on Naylor's novels, Gates refers to Peter Erickson's argument that "Naylor employs Shakespeare to thematize the split between white male and Black female literary traditions, as well as between 'white' high culture and 'Black' everyday experience" (1993: xii). Valerie Traub also presents the challenge facing Black women writers as "doubly problematic: how to negotiate a relationship to an Anglo-European language and tradition that doubly defines them as absence and lack – as black and as women" (1993: 151). Thus, Naylor's task as female revisionist of Shakespeare's play has a particular urgency.

During an interview with Virginia Fowler in *Gloria Naylor: In Search of Sanctuary* (Fowler 1996), Naylor attributes her inspiration by Shakespeare to Joe Papp's free performances of "Shakespeare in the Park." She saw *A Midsummer Night's Dream* – to which she alludes repeatedly in *The Women of Brewster Place* – *Macbeth*, and other plays featured in the New York Shakespeare Festival. Naylor "loved tragedies," a fact relevant to the tragic end cooked up for George at the end of *Mama Day*, but most of all there was "something about the way in which Shakespeare used language [that] resonated within me" (Fowler 1996: 149). Naylor's use of the word "resonance" is pertinent, suggesting perhaps that Shakespeare inspired a free range of overtones in her own novels, or that his language elicited a response beyond emulation and performance – the need to interrogate and signify on his plays. Peter Erickson discusses a brief but important allusion to Shakespeare in *Linden Hills*, Naylor's second novel (1985), which was written just before *Mama Day*. The struggling poet, Willie, asks his friend Lester, "why black folks ain't produced a Shakespeare. … You'd think of all the places in the world, this neighborhood had a chance of giving us at least one black Shakespeare." Lester responds, "But Linden Hills ain't about that, Willie. You should know that by now" (cited in Erickson 1993: 236). In *Mama Day*, however, Naylor does indeed play the "black Shakespeare," engaging canonical views of *The Tempest* and challenging, inverting, and controverting the blatant colonial assumptions of the play.

What interests me most about *Mama Day* as an important illustration of Africanist Shakespeare are:

1 the novel's sustained commentary on the plays of Shakespeare from a feminist and African American perspective;
2 the author's flat denial in lecture and interview that *The Tempest* was an influence on her, although characterization and structure in the novel clearly derive from that play;
3 *Mama Day*'s systematic feminization, "negrification," and fairly systematic inversion of *The Tempest*'s contrapuntal plots;
4 Naylor's concerted attempt to broaden the focus and especially the perspective of the play by introducing multiple speakers and thus dialogizing the single voice of Prospero; and,
5 the novel's articulate embodiment of the trope of signifying – that creative, spontaneous, playful mode of improvisation and adaptation that Gates ranks as the major figure of African American literature.

Mama Day, as Fowler, Traub, and Erickson have shown, is studded with references to *Hamlet*, *The Taming of the Shrew*, *Romeo and Juliet*, and *King Lear*, which broaden and reinforce Naylor's signifying on the narrative of *The Tempest.* The naming of the principal character in the novel, Ophelia/Cocoa, evokes the death by drowning of Hamlet's former lover, a role that Cocoa's husband George will assume in *Mama Day* in a way that is consistent with the pattern of gender inversions Naylor sets up in the novel. Early on in their relationship, Cocoa meets George on an "evening [when] I had left King Lear naked and wandering on a stormy heath" (Naylor 1989: 59), introducing yet another foreboding reference to cataclysmic meteorological and emotional tempests in Shakespeare. Later on, George and Cocoa meet to discuss his favorite play, which happens to be *King Lear*. With play copies in hand, they argue point for dramatic point, although *The Taming of the Shrew* seems to be the operative text in the lovers' relationship at that point. As Cocoa says of *King Lear* in one of her monologues addressed to George, "along with *The Taming of the Shrew*, this had to be Shakespeare's most sexist treatment of women – but far be it from me to contradict anything you had to say" (106). Apparently George, like Petruccio, Lear, and Prospero before him, perpetuates one of the most disturbing practices of Shakespearean misogyny, the silencing of potentially independent women such as Kate, Cordelia, and Miranda.

Peter Erickson makes a great deal of George's "attachment to Shakespeare," particularly *King Lear*, which "serves as a badge for his upward mobility" as well as his superiority as a male (1993: 242). George, who is an orphan, identifies openly with Edmund, the bastard son whose ambitions are fueled by his disadvantaged childhood, but he may also feel sympathy for Edgar, who is disowned, and therefore "orphaned," by his father Gloucester. Such a combination of ruthlessness and sensitivity aptly captures the polarity of George's character. He admits that *Lear* "had a special poignancy for me, reading about the rage of a bastard son, my own father having disappeared long before I was born" (Naylor 1989: 106). Traub notices that George and Cocoa's relationship is described, in an allusion to *Romeo and Juliet*, as "star-crossed" – in other words, as fated to materialize in some legendary memory as it indeed will be memorialized on the island of Willow Springs (1993: 157). Traub also suggests that Naylor has Cocoa playfully signify on the canonicity of Shakespeare. In order to express how alienated she feels from George, who has just asked her out again after a couple of bad dates, Cocoa exclaims to herself, "Surely, he jests" (referring to *Romeo and Juliet* 2.1.43), then concludes disparagingly that such a quotation "had to be something from my high school Shakespeare":

> "Just proves that Shakespeare didn't have a bit of soul – I don't care if he did write about Othello, Cleopatra, and some slave on a Caribbean island. If he had been in touch with our culture, he would have written somewhere, 'Nigger, are you out of your mind?'"
>
> (Naylor 1989: 64)

Naylor suggests here that Othello may not have been the "tawny Moor" that the majority culture, following Samuel Taylor Coleridge,[2] has claimed him to be for centuries; she also implies that Cleopatra and Caliban are Black as well as African, which again has not generally been granted in the tradition of Shakespeare scholarship.[3] Most of all, she playfully demonstrates the whiteness of Shakespeare. However concerned with African issues he may be in these and other plays, he is still a White European and his plays need "darkening."

Naylor's signifying on *The Tempest* in *Mama Day* begins fast and furiously with the naming of the titular character. If *The Tempest* is about Papa Prospero, Naylor may give Mama Day the name of Shakespeare's ingénue, Miranda, to signify that the daughter of Prospero is now in control of the text. Mama Day combines the qualities of Shakespeare's daughter and her wizard/father. Like her younger counterpart in *The Tempest*, Old Miranda wonders at the magical properties of the island – much more than Prospero ever does, for it is Caliban who is sensitive to its mystical beauty – and, initially at least, admires her grand-niece's choice of mate from the "brave new world" (*The Tempest* 5.1.186) of New York. But she is also Prospero's female counterpart. With her decidedly "sympathetic" magic, Mama Day calls down, or at least cannot call off, a fearsome tempest that isolates inhabitants and urban visitors alike on the island. She instructs the young couple from New York, George and Ophelia, in the art and obedience of love, as Prospero instructs Ferdinand and Miranda. Finally, she controls the magic, the marriages, and most of all, the reproductive activity on the island, including the fertilization, pregnancy, and delivery of one Bernice, who gives birth to a Black "little Caesar." But unlike Prospero, who has been deposed by and revenges himself on his brother Antonio, Mama Day has no quarrel with her sister, Abigail. They squabble from time to time over domestic chores but clearly love each other and are able to coexist on the island. Abigail also offers no challenge to Mama Day's magical powers or influence over her own granddaughter, Ophelia, who is only a grand-niece to Miranda. Sisters, Naylor seems to be suggesting, do not resort to the fratricidal struggles of "brothers and others" that W. H. Auden (1948) and various critics have identified as the disruptive energy that drives so many Shakespearean plays. On Naylor's island, family dynamics, like Mama Day's magic, are benign.

The island itself is an African American revision of Shakespearean geography. Willow Springs has preserved African cultural traditions and dialects, such as the Gullah speech and folk pastime so lovingly represented in Julie Dash's film, *Daughters of the Dust*, which was released in 1990, just a year after the publication of *Mama Day*. Dash's film is introduced with an ethnographic caption that Naylor herself might have written:

> At the turn of the century, Sea Island Gullahs, descendants of African captives, remained isolated from the mainland of South Carolina and Georgia. As a result of their isolation, the Gullah created and maintained a distinct, imaginative, and original African American culture.
>
> (Dash 1992: 27)

Similarly, Naylor's mythical island has not yet been invaded and occupied by the likes of Prospero. Willow Springs, sketched in a map prefacing the novel, is located somewhere between South Carolina and Georgia, and so legally exists "nowhere," much as the island of *The Tempest* is situated by Shakespeare somewhere between the Old World (between Tunis and Milan) and the New ("the still-vexed Bermudas" 1.2.230). It therefore becomes the property of the African American inhabitants: "So who it belong to? It belongs to us – clean and simple" (Naylor 1989: 5). Although Willow Springs has been and is periodically invaded and claimed by real estate interests, the African American Natives own it, "thanks to the conjuring of Sapphira Wade," who had enchanted her master and lover, Bascombe Wade, to pass the island down "to our daddies, and our daddies before them, and them, too" (5). As Caliban had declared 400 years before, "This island's mine, by Sycorax my mother" (*The Tempest* 1.2.334).

Not only the island, but also its maternal origins, are reconceived by Naylor in *Mama Day*. Traub suggests perceptively that "Sapphira not only invokes, but also newly configures Caliban's mother Sycorax, the original mother and conjurer of the uncharted island usurped by Prospero" (1993: 155). We might add that Sapphira is from Africa, but is brought, like Sycorax, to the New World against her will. Prospero relates to Ariel that "This blue-eyed hag was hither brought with child, / And there was left by th' sailors" (1.2.271–72). Naylor's choice of name for the great-great grandmother of Cocoa, Sapphira, may also signify on Willa Cather's neglected late novel, *Sapphira and the Slave Girl*, which Toni Morrison makes so much of in *Playing in the Dark*. Cather's Sapphira is the invalid mistress of a huge plantation who is dependent on slaves for "the most intimate of services" (Morrison 1992: 18 ff.). She suspects her "slave girl" Nancy of having an affair with her husband and takes that as an occasion to tyrannize all the slaves who serve her, particularly Nancy, who is innocent. Naylor's Sapphira, on the other hand, is a Black "conjurer" who manipulates her White master erotically to liberate the island's posterity from dependence on White authority.

There are other Shakespearean echoes in the novel. A rival witch and neighbor named Ruby makes trouble for George and Ophelia and challenges Mama Day's supremacy; drunk with her illegitimate power, Ruby may parallel Stephano. Even Trinculo seems to turn up in the story as an alcoholic doctor named Buzzard, who also mounts an innocuous challenge to Mama Day's magical dominance of the island. The most problematic character in the novel, however, is George (Ferdinand/Caliban), as we have been suggesting all along. Although there is nothing of the colloquial *bastard* in George, he does die of a heart attack after he is perceived as having failed to appreciate the enchantment generated on the island by Mama Day. Initially a Ferdinand, imagining himself the owner one day of the island, but drunk, exhausted, and filthy by the end of the novel, George comes to resemble Caliban more than the Prince of Naples. Neither Miranda nor Ophelia, it turns out, needs a Prospero or a Ferdinand, not to mention a Polonius or a Hamlet. The death of George, who as Ferdinand in Shakespeare's version would have continued Prospero's patriarchy back in Milan, completes Naylor's rewriting of *The Tempest*.

In form as well as content, *Mama Day* both controverts and extends the range of *The Tempest*. The impetus of African American signifying, according to Gates, is the search for the "black voice" in the "white written text."[4] Although Naylor's novel begins with the traditional visual and print icons of Western power – a map indicating ownership of the island by the female progeny of Sapphira Wade, a genealogy tracing the line of Sapphira, and a bill of sale for Sapphira – the novel speaks in many voices, as a drama does. It is clearly what Gates calls a "talking book," a speakerly text. In interview and lecture, Naylor insists that this book would simply not write itself in third-person narrative style, the way her earlier novels had. The form of *Mama Day* is overtly dialogical (that is, double-voiced) in the sense meant by Mikhail Bakhtin in *The Dialogic Imagination* (1981). In *The Tempest*, all characters are voiced, situations controlled, reconciliations rigged, and outcomes maneuvered by Prospero on what Gonzalo calls "the plantation of this isle" (2.1.143). Naylor displaces the monologic (single-voiced) voice of Prospero with multivocality and polyphony (or competing voices). A theme is announced in the map, genealogy, bill of sale, and synoptic introduction in the text. Then, as if in a jazz piece, the theme is voiced, re-voiced, controverted, and parodied by the three main characters. George and Cocoa converse through independent first-person narratives about their courtship, wedding, squabbles, and plans to visit Willow Springs. Mama Day's voice is introduced early in the novel – again, in her own narrative segments – and takes center-stage in the second part, but never assumes the dictatorial tone we detect in, say, Prospero's catechism of Miranda in the second scene of *The Tempest*. The icon for dialogism (awareness of competing meanings and of the fact that meaning is relative rather than authoritative) or even polyphony (multiple, sometimes competing voices) in *Mama Day* is what Miranda explicates as the "chicken coop" analogy. We live, she muses toward the end of the novel,

> "in a world where there ain't no right or wrong to be found. My side. He [George] don't listen to my side. She [Ophelia] don't listen to my side. Just like that chicken coop, everything got four sides: his side, her side, an outside, and an inside. All of it is the truth."
>
> (Naylor 1989: 230)

Miranda's analogy between communication and the chicken coop suggests that there is always another side, another perspective, another voice that needs to be heard. Sycorax, absent in the Shakespearean text, is given presence and posterity in the matriarchal figure of Sapphira Wade. Ophelia, never given a real voice in

Hamlet, muses on her future and the future of Willow Springs at the end of the novel. Even George, unlike Ferdinand when he is under the sway of Prospero, is free to reject Mama Day's benign dominion over his relationship with Ophelia and eventually does. Of course, he pays the price for his objections and convictions.

Like Prospero, Mama Day discourses on her magic: "'I can do more things with these hands than most folks dream of – no less believe'" (Naylor 1989: 294). But unlike her fellow magus, she depends on the sympathetic response of those for whom she works her magic. George, as a self-avowed rationalist, does not trust Mama Day's powers. George therefore becomes something of a tragic sacrifice, like so many of Shakespeare's tragic heroines who suffer – with little opportunity to respond verbally – fates cooked up for them by men. In lecture and interview, Naylor claims to have developed a real affection for George, and she wonders aloud about why she had "to kill him off." The union of Miranda and Ferdinand is imperative to Prospero, of course, for it unites Milan and Naples and reconciles him with Alonso, one of the former conspirators against his dukedom. Ferdinand is powerless against the magic of Prospero, as he learns when he draws his sword in resistance early on in the play (*The Tempest* 1.2.470), and therefore comes to respect Prospero's power. Westerner that he is, George dismisses as "mumbo-jumbo" the magic that would have allowed him not only to save Cocoa's life, but also to avoid his fatal heart attack (Naylor 1989: 295). He renounces Mama Day's magic, then tries desperately to assist with some of her exotic remedies to find a cure for the malady that afflicts Ophelia after the storm. Cocoa apologizes to him: "'I'm doubly sorry. 'Cause I know how serious this thing is that you can't believe'" (287). The magic of Mama Day is – to borrow a metaphor from Shakespeare – like that of Paulina in *The Winter's Tale*, as natural and "lawful as eating" (*The Winter's Tale* 5.3.11). Mama Day qualifies her magic by rejecting the dictatorial control Prospero wields with his book and staff over the inhabitants and visitors to his island, but she does not renounce her magical powers, as Prospero does. At the end of the novel, Mama Day, carrying Prospero's book and staff – in this case, the ledger with the Day family's historical record, essentially its deed to Willow Springs – moves through the night, "never allowing the book and the cane to stay in the shadows" (Naylor 1989: 293). Mama Day remains the benevolent – and, let us remember – the legitimate matriarch of Willow Springs.

John Edgar Wideman writes that

> race signifies something quite precise about power, how one group seizes and sustains an unbeatable edge over others. When the race wild card is played, beware, the fix is in ... [race] in its function as wild card is both a sign and an enabler of these shady transactions in a game only one player, the inventor of race, can win.
>
> (1994: xvi)

During the exploration of the New World, Shakespeare – however much he may have interrogated the norms of his own culture – was busy helping the West to invent alternative concepts of gender, territoriality, and race in *The Tempest* and kindred plays that deal with the "alien," in order to justify the systematic rape and exploitation of one race by another in the development of a "new" continent.

Gloria Naylor is busy in her turn signifying on these venerable colonial paradigms in *Mama Day*, as her contribution to a postcolonial, multicultural, multi-colored world. European Americans are all but invisible in the novel, perhaps because Naylor, like the playwright August Wilson, is interested in pursuing a program of cultural separatism and a return of African Americans to the rural South. Males are subordinated to females on the island, too, which restores a matriarchy that is nostalgically projected back into a distant African past as the dominant system of cultural control. There is, however, a strange, artificial isolation imposed on Naylor's mythical island community of Willow Springs, a cultural separatism that none of the islands off of the coast of South Carolina has enjoyed for decades, certainly not, for instance, the island where Naylor herself now lives half of the year, when she is not in New York. One suspects that Willow Springs enjoys the same rarefied atmosphere of science fiction that *The Tempest* has inspired in novels such as *Robinson Crusoe* and *Brave New World*, and in films and television series such as *Forbidden Planet*, *Lost in Space*, and *Star Trek.* What Daniel Defoe manages to show in his novel, however, is the European Crusoe's desperate but reluctant dependence on his Native man, Friday, a dependence that the South has never acknowledged with respect to African Americans during or subsequent to the period of slavery. While *Mama Day* sets the colonial record straight for African Americans, one suspects that European cultural hegemony, fictitious as it was from its roots in the slave trade, may be displaced by another, equally fictitious myth about racial independence and autonomy in the United States.

While ideologically *Mama Day* may be separatist and utopian, signifying as a literary methodology holds real hope for the canonical reconfiguration of race and class that any truly "new world" will demand in the twenty-first century. Signifying is all about words, about rearranging words and verbal patterns to configure new meanings and identities. As Jacques Derrida writes, "there's no racism *without* a language" (1986: 331, my italics). The point is not that acts of racial violence are only words, but rather that they have to have a word; racism "institutes, declares, writes, inscribes, prescribes" (331). For this reason, ethnic categories may and perhaps must be scrutinized, critiqued, and radically revised only *through* language and its cultural vehicles, such as the novel and the theater. In *Mama Day*, Gloria Naylor has clearly trumped Shakespeare's racist, colonial paradigm in *The Tempest* and has in the process sparked renewed interest in that dazzlingly inventive play.

Notes

1 I am not the first to make this comparison. Peter Erickson, in "Shakespeare's Changing Status in the Novels of Gloria Naylor," argues that "the effect of *Mama Day*'s exploration of Shakespearean heritage is critically to revise and decenter it" (1991: 139).

2 Coleridge writes: "Can we suppose [Shakespeare] so utterly ignorant as to make a barbarous negro plead royal birth? Were negroes then known but as slaves ... No doubt Desdemona saw Othello's visage in his [Othello's] mind; yet, as we are constituted, and most surely as an English audience was disposed in the beginning of the seventeenth century, it would be something monstrous to conceive this beautiful Venetian girl falling in love with a veritable negro. It would argue a disproportionateness, a want of balance in Desdemona, which Shakespeare does not appear to have in the least contemplated" (cited by Barnet 1986: 273–74).

3 For the argument about Othello's race and ethnicity, both as a character and an actor playing an African character, see Mythili Kaul (1996) and Virginia Mason Vaughan (1994).

4 As Gates writes: "[T]he curious tension between the black vernacular and the literate white text, between the spoken and the written word, between the oral and the printed forms of literary discourse, has been represented and thematized in black letters at least since slaves and ex-slaves met the challenge of the Enlightenment to their humanity by literally writing themselves into being through carefully crafted representations in language of the black self" (1988: 131).

7

Accommodating the virago: Nineteenth-century representations of Lady Macbeth

GEORGIANNA ZIEGLER

Lady Macbeth is a troubled character who continues to haunt our *fin-de-siècle* perceptions of women. The December 1994 issue of the British magazine *Tatler* featured a fashion spread entitled, "Dedicated follower ... If looks could kill," which proclaimed that "Richard Eyre's moody production of *Macbeth* at the National this year pioneered a heroine whose singular ambition and wardrobe of velvet were absolutely in tune with the Nineties" (Phillips 1994: 46–47). Three actresses, two former and one prospective Lady Macbeths, all slim and beautiful, modeled slinky red and black velvet evening dresses. The message conveyed by this advertisement is ambiguous and thus reflects the conflicted nature of contemporary society toward the position of women. On the one hand, they are still "dedicated followers" in a man's world, still dressing to attract male attention, still killing with their looks. On the other hand, they are allowed their own "singular ambition"; women in the nineties are assertive *and* attractive, the advertisement reassures us. But that in turn depends on the position of the woman. If she is too near "the throne," assertiveness can be seen as threatening. Take the case of America's First Lady, Hillary Clinton, whose early attempts to direct part of her husband's domestic agenda were met with surprisingly vehement opposition. In his London *Times* column of June 11, 1993 entitled, "Hillary Clinton Rejects Lady Macbeth Image," Martin Fletcher writes:

> Asked why her active involvement in her husband's administration provoked so much controversy, she said it was a reflection of the national debate over the role of modern women. "People are struggling to define what it means to be a woman, a mother, a wife," she said.
>
> (1993: 9)

Contemporary feminist thinking has taught us that notions of gender are culturally constituted and it invites us to destabilize the status quo. But redefining received cultural structures makes many people uncomfortable. We have inherited a number of these structures from the nineteenth century, a period that refined and idealized the notion of womanhood, while beginning to challenge and stretch its boundaries. Though Queen Victoria saw *Macbeth* at least eight times, praised the acting of Ellen Kean as Lady Macbeth,[1] and fell under the spell of things Scottish, neither she nor her subjects would have granted Victoria the unseemly political ambition of a Lady Macbeth. Quite the contrary. Idealized as wife and mother in both her domestic and national realms, "Queen Victoria offered the perfect solution to Britain's fears of female rule and of excessive monarchic power," as Margaret Homans has pointed out (1993: 3).

Nevertheless, Lady Macbeth could not be ignored. She was, after all, a major tragic heroine created by that nineteenth-century idol of British literature, Shakespeare. What does one do, however, with a wife who is strong-minded, ambitious, and given to evil in a period in which most women did not have careers, when a good nature and grace, not aggressiveness, were admired, and when husbands were expected to have the last say in matters concerning their married life? The twentieth century may turn Lady Macbeth into the smart professional woman, but the nineteenth century had other ways of appropriating her character. The discussion that follows uses pictorial representations as well as British and continental criticism to tease out these various methods of appropriation. First, however, I want to consider briefly and more broadly the moralizing function of Shakespeare's heroines, an approach that dominated much nineteenth-century criticism.

I Shakespeare's heroines and/as Victorian women

Queen Victoria's reign (1837–1901) corresponded to a heightened cult of womanhood that focused on the heroines of that other idol of the period, Shakespeare.[2] The phenomenon may be said to date from 1832, with the publication of Anna Jameson's *Characteristics of Women, Moral, Poetical, and Historical.* Jameson wrote magazine articles, biographies, travel narratives, and art guides in order to support her family. Her seminal work on Shakespeare was published about forty times until 1911 and was known to critics and popular readers alike. The title indicates that the book was conceived as being primarily "about" characteristics of women and only incidentally "about" Shakespeare's heroines. Jameson herself, through the character "Alda" in the introductory dialogue, professes to use Shakespeare as a teaching device "'to illustrate the various modifications of which the female character is susceptible, with their causes and results'" (Jameson 1854: xii). She prefers examples from Shakespeare rather than from history, for history is often not clear-cut, but Shakespeare's characters "combine history and real life; they are complete individuals, whose hearts and souls are laid open before us" (xix). The inspiration for Jameson's work, then, is not so much commentary on Shakespeare as it is a desire for the morally improving education of women.[3]

Jameson was not alone in her concern. Led by Victoria, who "said that her success as a queen depended in large part on the morality of her court and the harmony of her domestic life," the Victorian period generated a number of instructional books for women (Springer 1977: 125, 128–29). Among the most popular were those by Sarah Stickney Ellis. Her *Women of England*, which appeared in 1839, was the first of an often-reproduced series, including *Daughters of* … , *Wives of* … , and *Mothers of England*, which set about to improve "the majority of the female population of Great Britain" (Ellis 1839: 11). Focusing on the large number of women in the new middle class, Ellis strives to promote in them a sense of their moral responsibility as "domestic women," keepers of hearth and home. While Ellis does not deal specifically with Shakespeare, her emphasis on what constitutes Englishness finds its natural counterpart in the yoking of Shakespeare, considered that most English of authors, with the moral development of England's women. Mary Cowden Clarke, one of the first female editors of Shakespeare's works, wrote the immensely popular *Girlhood of Shakespeare's Heroines* (1850–52), as well as a series of articles published in *The Ladies' Companion* for 1849–50 and 1854.[4] In these articles and in a later piece written for *The Girl's Own Paper*, Cowden Clark puts forth the view that woman should not only see herself as she is in Shakespeare's heroines but also learn how to improve what she sees:

> [Shakespeare] has depicted women with full appreciation of their highest qualities, yet with accurate perception of their defects and foibles. … To her [the young girl] he comes instructively and aidingly; in his page she may find warning, guidance, kindliest monition, and wisest counsel.
>
> (1887: 562)

Most of Shakespeare's heroines could be used to illustrate womanhood's positive aspects, but can Lady Macbeth exemplify anything except its "defects and foibles"? Neither Jameson nor Cowden Clarke shies away from Lady Macbeth. Indeed, they and other critics throughout the century situate her character within the parameters of Victorian womanhood. Other critics refuse such appropriation, finding her either morally reprehensible or grand and terrible in a classical sort of way. I want now to consider in more detail these various approaches to Lady Macbeth's character, gathering evidence from a broad spectrum of criticism and artistic representation.

II Lady Macbeth: barbaric and passionate

In 1800, Richard Westall painted Lady Macbeth for the Boydell Shakespeare Gallery,[5] and the image was widely distributed through an engraving by J. Parker (Figure 3). Westall draws on several artistic and theatrical traditions to depict an Amazonian heroine, terrible in her defiance. Specifically, he represents Sarah Siddons, who first played the role in London in 1785 and whose performance was so powerful that references to it appear throughout the nineteenth century in England and abroad. Siddons is a commanding Lady Macbeth; she stands in a Gothic doorway against a cloudy sky, her white figure challenging the dark world of nature behind her. She frowns, and with her left hand clutches a letter to her breast. Her arms are muscular, and she holds the right one out in front of her with a clenched fist that seems almost to break through the picture surface, as though her passion is too great to be constrained. Siddons's costume is more oriental or classical than medieval; dark hair streams over her shoulders from beneath a turban, and she wears a white tunic and sandals.[6]

Most commentators note that while Siddons described Lady Macbeth as small and feminine in her written comments, on stage she depicted her with a "turbulent and inhuman strength of spirit" (Bell in Jenkin 1915: 36), as "something above nature" (Hazlitt 1817: 21). The literary essayist William Hazlitt, who was particularly impressed by Siddons's performance, writes:

Figure 3 "Mrs Siddons as Lady Macbeth," engraving based on an 1800 painting by Richard Westall for the Boydell Shakespeare Gallery. Courtesy of the Folger Shakespeare Library

> It seemed almost as if a being of a superior order had dropped from a higher sphere to awe the world with the majesty of her appearance. Power was seated on her brow, passion emanated from her breast as from a shrine; she was tragedy personified.
> (1817: 21–22)

Hazlitt may be thinking specifically of Reynolds's portrait of Sarah Siddons as *The Tragic Muse* (1784), but the effect of both paintings, as well as of Siddons's performance and Hazlitt's comments, is to allegorize the character of Lady Macbeth and make her larger than life.[7] Westall's painting belongs to the same tradition as George Romney's *Cassandra*, also painted for the Boydell Gallery, in which a large, statuesque woman, with sandled feet and muscular bare arms, raises a hatchet over her head. Both paintings foreshadow a figure such as the bare-breasted, muscular-armed female Liberty in Eugène Delacroix's *The 28th July* (1830), defiantly holding aloft the French tricolor flag, a painting that has been called "perhaps the best known visual image of revolution ever created" (Honour 1979: 234).

Hazlitt says of Lady Macbeth: "Her fault seems to have been an excess of that strong principle of self-interest and family aggrandisement, not amenable to the common feelings of compassion and justice, which is so marked a feature in barbarous nations and times" (1817: 21). He thus distances Lady Macbeth from contemporary mores – the "common feelings" – by suggesting that she inhabits an older, less civilized time. Such distancing became one of the ways by which the nineteenth century could feel comfortable about appropriating Lady Macbeth; as a larger-than-life figure of evil who appears out of the past, she can have nothing to do with "real" women and their emotions. Thus, in the Goethe-Schiller production of the play at Weimar in 1800, the witches were depicted "like the norns of Nordic mythology or the Roman sibyls," and any signs of conscience on the part of Lady Macbeth were cut, leaving her as "an unchanging figure of evil," or in Goethe's term, a "'superwitch' who enslaves her husband" (Williams 1990: 95, 98–99). Similarly, the German Shakespeare translator Schlegel says of the play, "in every feature we see a vigorous heroic age in the hardy North which steels every nerve" (1833: 334).

The French also place the play in an older, more barbarous era, or see its grandeur and terror in the context of classical drama. François Guizot, a French politician and writer on Shakespeare, says, in his "Introduction" to the 1821 edition of Shakespeare, that Macbeth "has only the qualities and the defects of a barbarian" and that Lady Macbeth is "the product of the same state of civilisation, and of the same habit of passions" (1852: 236–37).[8] Daniel O'Sullivan, editor of *Galerie des Femmes de Shakspeare* [*sic*] (1840s) remarks on the comparison of Lady Macbeth to the Clytemnestra of Aeschylus or Sophocles, or the latter's Electra, but declares that the only female character who *can* be analogous to her is Euripides's Medea (O'Sullivan [n.d.]: 177). Certainly anyone who saw Delacroix's disturbing 1838 painting of Medea, holding her squirming children beneath her bare breasts as she prepares to wield the knife, might recall Lady Macbeth's threat to have torn the nursing babe from her breast "and dashed the brains out" (*Macbeth* 1.7.58).

As the century progresses, the classical Lady Macbeth transforms into a Victorian virago. Two later actress portraits, obviously derived from the Westall painting, are those of Isabella Glyn (after 1850) and Charlotte Cushman (1858). The actresses wear almost identical black, modified Victorian dresses; one or both of their brawny arms are bare, and they stand in a medieval Scottish castle. Like Westall's Siddons, Glyn clutches the letter in one hand, while she clenches the other and stares intently out of the picture.[9] Cushman holds a dagger in each hand and also looks out with a ferocious stare. Both pictures in turn resemble the earlier heroine portrait of Lady Macbeth made for Charles Heath's first *Shakspeare Gallery* in 1836–37, which shows a well-built woman dressed in dark clothes, clasping her hands in front of her, while the letter from Macbeth is tucked snugly into her belt.[10]

All of these pictures were used many times as illustrations to editions of Shakespeare or, in the case of the series of Heath portraits, as illustrations to books about Shakespeare's heroines, such as O'Sullivan's *Galerie* in France. Such pictures visualize a critical tradition that saw Lady Macbeth as an inherently evil character. The poet Heinrich Heine (who had moved to France) castigates a recent German stage tradition that attempts to recuperate Lady Macbeth: "Whether men still defend in Germany the amiability of this lady, I do not know. … [I]t may be that even in Berlin they have learned to perceive that dear nice Lady Macbeth may be an awfully horrid beast [*Das die jute Macbeth eine sehr bese Bestie sint*]" (1891: 357, published in German 1839). Writing about the same time in *Shakspeare's Dramatic Art* (1846; published originally as *Shakspeare's Dramatische Kunst*, 1839), Heine's compatriot, the scholar Hermann Ulrici, sees *Macbeth* as a Christian tragedy, working out the problem of evil within human nature. Because of the Fall, man's natural tendency is toward evil rather than good. Macbeth therefore has the temptation of ambition within him, even before the witches awaken this thought; but Lady Macbeth has the "greater share of guilt," and her madness is an outward sign of the power of sin (Ulrici 1846:

208–9). The French novelist Victor Hugo, writing a bit later in the century, makes the implied analogy to the Fall explicit:

> Macbeth has a wife whom the chronicle calls Gruoch. This Eve tempts this Adam. Once Macbeth has taken the first bite, he is lost. The first thing that Adam produces with Eve is Cain; the first thing that Macbeth accomplished with Gruoch is murder. (1887: 240)

This association of the Macbeth story with the Temptation and Fall is made iconographically explicit in the popular line drawings by Kenny Meadows that were used to illustrate a number of editions of Shakespeare's plays from the 1840s onward.[11] The macabre quality of this particular set of illustrations is striking. The half-title page to the play shows two snakes, completely entwined in a circle around the blood-dripping word "Macbeth," their fierce heads crowned and made to look like Macbeth and Lady Macbeth (Figure 4). They are the embodiment of Ulrici's comment that both characters have surrendered to evil. The snake bodies reappear, twined around the three witches in the headpiece to Act 1, while in the background, a murky figure with bat wings raises powerful arms on high, each hand holding a dagger. The figure's face and body are left purposefully clouded, but in the pictorial heading to Act 2, we see a similar figure, now visible as a kind of "bat-man," hovering in the shadows behind Macbeth and handing him a dagger with one hand, while Lady Macbeth appears out of this same shadowy cloud to lay her hands on Macbeth's other arm, further goading him to commit the deed. She is thus shown as a partner of evil, and when she next appears in Act 2, Scene 2, Lady Macbeth is a dark, threatening figure, with only the whites of her eyes glowing as she stands in the shadow of a stone doorway, listening for Macbeth's return from the deed. A bat off to the side reminds us again of her connection with evil.

In his headpiece to Act 3, Meadows strengthens this implied connection between Lady Macbeth and the embodiment of evil. Here Macbeth lies on his back, one arm thrown over his face, his body clawed at by the dusky figure of Evil, the whiteness of whose eyes recalls the similar eyes of Lady Macbeth in Act 2. Just visible in the murky clouds that hover over Macbeth are the words, "Macbeth shall sleep no more." The final depiction of Lady Macbeth in Act 5, Scene 1 shows her as a powerful figure even in the midst of her guilt-ridden sleepwalking scene. Her large form faces out at us, hands

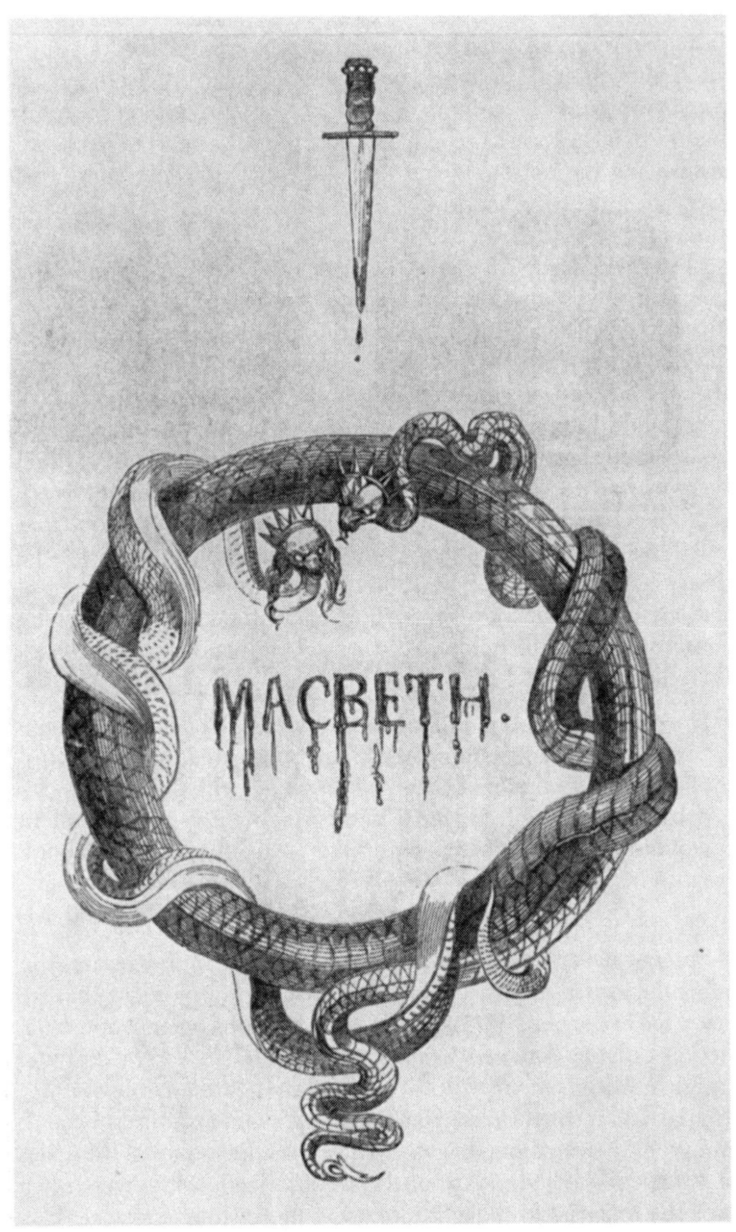

Figure 4 Kenny Meadows, half-title for *Macbeth* from *The Illustrated Shakespeare*, vol. 1, London: Tyas, 1840. Courtesy of the Folger Shakespeare Library.

clasped in a rubbing motion in front of her, eyes staring, not at us but at some internal vision. Meadows lights the figure dramatically from below with the oil-lamp on the table, creating a large looming shadow behind Lady Macbeth and over the upper part of her body, and leaving the bottom of her face only partly lit. Her continued association with the shadow of evil is thus brought to a dramatic climax.

Meadows's Lady Macbeth is woman as Other, as Demon, the dark side of womanhood that, as Nina Auerbach (1982) and Bram Dijkstra (1986) have shown, both fascinated and frightened the mid- and late-nineteenth century. The culmination of the iconography begun by Meadows is the serpent-woman of the turn of the century – the Lilith, Lamia, Salammbô figures – who are threatening and emasculating, as was the New Woman.[12] Sargent's portrait of Ellen Terry as Lady Macbeth (1889) grows out of this tradition. Terry wears her hair in long auburn braids entwined with ribbons that spill down over her shoulders. Her floor-length dress, made for the Henry Irving production of 1888, is slinky and shiny in shades of blue-green, and the long sleeves flow back off her elbows, catching sparks of light as she holds the crown triumphantly over her head. Terry herself wrote:

> It seems strange to me that anyone can think of Lady Macbeth as a sort of monster, abnormally hard, abnormally cruel, or visualize her as a woman of powerful physique, with the muscles of a prize fighter! … I conceive Lady Macbeth as a small, slight woman of acute nervous sensibility … on the terms of equals [with her husband].
>
> (1932: 160–61)

Sargent nevertheless paints Terry as a commanding figure who holds the crown aloft with defiant pleasure in a moment that we never see in the play. She becomes, as Auerbach cogently notes, the "icon of divine-demonic woman" (1982: 207).[13] Terry's costume designer, Alice Comyns-Carr, wrote that she "'was anxious to make this particular dress look as much like soft chain armour as I could, and yet have something that would give the appearance of the scales of a serpent'" (cited in Ashton 1980: 66). Beetle wings were sewn over the material to make it look even more shiny and scale-like, creating an imposing Eve-serpent figure who gleams out of the half-twilight of the painting.

The portrait of Ellen Terry marks the culmination of the lengthy tradition that depicted Lady Macbeth as a particular actress. That was another way for the nineteenth century to "tame" the figure of Lady Macbeth. If she could be seen as the creation of an actress on stage, then her threatening powers could be controlled as a theatrical presentation that had a beginning and an end. It is striking that Siddons and Terry, the two greatest interpreters of this role, both acted the part with more passion and power than their writings indicate. Terry, noting this difference in herself and Siddons, wrote:

> It is not always possible for us players to portray characters on the stage exactly as we see them in imagination. Mrs. Siddons may have realized that her physical appearance alone – her aquiline nose, her raven hair, her flashing eyes, her commanding figure – was against her portraying a fair, feminine, "nay, perhaps even fragile" Lady Macbeth.
>
> (Terry 1932: 163)

The idea of a feminine, "even fragile" Lady Macbeth evokes the alternate method by which the nineteenth century sought to appropriate her character. Siddons's notion that only a woman who was intelligent *and* beautiful, "respectable in energy and strength of mind, and captivating in feminine loveliness," could influence a man of Macbeth's stature, heralded the nineteenth-century attempt to fit Lady Macbeth's character into the model of acceptable womanhood (Siddons in Campbell 1834: 2: 11).

III Lady Macbeth: domesticated and caring

Writing her *Characteristics of Women* in 1832, Anna Jameson acknowledges that it is time to move beyond Siddons's stage conception of Lady Macbeth (1854: 322). She takes issue with the idea that Lady Macbeth should be seen primarily as a historical figure, the Gruoch "of an obscure age" (319). Rather, Jameson sees her as an evil but magnificent character with whom we sympathize "in proportion to the degree of pride, passion, and intellect, we may ourselves possess" (321). Lady Macbeth is a woman of superior intelligence, eloquence, and determination, dominated by ambition, who, "like an evil genius" goads her husband "to his damnation," yet is "never so far removed from our own nature as to be cast beyond the pale of our sympathies; for the woman herself remains a woman to the last – still linked with her sex and with humanity" (323). Jameson sees Lady Macbeth's references to her own sexuality, even in the midst of her savage determination, as ameliorating and humanizing her character: they "place the *woman* before us in all her dearest attributes, at once softening and refining the horror, and rendering it more intense" (327). This womanly nature is evidenced further in the ambition that Lady Macbeth has, not for herself, but for her husband, for whom she shows "no want of wifely and womanly respect and love," while unconsciously realizing "her own mental superiority" (328).

On the face of it, Jameson's reading of Lady Macbeth seems far removed from the view of Englishwomen given just a few years later by Sarah Stickney Ellis in her *Women of England* (1839). Men, Ellis writes, exist in the world of business, the marketplace where "envy, and hatred, and opposition" reign; "to men belongs the potent … consideration of worldly aggrandisement" (52, 51). Women, on the other hand, should provide in the home the peace and moral center that men need; they are "a kind of second conscience, for mental reference, and spiritual counsel, in moments of trial" (53). Lady Macbeth, by contrast, attempts to enter the "marketplace" herself when she meddles in politics and pushes her husband in his "consideration of worldly aggrandisement." In the end, however, even she is kept out of the public sphere by her own conscience and by Macbeth. Her scruples prevent Lady Macbeth from killing Duncan herself, and after that deed is done, Macbeth ceases to confide in her as before, leading to her isolation and madness. Jameson's insistence on Lady Macbeth's wifely "respect and love," the "entire affection and confidence" (1854: 328, 332) she has with her husband, especially in the early parts of the play, and the references to her womanly attributes of childbearing, place her – however flawed – within the accepted framework of Victorian womanhood.

Jameson's view was highly influential; we find it echoed later in the century by other Shakespeare critics such as M. Leigh-Noel, Mary Cowden Clarke, and Edward Dowden in England; and by Friedrich von Bodenstedt, Louis Lewes, and Georg Gervinus in Germany.[14] Pictorially, it is a view reflected in a counter-tradition of illustration running simultaneously with the one we have observed. As early as 1827, F. Howard completed a set of line drawings (probably influenced by the work of John Flaxman, a Wedgwood designer and illustrator of the *Iliad* and *Odyssey*) to illustrate *Macbeth*.[15] Several of them emphasize the companionship between Lady Macbeth and her husband. For the line, "My dearest love, / Duncan comes here tonight" (1.5.56–57), Macbeth stands frowning and resting on his sword, while Lady Macbeth tries to comfort him, leaning with her chin on his shoulder.[16] She bolsters Macbeth's confidence again in Act 2, Scene 2, standing close with one hand on the dagger he holds, while he looks at her worriedly. Howard also includes two scenes that do not appear in the play. One is Macbeth's crowning, where Lady Macbeth also sits crowned on a throne to the left, surrounded by her handmaids and looking on at Macbeth. The other depicts Lady Macbeth's deathbed, where she lies with a peaceful face surrounded by grieving ladies, one of whom comes to Macbeth at the head of the bed, as though to comfort him. Lady Macbeth and her women are thus shown in the supportive roles typically assigned to women in the nineteenth century.

The same Kenny Meadows who depicted a vampire-like Lady Macbeth in his book illustrations also contributed the fierce, but benign, portrait of her to Heath's second gallery of Shakespearean heroines (1848) (Figure 5). The picture shows the bust of a slender, beautiful, young woman, dark hair plaited with ribbons in rings at the sides of her head, which is encircled by a thin jeweled coronet. Though scowling and holding a bloody dagger in front of her, this Lady Macbeth – with her soft, finely-chiseled features and her delicate hand – evokes the cult of physical frailty which, by mid-century, "was a sign of respectable femininity" (Nead 1988: 29). This is the Lady Macbeth of Edward Dowden, who writes of "her delicate frame … filled with high-strung nervous energy," and "little hand" from which she tries to remove the stain of blood, at which "her delicate sense sicken[s]" (1901: 251, 254).

Later in the century, there appears in *The Royal Shakespeare* edition an illustration, by V. W. Bromley, for the lines "Look like the innocent flower / But be the serpent under it" (1.5.63–64). Bromley's interest in history painting is evident in his attempt at medieval costumes and setting, but in expression and gesture his Lady Macbeth is every inch the Victorian wife (Figure 6). Macbeth stands on the right, a dark armored figure deep in contemplation, with his arms folded across his chest. Lady Macbeth faces him, her profile, full of concern, that of a nineteenth-century lady, and she extends her right hand to rest comfortingly on his arm. Bromley's illustration might have called to mind the painting by George Elgar Hicks, which was exhibited at the Royal Academy in 1863, entitled *Woman's Mission, Companion of Manhood.* Hicks shows a Victorian woman holding her husband's arm and shoulder to comfort him in his obvious distress at having received a letter containing bad news. The paint-

Figure 5 Kenny Meadows, "Lady Macbeth," engraved by W.H. Mote for Charles Heath, 1848. Courtesy of the Folger Shakespeare Library.

Figure 6 Valentine Walter Bromley, "Macbeth and Lady Macbeth," engraved by G. Goldberg for Cassell & Company, London (n.d.). Courtesy of the Folger Shakespeare Library.

ing was part of a series of three, designed by Hicks with the title *Woman's Mission*; all three sold immediately.[17] The Howard and Bromley illustrations of Lady Macbeth show her enacting the role of *Woman's Mission*, and along with the Meadows portrait, they depict a woman "respectable in energy and strength of mind, and captivating in feminine loveliness" – what Sarah Siddons had written about Lady Macbeth (Siddons in Campbell 1834: 2: 11).

When John Ruskin, in his famous essay "Of Queens' Gardens" (1865), writes of the foolishness of "the idea that woman is only the shadow and attendant image of her lord, owing him a thoughtless and servile obedience" (1891: 115), we expect that he, like Siddons, Jameson, and others, might respect Lady Macbeth's "strength of mind." Not at all. While Ruskin appreciates Shakespeare's depictions of women ("Shakespeare has no heroes; he has only heroines"), he nevertheless denigrates Lady Macbeth along with Goneril and Regan, who, he says, "are felt at once to be frightful exceptions to the ordinary laws of life" (116, 121). Ruskin, like Ellis, wants a woman who keeps the home as a place of shelter and peace from the turmoil of the outside world, a woman whose "intellect is not for invention or creation, but for sweet ordering, arrangement, and decision" (136). His woman is the equal of her husband, but only as one sex complements the other. And though Ruskin makes her a queen, her rule is only within the restricted garden of her home.

On the one hand, Ruskin offers women a kind of power, but on the other he withdraws it, for a woman of Lady Macbeth's strength of character is too terrifying to contemplate. Other women, however, *can* contemplate her, and write her back into the script of Victorian womanhood. Anna Jameson, as we saw, appreciates her intellect, and Mary Cowden Clarke, in *The Girlhood of Shakespeare's Heroines*, tries to explain Lady Macbeth's willful temperament by making her the daughter of a woman who wanted only to produce a son, and who then neglects the daughter born to her and dies after a bout of postpartum depression, leaving the girl to grow up unrestrained and allowed to follow her own inclinations. The most powerful answer to Ruskin, however, comes from a relatively obscure monograph written by M. Leigh-Noel, author of the later volume *Shakspeare's Garden of Girls* (1885).[18]

Leigh-Noel's *Lady Macbeth: A Study* (1884) is the result of the kind of thoughtful reading that both Ruskin and Ellis recommend to women. A period of illness, which allowed Leigh-Noel to meditate upon the play, resulted in one of the most sympathetic assessments of Lady Macbeth's character ever made. Although she never says so explicitly, Leigh-Noel obviously accepts the parameters for a woman's role as set forth by Ruskin, but she understands Lady Macbeth within this role. Though she compares Shakespeare's play with "the sublime tragedies of ancient Greece" and notes that the play takes place in an age "far removed from our scrupulous times," she is not content to use classicism or medievalism as a distancing device (Leigh-Noel 1884: 2, 3). Leigh-Noel draws upon her own sympathies and assumptions as a Victorian woman to create the portrait of a lonely woman, deprived of the love of a child and often solitary, lacking the companionship of her lord. Leigh-Noel characterizes the relationship between Lady Macbeth and her husband in a manner that shows she accepts traditional gender roles within Victorian marriage:

> He, brave in the field, and favoured by fortune and nature alike, ambitious and yet scrupulous, bold in aspiration, but in action held in check by conscience; she, blind in her wifely devotion, owning no law but the advancement of her husband, and acknowledging no ties but those which bound her to him.
>
> (5–6)

It is the witches, not Lady Macbeth, who give Macbeth the notion of murdering Duncan. She is ambitious for him and thus is prepared "to lay aside her womanhood, or rather all its sweeter and softer features, in order to place on her husband's brow the crown he would never achieve for himself" (9). After Macbeth achieves the crown, however, their relationship dissolves, and Lady Macbeth is left solitary, unable to share the burden of her guilt. Accepting the Victorian assumption that a woman's natural instincts are to comfort and support her husband and to bear and nurture children, Leigh-Noel fantasizes that at this time, Lady Macbeth would have ached to hold a child at her breast to alleviate her awful loneliness. The thought that she might have been partially responsible for the deaths of Macduff's children would have been a shock that "must have hastened her end" (70).

Leigh-Noel's final assessment of Lady Macbeth places her within the context of the "fallen woman," a figure that haunted the edges of Victorian society:

> [S]he remained a woman singled out by destiny to become an example of the torture of unconfessed sin and the bitterness of

> unlawful ambition, standing a mute and awful figure, distinct and prominent against the storm-swept horizon. Could any lesson be more salutary? Does not one feel intense commiseration for the criminal? Who amongst us can cast the first stone? She had loved, had sinned, had suffered, and now she dies in complete desolation and despair.
>
> (1884: 75)

Leigh-Noel writes here out of an increased notion of "woman's mission to women," characterizing "the role of respectable women in the reclamation of the fallen" that developed from mid-century on (Nead 1988: 196). Yet Lady Macbeth has not committed adultery; she is "fallen" only in the Victorian sense that her assertiveness and single-minded willingness to assume that the ends justify the means remove her from acceptable womanly behavior. Leigh-Noel herself ultimately looks beyond her own social conventions and understands that Shakespeare has created a character of tragic power. She sees in Shakespeare's play a terror and sublimity beyond the merely ordinary: "there are degrees of suffering, and a light and facile spirit cannot grasp the thunderbolt that may shake a human soul" (Leigh-Noel 1884: 85).

Perhaps the terribleness of depicting the shaken soul kept Dante Gabriel Rossetti from executing his planned painting of *The Death of Lady Macbeth.* He made at least four studies for this painting, one of which (1876), now at the Carlisle Museum and Art Gallery (Cumbria), draws on the tradition of history painting in its overall design and on that of the fallen/mad woman in its uncompromising portrayal of Lady Macbeth in the last throes of mental agony, staring fixedly at the hands that she cannot wipe clean.[19] She is surrounded by three of her handmaids, one of whom lies exhausted in sleep at her side, the sleep that will never more come to her mistress, except in death. A holy friar prays at the foot of her bed, while a kindly-faced doctor wipes her brow and an old crone, perhaps her nurse, stands worriedly at Lady Macbeth's pillow. The two focal points of the painting are the praying friar and the mad woman, suggesting that Lady Macbeth needs the divine more than the physician (see *Macbeth* 5.1.64). The agony on the face of this tortured soul terrifies the viewer, who becomes a voyeur to this scene where the mental and spiritual are held in tension, waiting for the drama to be played out.

Though we are profoundly disturbed by her, Rossetti's Lady Macbeth lives in the neo-medieval world of the pre-Raphaelites, somewhat removed from everyday life. I want to conclude, therefore, by juxtaposing Rossetti's drawing with another image that completely domesticates the character and the play; together, drawing and painting represent the interpretive polarities given to Lady Macbeth in the nineteenth century. In 1864, Charles Hunt exhibited a painting of *The Banquet Scene: "Macbeth"* at the Royal Academy. That painting is now lost, but the previous year he completed another painting, *My "Macbeth."* In it, we see Hunt standing with his wife and son in their comfortably furnished parlor, contemplating with pride *The Banquet Scene*, which stands on an easel to the right. Hunt points to the painting, his gesture echoing that of the "witch" within the painting (see Altick 1985: 317). Not only is the story of *Macbeth* framed by and brought within the compass of the family home, but the scene depicted by the painting on the easel is actually a schoolboy performance of the play, in which all of the characters, including Lady Macbeth, are played by children. Altick suggests that Hunt's son himself may be the "witch" who points back at his father from the inner painting. This miniaturization of the play, achieved both through the size of the painting-within-the-painting and the age of the actors, diffuses the sense of sublime struggle and makes it a work of Shakespearean "Literature," co-opted by the educational system. In the larger painting, Hunt's wife stands behind their son, her hand protectively on his shoulder, reminding the viewer of the role of woman as mother and moral nurturer of her children. It is she, not the childless and dangerous Lady Macbeth, who will guide her son's future.

These two images of Lady Macbeth – as barbaric and passionate or domesticated and caring – figure the conflicted notions about women's roles in the nineteenth century. All around the constructed view of the "Angel in the House" promulgated by Coventry Patmore's wildly successful poem (1854–62), resistant forces were at work within society to reshape the idea of woman's position and rights: the Married Woman's Property Acts (1870–93), the admission of women to university education, the movement for women's suffrage, and the gradual entrance of women into professions.

A hundred years later, we have inherited both the traditional values and the reactionary behavior of our ancestors. Halfway into her husband's second term of office and bravely outfacing the role of "wronged woman" after his sex scandal, Hillary Clinton appears on the cover of the November 1998 U.S. *Vogue* magazine. Sitting queenly and poised in the Red Room of the White House, she is dressed in a dark red velvet gown similar to those modeled by the aspiring Lady Macbeths in *Tatler*. Writing about this image, reporters use the words "elegant," "regal," and "glamorous." Robin Givhan of *The Washington Post* says,

> It is a portrait loaded with subtext: a scorned woman victorious. ... This cover, which combines statesmanlike grandeur with womanly elegance and restrained chic, suggests self-assurance – politically, personally, and physically.
>
> (1998)

Quoting Givhan, Hugh Davies of the London *Daily Telegraph* notes that "becoming a cover woman was also a natural progression for the former bespectacled 'policy wonk' once described as 'the Lady Macbeth of Little Rock'" (Davies 1998). Lady Macbeth continues to figure our society's conflicted admiration for and fear of women's rights, power, and professional success. She frightens us, as she frightened our forebears, because of her perceived ability to empower the feminine while disempowering the masculine. Looking at cultural perceptions of a figure like Lady Macbeth over a period of years helps us to tease out notions of gender that construct us as much as we have constructed them.

Notes

1 See Rowell 1978: 57 and Appendix.

2 For an intelligent discussion of the nineteenth-century canonization of Shakespeare and the idealization of his female characters, see Tricia Lootens 1996. My own work has developed independently, along parallel lines with that of Lootens. See the two introductory essays in Ziegler 1997: 11–31.

3 Jameson is gaining wider recognition as an important early "feminist" critic. Anne E. Russell (1991) discusses some of the tensions that arise as Jameson tries to define Shakespeare's heroines within the context of nineteenth-century "womanliness," while Christy Desmet (1990) views Jameson's Shakespearean criticism against its background of the Romantics' views on Shakespeare.

4 Technically, the honor of being the first female editor must be given to Henrietta Bowdler, who did much of the work on the famous "sanitized" version of Shakespeare (1807) that was popular throughout the nineteenth century. The efforts of Mary Cowden Clarke, however, are closer to our modern notion of editing. See Thompson and Roberts 1997: 46–47.

5 The Boydell Shakespeare Gallery was an exhibition of paintings by prominent British artists that had been commissioned by John and Josiah Boydell with the idea of making money from selling a special edition of Shakespeare's plays illustrated with engravings of the paintings. In 1789, thirty-four of the paintings went on display in a gallery on Pall Mall in London. By the time the gallery closed in 1805, there were 163 paintings. Unfortunately, the Boydells lost money on the expensive venture.

6 Westall's painting draws not only on the important eighteenth-century tradition of full-length portraiture, practiced by such English artists as George Romney, Thomas Gainsborough, Sir Joshua Reynolds, and Sir Thomas Lawrence, but also on the contemporary traditions of neoclassicism, encouraged by the discovery and importation of Greek and Roman antiquities (e.g., the Elgin Marbles), and of history painting.

7 On the pictorial representations of Siddons as Lady Macbeth, see the forthcoming article by Heather McPherson in *Studies in Eighteenth-Century Culture*. I am grateful to McPherson for the opportunity to read and cite her essay.

8 Reprinted and translated in *Shakespeare and His Times* (London 1852).

9 For a discussion of the Glyn portrait, see Pressly 1993: 240–41.

10 The publisher Charles Heath produced two sets of engravings of Shakespeare's heroines. The first, in 1836–37, comprised forty-five portraits with a passage from each play quoted on the facing pages; the second set, in 1848, was even more popular, going through five editions until 1883. It was a series of engravings based on paintings by artists such as Frith, Egg, Meadows, Hayter, Wright, and Corbould. These sets belonged to the popular tradition of "beauties" portraits that depicted heroines from other admired authors such as Byron and Scott, or the ladies of Victoria's court.

11 Nearly 1,000 wood engravings by Kenny Meadows first appeared in Shakespeare's *Works*, edited by J. Ogden and published in three volumes by R. Tyas (London 1839–43). Like many Victorian novels, the edition first appeared in paper-bound parts, issued serially.

12 Lilith was Adam's first wife, according to Rabbinical literature, and Lamia is a witch from classical literature; they are the subjects of poems by Dante Gabriel Rossetti and John Keats, respectively. Salammbô is a priestess in a novel of ancient Carthage by the French writer Gustave Flaubert. All three women are associated with serpents. The New Woman is a term used to denote those who advocated voting and educational rights, as well as more social freedom for women in the latter part of the nineteenth century.

13 In her biography of Ellen Terry, Nina Auerbach discusses in some detail Terry's approach to the role of Lady Macbeth. Despite Sargent's portrayal of Terry as a virago, Terry actually depicted Lady Macbeth as "the feminine woman" (Auerbach 1987: 255). "In her notes, Lady

Macbeth smiles incessantly. … She wins [Macbeth] to murder not by bullying, but by pleasing" (254). Terry's stage portrait of Lady Macbeth is thus closer to attempts to accommodate her into Victorian womanhood than is Sargent's painted portrait.

14 Friedrich von Bodenstedt, writing first in 1874, suggests that because she is childless, Lady Macbeth has only one aim – "her husband's greatness." In order to achieve this end, "only once can she collect all her power and negate all her femininity"; afterwards, "she is not able to wade any farther into blood" and "her womanhood claims back its rights" (Bodenstedt 1878: 307). (I am grateful to Dr. Christa Jansohn for the translation of Bodenstedt.) Georg Gervinus, in 1850, insists that Lady Macbeth "is far more a dependent wife than an independent masculine woman, for she wishes the golden circlet rather for him than for herself. Her whole ambition is for him and through him … she lives only in him and in his greatness" (Gervinus 1883: 598). Similarly, Louis Lewes says of her: "She desires the throne, not for herself, but for her husband" (Lewes 1895: 264). He finds the pair "endurable" because of their "warm and tender" love, but he finds that in Lady Macbeth, "the weakness of woman, which is a great part of her charm, gives way under a burden which a man, though he may seem weaker, can easily bear" (271, 273).

15 The outline drawings by the German artist Friedrich August Moritz Retzsch did not begin to appear until the first publication of his Shakespeare Gallery in 1828. These became enormously popular, both on the continent and in England. See the article on Retzsch by W. H. T. Vaughan 1996.

16 A picture from mid-century with very similar iconography is the painting by George Hicks, *Woman's Mission: Companion of Manhood* (1863). Here we see a woman leaning on her husband's shoulder with her hand on his arm, trying to comfort him in his grief. But she looks up at him in sweet adoration, while Lady Macbeth in Howard's drawing is about the same height and looks at Macbeth more as a companion. For a discussion of Hicks's painting, see the article by Helene E. Roberts 1972.

17 Sounding like a reprise of the conduct books of Sarah Stickney Ellis, the other two paintings in the series were titled *Guide of Childhood*, and *Comfort of Old Age*, thus covering the total supportive role of women in the family. On these paintings, see Roberts 1972; Nead 1988: 13ff and Treuherz 1993: 114. On the relationship of the Hicks's series to Ruskin's description of an ideal wife and helpmate, see Casteras 1987: 50–52.

18 Not much is known about Madeline Leigh-Noel, later Mrs. M. L. Elliott. See Thompson and Roberts 1997: 173–74.

19 Another version in pen and sepia ink is at the Ashmolean Museum in Oxford. Rossetti tried another painting of a fallen woman entitled

Found. This work, too, he never finished, and his poem "Jenny" also distances the reader from its title figure, a prostitute, as the scholar narrator, while seeming to speak directly to Jenny, in fact, never approaches her. While obviously compassionate toward such women, nevertheless Rossetti seems blocked by contemplating their plight. See the discussion of the painting by Nina Auerbach (1982: 172–74), of the poem by Amanda Anderson (1993: chapter 4), and of both by Helene E. Roberts (1972: 67–72). Earlier depictions of the apocryphal scene of Lady Macbeth's death were made by F. Howard in 1827, as part of his set of illustrations for the play, and by Theodor von Holst in an 1838 painting, perhaps influenced by Fuseli (on Holst, see Altick 1985: 318). By far the most frequently reproduced scene, however, is Lady Macbeth's sleepwalking scene. There is often a voyeuristic quality about this scene, as the doctor and lady-in-waiting look on, registering in their faces the fear, horror, or concern which we as fellow viewers may also feel.

8
The Shakespeareanization of Robert Browning

ROBERT SAWYER

In June of 1879, Robert Browning appeared as a witness in a libel hearing. A freelance editor, who was suing *The Athenaeum* for damages, charged that the magazine had committed slander by referring to him as a "literary vampire" for his republication of Elizabeth Barrett Browning's poetry without her family's permission. As Browning stepped into the witness box, the defense counsel, Mr. Parry, decided to forgo the custom of asking the witness to identify himself. Instead, Parry announced, "I need not ask who you are; I would as soon ask William Shakespeare." According to the *Daily Telegraph*, Browning ceremoniously "bowed" and confessed, "I have been before the public for some years now" (16 June 1879: 2).

For at least twenty years prior to this court appearance, Robert Browning had carefully manipulated his public image in order to borrow Shakespeare's cultural authority for his works. After his much-maligned attempts at Shelleyan subjective poetry in the 1840s, Browning began a public relations campaign to link his name and work with Shakespeare's.[1] His "Essay on Shelley" (1852) represents Browning's first successful attempt in this enterprise, and his poem "House" (1876) signals one of the last. In the years between publication of these two works, many critics of the mid-Victorian era begin to speak of Browning's work in Shakespearean terms.

By combining reception study with close reading, and by considering the cultural context of the mid-Victorian period, I will show

how one poet defines himself in relation to Shakespeare. Browning distances himself from the Romantics and their particularly subjective poetry by perfecting the dramatic monologue, a genre that calls to mind the "objectivity" of Shakespearean drama. Moreover, Browning insists on a distinction between the private lives of poets and the public works they create. A second level of appropriation also occurs in the 1880s, when the Browning Society promotes Browning as a Victorian bard, more masculine and more religious than Shakespeare – in short, a more wholesome national poet.

I Objective and subjective poetry

At the beginning of the 1850s, Browning began carefully to distinguish between the art of Shelley and that of Shakespeare. While residing in Paris during the winter of 1851, Browning was asked to write an introduction for a new collection of what were believed to be Shelley's letters. Although the letters were later discovered to be spurious, the "Essay on Shelley," as it has come to be known, represents one of the few pieces of literary theory ever written by Browning.[2] In the "Essay," Browning carefully outlines the distinctions he sees between an "objective" poet such as Shakespeare and Shelley as a "subjective" poet. In so doing, Browning works out his own role as a poet.

Browning defines the objective poet as a person "whose endeavour has been to reproduce things external (whether the phenomena of the scenic universe, or the manifested action of the human heart and brain) with an immediate reference, in every case, to the common eye and apprehension of his fellow men" (Browning 1997: 574). The objective poet explains the world in terms understood by many, because he sees "external objects more clearly, widely, and deeply, than is possible to the average mind" (574). Being "in sympathy" with the "narrower" conception of the object under consideration and "careful to supply it with no other materials than it can combine into an intelligible whole" (574), the objective poet such as Shakespeare is attracted to the drama as a medium. His works are intelligible in part because his characters are both complete and concrete. Thus, while the abstract notion of "intellectual paralysis" may seem remote and incomprehensible, when viewing a character such as Hamlet we understand the concept because the character seems finished. Browning calls the objective poet a "fashioner" (574): "the thing fashioned, his poetry, will of necessity be substantive, projected from himself and distinct" (574–75). For this reason, poetry has nothing to do with the biography of the poet; though biographies may be "fraught with instruction and interest," they are ultimately dispensable, because the "man passes, the work remains" (575). In the "Essay on Shelley," Browning even refuses to name Shakespeare; in the single reference he makes, Browning calls him, instead, the "inventor of 'Othello'" (575).

While the objective poet deals with "humanity in action," the subjective poet struggles with "the primal elements of humanity" (576). The subjective poet, then, is a "seer," a prophet rather than a "fashioner," and what he "produces will be less a work than an effluence" (576). His biography, unlike the objective poet's life story, is important because "that effluence cannot be easily considered in abstraction from his personality, – being indeed the very radiance and aroma of his personality, projected from it but not separated" (576). A knowledge of the personality of the subjective poet is essential: "in apprehending it we apprehend him, and certainly we cannot love it without loving him" (576).

Browning remained troubled over which kind of poetic model was best, concluding in the "Essay" that there is no way to judge which of these poetic gifts is the greater, as there is a need for both types of poetry and poets. While it might seem that the subjective poet is "the ultimate requirement of every age," Browning regards the objective poet as equally important, "[f]or it is with this world ... that we shall always have to concern ourselves: the world is not to be learned and thrown aside, but reverted to and relearned" (577). Thus, Browning suggests a cyclical view of poetic history: after the lofty insight of seers and prophets, there will come an "imperative call for the appearance of another sort of poet, who shall at once replace this intellectual rumination of food swallowed long ago, by a supply of the fresh and living swathe" (578). It seems in these lines that Browning defends his own attempts to create new, "fresh" ways of looking at the world, to distinguish himself from the dominating influence of Shelley and other Romantic predecessors and to associate himself with Shakespeare. The poetic result is Browning's dramatic monologue.

While a single definition of the dramatic monologue is impossible, the form usually contains a speaker who unconsciously reveals more about himself than he intends. Unlike many of the Romantics, who purportedly drew their inspiration from solitude and isolation, Browning writes about "men among men," combining the perspective of the subjective, philosophical speculator with dramatic action concerning people of this world. Joseph Milsand, a contemporary of the poet, suggests that Browning sought "to reconcile and combine" the subjective and the objective, "in order to find a way of being, not in turn but simultaneously, lyric and dramatic, subjective and pictorial" (Milsand 1856: 545). In *Men and Women* and *Dramatis Personae*, Browning attempts this fusion with the dramatic monologue.

II Performing appropriation

Browning's effort to fuse objective with subjective perspectives manifests itself in two poems that appropriate Shakespeare: "Childe Roland to the Dark Tower Came," which was composed (January 1852) soon after the "Essay on Shelley" and was based on *King Lear*; and the later poem "Caliban upon Setebos" (published 1864), which rewrites Shakespeare's *Tempest*. In these two poems, we see Browning struggling with his role as poet; in "Childe Roland" he aligns himself firmly with the goals of objective poetry, yet in the later poem, Browning seems to return to the agonistic stance of the Romantic or subjective poet, competing with Shakespeare even as he empathizes with Shakespeare's maligned character.

"Childe Roland to the Dark Tower Came" involves a young knight, a "Childe," on a quest to find the mysterious "Dark Tower." At the beginning of the poem, the quester watches as a "hoary cripple, with malicious eye" (Browning 1997: p. 194, l. 2)[3] points him in the direction of what may or may not be the "ominous tract" leading to the Dark Tower (l. 14). At the conclusion of the poem, Roland "[b]urningly" realizes, "all at once," that he has reached his goal (l. 175). In front of him lies the "Tower itself / The round squat turret, blind as the fool's heart" (ll. 181–82). At this point, Roland recalls the names "of all the lost adventurers," his "peers" who have struggled to reach the same place (l. 195). As their images surround him, Roland puts his trumpet to his lips and blows "Childe Roland to the Dark Tower came" (l. 204).

The most important point of intersection between "Childe Roland" and *King Lear* is the landscape's function as the locale for a rite of passage. Both protagonists learn to go beyond themselves "by acts of sympathetic imagination" to a sense of "the intrinsic nature of inanimate objects" (Shaw 1968: 129). On this route, Lear's empathy shifts from the inert landscape to various animals, and then, finally, to other human beings. The King sees in the storm another person who resembles himself or one of his family. Yet Lear sympathizes with and forgives the storm's fury because he never "gave [it] kingdom" nor "call'd [it] children" (3.2.16).[4] Therefore, the storm "owes" Lear "no subscription" as daughters do (3.2.17). Indeed, Lear's daughters seem even less worthy than beasts, as Lear at least feels some identification with animals. He states, for instance, that "man's life's as cheap as beast's" (2.4.262), and compares "unaccommodated man" to a "poor, bare, forked animal" (3.4.98, 100). Eventually, when Lear totters toward insanity, he himself becomes, in essence, like "a beast, that wants discourse of reason" (*Hamlet* 1.2.150) and loses his reason to wander madly on the heath. Finally, Lear learns to sympathize with others, including Kent and the Fool. In the hovel scene, for instance, Lear invites others to go in first. "Prithee go in thyself," he says to Kent, "seek thine own ease" (*Lear* 3.4.24). Lear then turns to the Fool, asserting, "In boy … You houseless poverty / Nay get in" (3.4.27–28). As the two precede him into the shelter, Lear remains alone on the heath, prayerfully proclaiming the words that signify his epiphany: "O, I have ta'en / Too little care of" others less fortunate (3.4.33–34).

Roland goes through a similar progress toward selfless empathy, an initiation signaled in part by the title of "Childe," bestowed on a young warrior awaiting knighthood. His journey also begins through an identification with inanimate objects, which he endows with human characteristics: the "desperate" earth (l. 147), the "blotches" of soil that look like "boils" (ll. 151, 153), which might recall Lear's descriptions of his daughters as "boil[s], and "embossed carbuncle[s]" (2.4.218–19). Even the "willows" growing by the "wrath[ful] … black eddy" on Roland's path seem to fling themselves, like a "suicidal throng," downward "in a fit / Of mute despair" (ll. 117, 113–14, 117–18). Roland's empathy at this point grows so strong that even the animals take on human qualities. The "water-rat['s]" cry (l. 125) sounds "like a baby's shriek" (l. 126), while the "stiff blind horse" is full of "grotesqueness" and "woe" (ll. 76, 82). By the end of the journey, Roland himself feels hunted like an animal, caught "[a]s when a trap shuts [and] you're inside the den" (l. 174). Roland achieves a level of sympathy comparable to that of Lear when he recalls other humans, addressing them with understanding in spite of their failures and dishonor. Roland recalls "all the lost adventurers my peers," and remembers "[h]ow such a one was strong, and such was bold" (ll. 195, 196). Like Lear, Roland sympathizes with the precarious nature of the human condition.

The most obvious intertextual relation between play and poem is Edgar's song, which Browning appropriates for the epigraph of "Childe Roland." By telling the reader to "See Edgar's song in 'Lear'," Browning overtly seeks the cultural authority that this Shakespearean reference can grant to his poetry. After the storm scene on the heath, Edgar, still in disguise, speaks these lines as the party heads toward Gloucester's castle:

> Child Rowland to the dark tower came,
> His word was still – fie, foh, and fum,
> I smell the blood of a British man.
>
> (3.4.170–73)

On the most literal level, the "dark tower" in Edgar's song probably represents Gloucester's castle, where evil lurks after Lear's banishment to the heath. The lines may also suggest Edgar's fear of death, if he, as Gloucester's "child," returns home. In addition, the lines foreshadow the bloody blinding of Gloucester by Cornwall and Regan two scenes later. As Cornwall plucks out the "vile jelly" of Gloucester's eyes, the blind man becomes a "dark and comfortless" tower who is expelled from his own castle, condemned to "smell / His way to Dover" (3.7.68, 88, 96–97). Certainly Edgar's lines express the potential for numerous dangers on the path to enlightenment. The dark tower, which is at once (in Shakespeare) the father Gloucester and (in Browning) the goal of Roland's quest, symbolizes the conflation of inanimate and human. In reaching the tower, Childe Roland reaches the state of complete empathy that both Lear and Edgar have achieved before him.

The conclusion of Browning's poem returns us to the title and the beginning of his journey. As Roland reaches the "Dark Tower," he hears "toll[ing] / ... like a bell" the "[n]ames in [his] ears / Of all the lost adventurers [his] peers" (ll. 193–95), and in this "one moment knelled the woe of years" (l. 198). As the images of his former companions are "ranged along the hill-sides," creating a "living frame," Roland declares, "I saw them and knew them all" (ll. 199, 202). "Dauntless[ly], Roland raises the "slug-horn" to his lips and blows "Childe Roland to the Dark Tower came" to announce his presence (ll. 203–4). Roland describes the Tower as "blind as the fool's heart" (l. 182) echoing, perhaps, the biblical passage the "fool hath said in his heart, / 'There is no God'" (Psalms 14.1–2). Anne Williams's characterization of Roland as "the archetypal 'wise fool' who is wiser than he knows" (1983: 40) leads us back to

King Lear and the wise Fool in the play who knows much more than the "blind" Lear or Gloucester. The impossibility of a single interpretation may be suggested by Roland's lines preceding the conclusion, when the speaker seems to challenge the reader: "Solve it you!" (l. 167). Still, the blowing of Roland's horn recalls the scene in Act 5 of *Lear* in which Edgar appears on the "third sound of the trumpet" (5.3.113) to reclaim his real identity and to triumph over his evil brother Edmund in battle. Further, Roland's lines "I saw them and knew them all" (l. 202), coming as they do in the last stanza, signal a new perspective, whether it be the recognition of death or the emergence of a new empathy with mankind, or both. In "Childe Roland" Browning achieves the dramatic vision of his own construction of the objective Shakespeare.

Browning stated later that "Childe Roland came upon me as a kind of dream. I had to write it, then and there, and I finished it the same day, I believe. But it was simply that I had to do it" (cited in De Vane 1955: 229). Not only does Browning suggest that his Shakespearean appropriation had entered his unconscious, but he also may be thinking of Shakespeare's line from *The Tempest* (a play from which he would soon substantially borrow), which describes life as "such stuff / As dreams are made on; and our little life / Is rounded with a sleep" (4.1.156–58). Thus, not only literary composition, but also life may be no more than a mere dream, or in Childe Roland's case, a disturbing nightmare. In focusing on Childe Roland's replication of Lear's journey from blindness to self-knowledge, Browning's poem focuses on the drama of "men among men," prefiguring a strain of humanist criticism that focuses on the heroic journey toward enlightenment of Shakespeare's "great" tragic heroes.[5] Only a hint of the unconscious, the nightmare recognition of life's insubstantial status, disturbs the careful and complete delineation of Roland's quest and growing awareness of the human condition. The relation between the objective poet's subordination to the world and the subjective poet's assertion of self coheres less smoothly, ironically enough, in the later poem "Caliban."

A second way to claim Shakespearean authority and yet ward off notions of influence is to write what today would be called a prequel. Long before materialist and postcolonialist critics attended to his situation, "Caliban upon Setebos" portrays the Caliban of Shakespeare's *The Tempest* in the moments before the play begins. Hence, Browning inverts the idea of literary authority by turning Shakespeare into Browning's literary heir. The intertextual struggle between poem and play not only concerns the "evolutionary creature" Caliban, but also demonstrates the evolution of Robert Browning as a poet. As Harold Bloom argues, a poet "'completes' his precursor" by borrowing from the "parent-poem," but then altering or extending the meaning "as though the precursor had failed to go far enough" (Bloom 1973: 14). Hence, Browning ups the ante by "completing" Caliban, transforming the creature to reflect Browning's own ideas.

Browning endows his Caliban with a sophistication lacking, as he saw it, in Shakespeare's original conception. Browning examines Caliban as an evolving creature whose idea of God/Setebos, like the reader's perhaps, is evolving as well. In Shakespeare's play, Caliban learns language from Miranda, who "pitied" him, and took "pains to make [him] speak, taught [him] each hour / One thing or another" (1.2.356, 357–58). Shakespeare's Caliban acknowledges her role in his acquisition of language, admitting that he was taught "how / To name the bigger light, and how the less, / That burn by day and night" (1.2.338–39), but concludes angrily that "You taught me language, and my profit on't / Is I know how to curse" (1.2.363–64). In Browning's version, Caliban also learns speech from his masters, but employs it to contemplate the nature of Setebos, "whom his dam called god" (1997: l. 16). These thoughts bother Caliban, "[b]ecause to talk about Him, vexes" (l. 17).

Browning's Caliban uses his language in a more philosophical, and by extension, more profitable manner than Shakespeare's Caliban. His words reflect his sophisticated understanding of the isle, and the "sea which sunbeams cross / And recross till they weave a spider-web" (ll. 12–13). Although Shakespeare imparts some poetical language to his Caliban, Browning's creature employs language to contemplate existence rather than to curse his captors. Caliban also recalls the creativity of Setebos, who, like Shakespeare, "[m]akes this a bauble-world to ape yon real" (l. 147). Perhaps Browning's appropriation also cheats Shakespeare out of his mastery, just as Caliban discovers it "good to cheat" Miranda and Prospero (l. 22). Like Caliban, who "[p]lays thus at being Prosper in a way" (l. 168), Browning plays at being Shakespeare. Browning's "Caliban upon Setebos," which concerns the evolution of man, also reveals the evolution of an appropriating poet, Robert Browning. Thus, Browning's second method of mitigating influence is to write a prequel to Shakespeare's play, and to replace Prospero with Caliban. This move allows the auditor to "see" through Caliban's eyes, the goal of the "objective" poet, and to sympathize with a creature held captive against his will. At the same time, however, Browning competes with Shakespeare: if Caliban is as much a philosopher as Prospero, then perhaps Browning, the poet whose empathy transforms Caliban into an intelligent being, is superior to Shakespeare in his understanding. In this way, Browning also insists on his "genius," the hallmark of the "subjective" poet. Although intellectually Browning is committing himself to dramatic poetry, the influence of the same Romantic models that inform Bloom's account of literary influence have their place in Browning's relation to Shakespeare.

III The Shakespeareanization of Robert Browning

Although a somewhat muted reception greeted "Childe Roland" and the other poems collected in *Men and Women* (1855), a shift in critical response demonstrates Browning's successful appropriation of Shakespeare and his cultural authority. Following the publication of *Men and Women*, Browning's name was often evoked with Shakespeare's by the critics as well as by Browning himself. Some critics even began to equate Browning's art with Shakespeare's. Defending Browning against the charge of "obscurity," William Morris writes:

> Now, I know well enough what [the critics] mean by "obscure", and I know also that they use the word wrongly; meaning difficult to understand fully at first reading, or, say at second reading, even: yet, taken so, in what cloud of obscurity would "Hamlet" be!
> (1856: 172)

Morris, defending Browning's alleged obscurity by yoking it with the "obscurity" of the author of *Hamlet*, establishes the movement to Shakespeareanize Browning.

In private, Browning also positioned himself as a misunderstood artist, an heir to other complex artists such as the creator of *Hamlet*. In a letter to John Ruskin (Dec. 10, 1855), Browning first defends his lack of critical acclaim, stating, "A poet's affair is with God, – to whom he is accountable, and of whom is his reward; look elsewhere and you find misery enough" (cited in Woolford and Karlin 1996: 258). Then Browning participates in his own Shakespeareanization:

> Do you believe people understand *Hamlet*? The last time I saw it acted, the heartiest applause of the night went to a little by-play of the actor's own – who, to simulate madness in a hurry, plucked

> forth his handkerchief and flourished it hither and thither: certainly a third of the play, with no end of noble things, had been (as from time immemorial) suppressed, with the auditory's amplest acquiescence and benediction.
>
> (258)

Thus, Browning, as well as critics such as Morris, begins to position the poet as a Victorian Shakespeare – objective, dramatic, and, like Shakespeare, difficult to comprehend on occasion.

In favorable reviews, poems such as "Caliban" were used to demonstrate Browning's relationship to Shakespeare. *The Athenaeum*, which had not exactly been Browning's ally in the past, wrote that "Caliban" is a "striking example" of Browning's creativity. The writer adds that the "revelation of what Caliban 'thinketh' would have delighted Shakespeare himself, who would have been the first to have acknowledged that it faithfully represented the inner man of his original creation" (*The Athenaeum* 1864: 766). The reviewer concludes that "only a great dramatic poet could have written this poem" (766). Twenty-six years later, Oscar Wilde fashions a similar connection between Browning and Shakespeare. He claims that from "ignoble clay" Browning created "men and women that live," concluding that Browning "is the most Shakespearian creature since Shakespeare" (Wilde 1890: 127) and "from the point of view of a creator of character [Browning] ranks next to him who made Hamlet" (127). Unlike Shelley, Browning writes dramatically about real "men and women." In his irrepressible manner, Wilde adds: "If Shakespeare could sing with myriad lips, Browning could stammer through a thousand mouths" (127). The equation between Browning and Shakespeare confirms Browning's successful positioning of himself in the Shakespearean poetic line.

Ironically, the private Browning began to chafe at the invasion of privacy brought on by the enormity of his success, an accomplishment due in great measure to his Shakespearean appropriation. In the poem "House" we see Browning's new use of Shakespeare, this time to defend rather than to extend his public image. The publication of *Dramatis Personae* was deliberately delayed for a year as his other works continued to sell (Litzinger and Smalley 1970: 17). It appears that Browning, like many artists, desired the recognition of others, but disdained the attendant celebrity. In one of his last appropriations of Shakespeare, Browning returns to the theme of the "Essay on Shelley," arguing that Shakespeare is the central dramatic and objective poet; more importantly, in this same poem, Browning seems to identify himself with Shakespeare completely. As John Maynard points out, "on the rare occasions when he used a poet as an image for himself," such as the poem "House," it was "Shakespeare, not Shelley, with whom Browning would identify" (Maynard 1977: 232). As Browning successfully redefines himself as the objective poet, relinquishing in his retreat the ambitions of the Romantic, subjective poet who wants to supplant Shakespeare as a literary authority, he achieves greater resemblance to Shakespeare and greater authority.

In "House" (1876), Browning denounces subjective poetry such as that of the Romantics, while maintaining a poet's right to privacy. Although James F. Loucks detects in this poem a "rather shrill defense of the author's right to privacy" (1979: n. 1, 415), the poem, instead, emphasizes Browning's choice of Shakespeare as his poetic model at the expense of his Shelleyan connection; this alignment would culminate in Browning's refusal to preside over F. J. Furnivall's Shelley Society and his willingness to accept the presidency of the New Shakspere [*sic*] Society.

The idea that a house could provide allegedly important clues about the author's state of mind finds its comically exaggerated conclusion in Browning's poem. Employing the image of the open house on display for all to see, Browning asks:

> Shall I sonnet-sing you about myself?
> Do I live in a house you would like to see?
> Is it scant of gear, has it store of pelf?
> "Unlock my heart with a sonnet-key?"
>
> (Browning 1997: ll. 1–4)

In the last line of this first stanza, Browning paraphrases Wordsworth's poem, "Scorn not the Sonnet," which chastises those critics who have "frowned" on the sonnet form, "mindless of its just honours" (Wordsworth 1917: l. 2). Yet Wordsworth, like many Romantic poets, believed that the sonnet was the "key" with which "Shakespeare unlocked his heart" (l. 2–3). In "House," however, Browning continues to resist the pull of confessional poetry, wondering whether he should "[i]nvite the world, as [his] betters have done" to view his "private apartment and bedroom too" (Browning 1997: 507, ll. 5, 8). "No," he responds, "thanking the public, [he] must decline" (ll. 9–10). While he may grant "a peep through [his] window, if folk prefer," Browning pleads for his privacy: "But, please you, no foot over the threshold of mine!" (ll. 11–12). This disturbing image of the author's life laid bare obviously troubled Browning, and the poem articulates his plea for personal privacy.

Browning begins the conclusion of "House" by again paraphrasing Wordsworth: "'*With this same key / Shakespeare unlocked his heart,' once more!*" (ll. 38–39). In Wordsworth's poem, the poet suggests that Shakespeare, like many others, has revealed himself in his sonnets. Browning therefore challenges Wordsworth's assertion, exclaiming, "Did Shakespeare? If so, the less Shakespeare he!" (l. 40). For if Shakespeare were revealing himself, it would completely undermine Browning's depiction of Shakespeare as the dramatic, purely objective poet, one central argument in the "Essay on Shelley." It is clear that Browning refused to equate Shakespeare with any Romantic display of autobiographical poetry, particularly in relation to the sonnets.

The debate concerning the homoerotic quality of Shakespeare's sonnets began to intensify at about the same time as Browning's "House," and in part this debate compelled Browning's more ardent followers to begin disassociating Browning's image from Shakespeare's. The controversy had, however, been ongoing for some time. George Stevens, for example, writing on Sonnet 20 in the late eighteenth century, had claimed: "It is impossible to read this fulsome panegyric, addressed to a male object, without an equal mixture of disgust and indignation" (cited in Pequigney 1985: 30). In the very same year that Browning was composing "House," other writers were delicately distancing both Robert and Elizabeth Barrett Browning's works from those of Shakespeare. As Tricia Lootens (1996) has convincingly argued, the Brownings' marriage came to be considered a kind of corrective to troubling questions regarding sexuality in the last part of the nineteenth century.[6] While Browning resisted the biographical reading of Shakespeare's sonnets – "[i]f so, the less Shakespeare he" – Browning's contemporaries began to promote him as a more masculine and sanitized bard than Shakespeare himself.

Browning's appropriation of Shakespeare grants him such cultural authority that he begins to crowd Shakespeare himself in the center of the Victorian literary canon. One might even conclude that Browning "out-Shakespeares" Shakespeare by the close of the nineteenth century. A final example of the success of Browning's Shakespearean appropriation concerns his appointment to the presidency of the New Shakspere [*sic*] Society in 1879, three years after

"House" was published. A year later F. J. Furnivall, the founder of the Shakspere Society, joined Emily Hickey to found the Browning Society. The Society's Prospectus carefully explains its purpose:

> This society is founded to gather some, at least, of the many admirers of ROBERT BROWNING, for the study and discussion of his works, and the publication of Papers on them, and extracts from works illustrating them.
>
> (*Browning Society Papers* 1966: 1: 19)

Immediately following these statements, one sees the initial shaping of Browning's new status as the Victorian bard. After the writers of the Prospectus cite a paragraph-long analysis by Professor Spalding on Shakespeare, they outline similarities between the two poets, claiming that Browning possesses the same "leading note" as Shakespeare, which Spalding defines as "a spirit of active and inquiring thought" that can be seen "on every object which comes under his notice," as well as an "imagination [that] is active, powerfully and unceasingly" (19). In addition, both Shakespeare and Browning possess an "'active and piercing understanding'" (19). The Prospectus concludes that Browning is "profound enough in thought, noble enough in character and feeling, eloquent and interesting enough in expression, to deserve more thorough study, and a far wider circle of readers, than he has yet had" (20). The justification for Browning's ascendancy to Shakespearean status has been made.

Throughout the Society's existence, Shakespeare and his works are almost always the central touchstones for measuring Browning's achievement. There are comments comparing both on the topics of reason, thought, and characterization. Yet the Society goes one step further in the process of appropriation by elevating Browning *above* Shakespeare, because, for them, Browning is not only more religious in belief than Shakespeare, but also more masculine in his writing. The "Introductory Address" for the first meeting of the Browning Society, given by the Rev. J. Kirkman at University College, London, formalizes the effort to Shakespeareanize Browning. Kirkman proclaims that "Browning is undoubtedly the profoundest intellect, with widest range of sympathies, and with universal knowledge of men and things, that has arisen as a poet since Shakespeare" (*Browning Society Papers* 1966: 1: 172). He adds that Browning's "truly Shakespearian genius preeminently shines in his power to throw his whole intellect and sympathies into the most diverse individualities" (172). Kirkman concludes that "Browning is our nearest to Shakespeare" (172). James Thomson, at the third meeting, puts Browning in the company of those who "have learned everything and forgotten nothing," including Chaucer, Shakespeare, and Goethe (239). At the eighth meeting, Hiram Corson, speaking on "The Idea of Personality," comments: "the range of thought and passion which [Browning's poetry] exhibits is greater than that of any other poet, without a single exception, since the days of Shakspere [*sic*]" (293).

Another similarity between the two authors involves their portrayal of dramatic character. In the notes on Browning's poems contained in the Society bibliography for 1881, Furnivall suggests that

> Browning culminated in characterization in that 2nd period, as Shakspere did in his second period *Henry IV*. But *Dramatis Personae* and *Ring and the Book* are greater than *Men and Women*, as *Hamlet* is greater than *Henry IV*.
>
> (*Browning Society Papers* 1966: 1: 157)

At the twenty-fourth meeting, J. Cotter Morrison makes a number of connections between Shakespeare's Caliban and Browning's "Caliban upon Setebos." The forty-fourth meeting features a paper entitled "Browning's Jews and Shakespeare's Jews." Arthur Symons ponders the question, "Is Browning Dramatic?," at the twenty-fourth meeting. In this essay, Symons makes a slight distinction between the two: "Shakspere [*sic*] makes his characters *live*; Browning makes his *think*" (2: 6). A respondent disputes even this difference at the eighty-third meeting, arguing that Browning's characters are as "living and real as Richard the 2nd or Hamlet," and further concludes that "Shakspere's [*sic*] characters seem quite as full of thought as any of the creations of Browning (3: 141).

There was also a movement to distinguish the two poets from one another, usually at Shakespeare's expense. E. D. West, as early as the fifteenth meeting of the Browning Society, claimed:

> Shakspere, innately a positivist, can let any phenomenon be to him as an ultimate fact, which he does not care to go beyond. Browning, born a speculator, cannot and will not forgo the attempt to get at what lies behind the visible things of the world's order.
>
> (1: 417)

Just as Browning's character Caliban had outshone Prospero as a philosopher, Browning becomes even more philosophical than Shakespeare. In comparing the subjectivity of the two, according to W. A. Raleigh, one also sees a distinction: "If we try to form some idea of the personality of William Shakspere [*sic*], we are checked, and find it difficult to get further than the characters of his creations" (1: 479). On the other hand, "in trying to reach the personality of Browning," we get "a sense of personal acquaintance with him" (479). The author concludes that Browning's sympathy keeps this "intense subjectivism perfectly free from egotism" (479). Here, perhaps, we most clearly see the effect of the "Essay on Shelley," as Browning, at least for this critic, embodies the two kinds of poet, combining the dramatic poet with one who also gives us glimpses of his or her own nature. Thus, Browning displays an ability to retain "subjectivism," although one free from egotism, even in the presence of Shakespearean "objectivity."

The Browning Society members considered religion to be a major difference between Shakespeare and Browning. Although the Society itself was composed of a wide range of members, so much so as to contain both "pious spinsters" and "militant agnostics" (Peterson 1969: 6), many of the members believed in Browning as a spiritual teacher. This religious fervor can be seen as early as the Society's inception, as the co-founder Emily Hickey saw Browning "as a religious poet whose ethical teachings were of supreme value" (Peterson 1969: 19). At a time of challenges to traditional Christianity, many writers, including Browning, became secular prophets. Some members clearly saw Browning as a means of salvation, or in one member's case, a means of rediscovering his faith. A Dr. Berdoe, who had dismissed Christianity after his medical training, later, while a member of the Society, found a reaffirmation of his faith in Browning's works. In his book on Browning, he wrote that "the feeling came over me that in Browning I had found my religious teacher, one who could put me right on a hundred points which had troubled my mind for many years, and which ultimately caused me to abandon the Christian Faith" (Berdoe 1896: viii–ix). Even Browning's name was deified, as the "Browningites always capitalized Browning's nickname: Master" (Peterson 1969: 64). The religiosity surrounding Browning would play an important role in his literary canonization.

Obviously, Browning's cultural currency was taking on new value, becoming at the very least equal to Shakespeare's in some people's eyes. Most importantly, for the Browning Society and Victorian society at large, Browning came to represent a more decorous, less coarse Shakespeare, a Victorianized Bard. Shakespeare was a bit vulgar for some Victorian tastes. Emily Hickey, for example, read Browning's poetry in part because her father absolutely forbade her to read Shakespeare (Peterson 1969: 17). Unlike Shakespeare and his "unwholesome" sonnets, Browning and his works begin to symbolize the perfect, "normal" heterosexual poet. Further, Browning becomes an antidote to the "femininity" of French writers and English poets such as A. C. Swinburne and the vestiges of the Pre-Raphaelite Brotherhood. Furnivall believed that a "poet should be strong, manly, unpretentious, and Browning was all these" (Peterson 1969: 26). And Furnivall was not alone. Another prominent member of the Society, the poet James Thomson, had praised Browning as a poet "[w]ith a masculine soul for passion, a masculine intellect for thought, and a masculine genius for imagination" (*Browning Society Papers* 1966: 1: 247). Browning himself seems to have bought partly into this idea; a letter to Isa Blagden appears particularly revealing:

> Yes, – I have read Rossetti's poems ... you know I hate the effeminacy of his school, – the men that dress up like women – that use obsolete forms, too, and archaic accentuations to seem soft ... Swinburne started this with other like Belialisms.
>
> (Browning 1951: 336)[7]

Anxiety over homosexuality was beginning to spread in England at this time, and Browning, because of his highly publicized union with Elizabeth Barrett Browning, represented a safer, more traditional, "saintly" poet than even Shakespeare.

By 1888, Browning societies in Britain and America were growing in popularity, sometimes at the expense of Shakespearean study groups. One writer in America observed that "the Shakespeare clubs have been gradually elbowed to the wall" by the Browning societies (Hersey 1890: 543). Browning's literary reputation was also "elbowing" Shakespeare out of the center of the Victorian literary canon, as he becomes the nineteenth-century equal of Shakespeare. This movement results at least in part from Browning's appropriation of Shakespeare, which begins with the "Essay on Shelley" and continues through the poem "House." As early as the "Introductory Address" to the Browning Society, Kirkman had stated that while Browning and Shakespeare are equal in thought and reason, "[i]n knowledge of many things [Browning] is necessarily superior to Shakespeare as being the receptive child of the century of science and travel" (*Browning Society Papers* 1966: 1: 172). In essence, Browning's Shakespearean appropriation worked all too well. Like the sacred literary monument of Shakespeare, Browning was likewise sanctified as a poet-saint of England. By the close of the century, Browning becomes even more Shakespearean than Shakespeare himself, so that pseudo-religious Bardolatry gives way to even more infectious "Browning Fever."

Notes

1 Browning modeled his first poetic attempts on the Romantic notion of subjectivity, particularly Shelleyan subjectivism – introverted, personal, prophetic. Browning's first poem, "Pauline" (1833), was panned by most critics for its confessional mode. The most famous example is the unpublished review by John Stuart Mill. Mill was preparing a rather negative critique for *Tait's Magazine* when another review appeared first; consequently, Mill returned his copy of the poem to Browning with scathing comments scribbled in the margins. Mill wrote that Browning's fictional hero-narrator (and perhaps Browning himself) was "possessed with a more intense and morbid self-consciousness than I ever knew in any sane human being" (cited in Maynard 1977: 43). The reading public must have felt the same, for no copies of the original printing were sold.

2 Ross Murfin calls the "Essay" a part of Browning's work that has been "scandalously ignored" (1978: 3). Irvine and Honan hyperbolically refer to the piece as a "history not so much of Shelley's poetry as of Browning's soul" (1974: 285). Park Honan claims that the piece is Browning's "most important prose work" (1964: 31).

3 All citations of Robert Browning's poetry refer to line numbers rather than page numbers in *Robert Browning* (1997), Adam Roberts (ed.).

4 All references to *King Lear* are to the conflated version in the *Norton Shakespeare*.

5 For a good example of a critical analysis that traces Lear's gradual "self-discovery," see Jorgensen 1967.

6 See Lootens 1996, which articulates this point concerning the Brownings' marriage.

7 Swinburne and Browning had a curious and contradictory relationship. As an undergraduate at Oxford, Swinburne admired Browning; Rikky Rooksby claims Swinburne "imitated" the other poet's works (1997: 54). But after Browning called Swinburne's poems "moral mistakes, redeemed by much intellectual ability," their relationship became strained (cited in Rooksby 1997: 84). The dispute escalated when Browning accepted the position of titular head of The New Shakspere [*sic*] Society in 1879. Swinburne, at odds with the founder F. J. Furnivall

for years, wrote to Browning asking him to resign, but Browning weathered the storm and served out his two-year term. On the occasion of Browning's death, however, Swinburne composed seven laudatory verses, entitled *A Sequence of Sonnets on the Death of Robert Browning.* On Swinburne's own appropriation of Shakespeare, see Sawyer 1997.

9

The displaced body of desire: Sexuality in Kenneth Branagh's *Hamlet*

LISA S. STARKS

> The tragedy of *Hamlet* is the tragedy of desire.
>
> (Jacques Lacan 1993)

Psychoanalytic theory and contemporary performances of *Hamlet* are inextricably linked. Beginning with Freud, psychoanalysis has appropriated the tragedy for its own theoretical ends, leaving its mark indelibly on the history of cultural and cinematic appropriations of *Hamlet* in the twentieth century.[1] The tradition of *Hamlet* on screen necessarily emerges from this history, refiguring and recreating our current conceptions of Shakespeare's tragedy. Beginning with Laurence Olivier's influential screen adaptation (1948), these films chart the shifting connections between psychoanalysis and *Hamlet* that have underwritten popular and critical conceptions of the play. In contrast to directors who have openly positioned themselves within this psychoanalytic tradition, such as Olivier and Franco Zeffirelli (1991), Kenneth Branagh avoids any explicit reference to this inherited legacy in his 1996 cinematic epic *Hamlet* (1996a). Despite its resistance to psychoanalytic interpretation – or perhaps because of this resistance – Branagh's *Hamlet* provides the most "Oedipal" of all filmed *Hamlet*s, ironically replicating Freud's own repression of the maternal through symptomatic denials and displacements in its representations of desire and sexuality.

I Appropriations of *Hamlet* in psychoanalysis

Initially, *Hamlet* was appropriated by psychoanalytic theory as it developed, not the other way around. In his letter to Wilhelm Fliess dated October 15, 1897 (Freud 1985: 270–73), in "Mourning and Melancholia" (Freud 1974: 14: 246), and in *The Interpretation of Dreams* (Freud 1974: 4: 264), Freud draws on *Hamlet* and its melancholy hero for his theories of mourning, Oedipal desire, and the unconscious. Through his discussion of the play simultaneously as literary meditation, cultural artifact, and autobiographical text, Freud uses *Hamlet* to theorize both mourning and the Oedipal complex, though the latter eventually results in the expulsion of the former, resulting in the permanent linkage of *Hamlet* with Freud's theory of repression and the family romance.

In Freud's writings, the character Hamlet becomes the emblem of parental loss whose melancholy provides a model for a psychoanalytic theory of Oedipal desire and rivalry.[2] In "Mourning and Melancholia," Freud bases his concepts of mourning and melancholia on the example of Hamlet. In mourning, the subject takes in or "introjects" the lost loved one (or entity) for which it grieves; through "projection," the subject ejects the painful aspects of that loss outward into the world. Hence, mourning involves a taking in and a letting go, a process through which the subject can deal successfully with grief by accepting death. Melancholia, like mourning, may result from the subject's loss of a loved one through death, but it can also ensue from the subject's loss of a loved one or entity through separation only (Freud 1974: 14: 245). In melancholia, the subject internalizes an idealized lost object, and rather than projecting pain outward into the world, turns it inward upon the self. Consequently, the melancholic seeks to inflict punishment on his or her own ego. As Freud succinctly puts it, "In mourning it is the world which has become poor and empty; in melancholia it is the ego itself" (246). Internalizing all the grief and blame, the melancholic "represents his ego to us as worthless, incapable of any achievement and morally despicable; he reproaches himself, vilifies himself and expects to be cast out and punished" (246).

Not surprisingly, Hamlet becomes Freud's example of a melancholic, one who exhibits this self-denigrating behavior to a large degree, one whose disillusionment with the world and contempt for his own ego exemplify the characteristics of the melancholic patient. As a literary case study, Hamlet suffers from two kinds of failed mourning: the loss of his father, whose murder and subsequent ghostly presence inhibit the process of mourning, and the loss of the maternal object through Gertrude's marriage to Claudius.

Freud shifts away from this emphasis on melancholy in his writings on *Hamlet*, however, when he employs the play in the development of his theory of Oedipal desire and the unconscious. This movement can be detected within his letter to Fliess, in which Freud first works through his interpretation of *Hamlet*, as Julia Reinhard Lupton and Kenneth Reinhard have discussed at length (1993: 18–26). In his letter to Fliess, Freud moves from a discussion of grief to one of Oedipal conflict in *Hamlet*. In the first part of the letter, Freud narrates a dream in which he visualizes his mother lying dead in a casket. Analyzing this dream, Lupton and Reinhard point out its relationship to the role of introjection in mourning, in which the subject "interiorize[s] emptiness in the effort to make the absent [object of loss] present" (18). The dream allegorizes the subject's internal grief upon separation from the mother, for "the child experiences the mother's absence as a sealed box or casket (*Kasten*), an image of interiorization, at once womb and tomb, commemorating the lost mother by preserving her as lost" (18). Within the same letter, Freud switches from this scene of primary traumatic loss (the emblematic moment in which the infant's separation from the mother is envisioned), to one of the subsequent Oedipal dynamic (or triangle), in which the male child's desire for his mother results in hostility directed at his rival, the father (Freud 1985: 272). Perhaps unconsciously to avoid the painful scene of traumatic loss it suggests or to emphasize the paternal over the maternal in his theories, Freud ends up neglecting the role of mourning in his later writings on the Oedipal complex and in his reading of *Hamlet* in *The Interpretation of Dreams* (see Lupton and Reinhard 1993: 15–26).

In his famous commentary on *Hamlet* from *The Interpretation of Dreams*, Freud argues that Shakespeare's tragedy epitomizes Western civilization's movement in the direction of repression.[3] After discussing Sophocles' *Oedipus Rex* and the Oedipus myth as "primeval dream-material," Freud examines *Hamlet* as a similar type of text, but one that demonstrates a deviation from the overt Oedipal desires exemplified in Greek tragedy and myth. In *Oedipus Rex*, Oedipus literally, though unknowingly, kills his father and marries his mother, crimes that are eventually made public. In *Hamlet*, however, the prince unconsciously *desires* what Oedipus actually *does*, and these desires remain secret and private. Freud concludes that *Hamlet*, written at a much later point in the development of European culture, indicates the movement of Western civilization toward the repression of such transgressive longings. Comparing Shakespeare's tragedy with Sophocles', Freud argues that the Oedipus myth appears in a latent (present but not evident) rather than manifest (present and evident) form in the cultural dream-text of *Hamlet*. Viewed in comparison with *Oedipus Rex*, *Hamlet* thus provides the "intertextual lens through which the 'Oedipal' in *Oedipus* comes into – and goes out of – focus" (Lupton and Reinhard 1993: 32). Freud writes:

> Another of the great creations of tragic poetry, Shakespeare's *Hamlet*, has its roots in the same soil as *Oedipus Rex*. But the changed treatment of the same material reveals the whole difference in the mental life of these two widely separated epochs of civilization: the secular advance of repression in the emotional life of mankind. In the *Oedipus* the child's wishful phantasy that underlies it is brought into the open and realized as it would be in a dream. In *Hamlet* it remains repressed; and – just as in the case of a neurosis – we only learn of its existence from its inhibiting consequences.
>
> (Freud 1974: 4: 264)

For Freud, because Hamlet's Oedipal desires (to eliminate the father and sexually fulfill the mother) are unconscious and covert, they indicate the increased role of repression in the modern subject and civilization. As Jacques Lacan later puts it in his own interpretation of *Hamlet*, "Freud himself indicated, perhaps in a somewhat *fin de siècle* way, that for some reason when we lived out the Oedipal dream, it was destined to be in a warped form, and there's surely an echo of that in *Hamlet*" (1993: 44). Accordingly, Lacan continues, Freud's reading of Shakespeare's play "justifies and deepens our understanding of *Hamlet* as possibly illustrating a decadent form of the Oedipal situation, its decline" for "[i]t's not simply that the subject wanted, desired to kill his father and to violate his mother, but that that is in the unconscious" (45). For Lacan, Freud's analysis of *Hamlet* tells us a great deal about Freud's Oedipal theory itself. Lacan suggests that the main emphasis in Freud's Oedipal theory is the notion of the unconscious. Freud's reading of Shakespeare's tragedy stresses that modern Western civilization has repressed Oedipal desire and relegated it to the unconscious.

Following his discussion of *Hamlet* as cultural dream-text, Freud analyzes Hamlet's character and actions to explore his unconscious longings, which underlie the tragedy. In Freud's reading, Hamlet's reluctance to fulfill the Ghost's demand to kill his uncle stems from his identification with the murderer, "the man who did away with his father and took that father's place with his mother, the man who shows him the repressed wishes of his own childhood realized" (Freud 1974: 4: 265). Freud then relates Hamlet's unconscious to Shakespeare's through biographical speculation, positing that Shakespeare identified with both the Ghost in grieving for his lost son, Hamnet, and with Hamlet himself in mourning the loss of his father (265–66). In the second preface to the 1908 edition of *The Interpretation of Dreams*, Freud extends this analysis to himself, drawing a parallel between Hamlet's bereavement and his own grief upon his father's death (Freud 1974: 4: xxvi).[4] Despite this emphasis, the issue of mourning disappears in Freud's discussion of the Oedipal triangle, just as it does in his reading of *Hamlet* alongside *Oedipus Rex*. Consequently, the Oedipal reading of *Hamlet* comes to replace the melancholic one (Lupton and Reinhard 1993: 18–19, 26).

II Appropriations of psychoanalysis in filmed *Hamlets*

Interestingly, appropriations of psychoanalysis in the history of *Hamlet* on screen follow this same trajectory, a gradual move away from a melancholic interpretation to one that highlights the father–son Oedipal rivalry, which can be detected in the three representative, popular screen adaptations of *Hamlet* directed by Olivier, Zeffirelli, and Branagh. Olivier's self-pronounced "Oedipal" *Hamlet*, though ostensibly based on Ernest Jones's *Hamlet and Oedipus* (1954; first published in 1949), can be read as a meditation on melancholy, one more in tune with Freud's "Mourning and Melancholia" than with Jones's elaborations on Freud's Oedipal interpretation. Zeffirelli's film, although it may appear at first glance to be oriented in a Freud/Jones Oedipal interpretation, more closely resembles Lacan's reading of *Hamlet*, which emphasizes the interplay of desire and signification (see Lupton and Reinhard 1993: 82–83). It is Branagh's *Hamlet* that emerges at the end of the twentieth century as the most fully Oedipalized version, in which the father–son conflict and the onset of the paternal law completely overtake the melancholic and the maternal that are evident in both Olivier's and Zeffirelli's versions.

In this sense, Branagh's *Hamlet* realizes Freud's thesis concerning *Hamlet* and repression, much more so than earlier films that have attempted to depict, through cinematic conventions, the workings of the unconscious on a visual and often literal level.

In the shadow of psychoanalytic appropriations of *Hamlet* since Freud, all screen adaptations have necessarily had to position themselves either within or against a psychoanalytic reading that tends to resist visual representation. It is Ernest Jones's elaborations on Freud's analysis of Hamlet's repressed Oedipal complex, however, not Freud's own writings, that have had the most direct impact on the cinematic adaptations of Olivier and others. Ironically, the realization of this directorial concept can be seen as ultimately counter-psychoanalytic, for to visualize unconscious desire is potentially to render it conscious and to disavow the very existence of the unconscious as that which constantly disrupts the stability and unity of the subject. Since the unconscious is an effect of repression, a literal representation of the unconscious in *Hamlet* contradicts Freud's own reading of the play as an emblem of societal and individual repression.

In contrast to later directors, Olivier openly positions his film adaptation of *Hamlet* in relation to psychoanalytic literary criticism of the play. As an *Essay on Hamlet*, which the film was initially titled, Olivier's *Hamlet* proclaims itself to be a cinematic appropriation not only of Shakespeare's *Hamlet*, but also of psychoanalytic interpretations of the play, particularly those elaborated on by Jones (see Donaldson 1990: 37). When preparing his *Hamlet*, Olivier visited Jones, whose Freudian views on *Hamlet* provide the initial "Oedipal" concept of the film, namely that Hamlet's inability to kill Claudius results from his guilty conscience, for unconsciously, Hamlet longs to do what Claudius did – kill his father and fulfill his sexual longings for his mother (Olivier 1982: 102; see also Donaldson 1990: 31–34). Notwithstanding this influence, Olivier made many directorial decisions that directly countered Jones's suggestions for an ideal "Freudian" production of *Hamlet*, as detailed in his *Hamlet and Oedipus*. Jones thought that, contrary to popular stage practice, the actress playing Gertrude should be a mature forty-five year old, five years older than the actor playing Claudius and twice as old as Hamlet. In Jones's view, both Gertrude and Ophelia, whom he links as objects of desire, should be "unmistakably sensual," Ophelia never docile or "innocent." Jones recommends that Hamlet be "bawdy in a forced fashion but … never sensual – especially towards his mother"

(Jones 1954: 182), as his incestuous longings reside in the unconscious and therefore can only be manifested in a distorted manner. Olivier most likely would have known of Jones's preferences, as he notes that the analyst clearly emphasized the unconscious nature of Hamlet's Oedipal complex during their talk (Olivier 1982: 102). Nevertheless, Olivier cast twenty-seven-year-old Eileen Herlie as Gertrude and directed Jean Simmons to play Ophelia as a delicate, naive girl. And, contrary to Jones's advice, Olivier's Hamlet and Gertrude openly display erotic and loving feelings for one another.

Olivier's film departs from Jones's interpretation in other ways as well. As Peter Donaldson explains,

> the Freud/Jones interpretation of *Hamlet* is a central, structuring presence, the contours of which may be clearly discerned. At the same time, the Oedipus complex, so evident and even intentional in Olivier's *Hamlet*, serves partly as a mask or screen for other, perhaps deeper issues.
>
> (1990: 34–35)

Donaldson interprets these issues as Hamlet's narcissistic tendency, his difficulty in relating to his father, and his fused identification with his mother, which result in his low sense of self-worth. Hence, Olivier's Hamlet fluctuates between passive and violent behavior, which Donaldson relates to biographical accounts of the actor/director's own sexual abuse as a child (35–63). Although I agree with Donaldson on Hamlet's symptoms, I would argue that they indicate more than an identity conflict. In my view, they relate to melancholia, which permeates the film on multiple levels. Melancholia, the repressed within the Freud/Jones interpretation, thus returns with a vengeance in Olivier's film text.[5] Although perhaps not deliberate on Olivier's part, melancholia emerges as the underlying impetus of the Oedipal complex, a malady that at once connects to Shakespeare's own "melancholy Dane" and to the subtext of the Freudian treatment of the unconscious, trauma, and the repression of Oedipal desire.[6]

In his endeavor to film this psychoanalytic *Hamlet*, Olivier took on the formidable task of attempting to depict unconscious desire through the cinematic medium. To achieve this effect, he relies on the visual language of film through the use of particular camera shots. As Olivier stares out into the sea and his voice-over reads Hamlet's "To be or not to be" soliloquy (*Hamlet* 3.1.58–90), the camera zooms in from behind and appears to shoot through Olivier's head, through a superimposed image of the human brain. In this shot as in others, Olivier attempts to bring the viewer into Hamlet's unconscious, indicating that the perspective of the film is Hamlet's interior life, his mind. The many emblems that recur throughout the film – particularly the bed, Ophelia's chamber, the empty rooms, and Hamlet's chair – all represent Hamlet's own unconscious desires and anxieties. Through this valiant and brilliant attempt to make visible the workings of the unconscious, Olivier ends up uncovering what had been conspicuously buried within Freud's and Jones's Oedipal interpretations of *Hamlet*: failed mourning and melancholia.

Roger Furse's art direction for the film – the narrow, winding staircases; the dark, gloomy, foreboding sky; the play of light and shadow, whites, grays, and blacks – represents the world of Elsinore from Hamlet's perspective, as projections of his own internal torture and grief. Visual emblems, such as the deserted rooms and Hamlet's empty chair, serve to reinforce the sense of absence, and also to forge a symbolic link between that loss and Hamlet's own ego, an association that is further accentuated by Olivier's physical presence and line delivery throughout the film. In the opening court scene, seated in the chair that comes to represent the emptiness of grief, Olivier positions himself as the alienated mourner, whose dejection and self-deprecation appear to have no reasonable cause. In various shots, Olivier strikes a traditionally melancholic pose to stress the prince's grief and self-absorption, and he delivers Hamlet's soliloquies with pronounced emphasis on the word "mourned" in the line "a beast that wants discourse of reason / Would have *mourned* longer" (1.2.150–51) and on any references to loss.

Through this iconography, the film represents instances of Hamlet's failed mourning for both the lost mother and the father, which despite its Oedipal trappings, become among the most prominent features of Olivier's *Hamlet.* When Hamlet's father appears in his ghostly form – a large, shadowy figure clad in armor – he seems to dominate his son, who falls to the ground as if thrust down into submission by the specter's threatening presence, suggesting abuse and violation (Donaldson 1990: 31–67). These scenes dramatize the melancholic's desire to inflict pain on his or her own ego in retribution for the internalized loss. The melancholic, who assumes blame for the loved one's death, thus seeks self-punishment and degradation in response to the inner emptiness that cannot be mourned successfully.

Hamlet's ambivalent identification with the Ghost, who haunts his psyche and causes him to lash out at himself and others, is evidenced as well in his treatment of both Ophelia and Gertrude. Although in Oedipal readings of the play Ophelia and Gertrude are united as objects of Hamlet's desire, in Olivier's film Simmons's Ophelia mirrors Hamlet, not Gertrude, which suggests Hamlet's connection with femininity, and therefore a melancholic reading of his character. Throughout the film, Hamlet and Ophelia are associated exclusively with each other through various ocular effects. On an obvious level, the two are physically strikingly similar with their white-blond hair, chiseled facial features, graceful movements, and white, billowy shirts and gowns. Both are followed by the tracking camera as they wander through the narrow passageways of the castle. Ophelia, in her mad scenes, and Hamlet, in numerous scenes, are shown in identical body positions; for instance, the two appear with book in hand in the opening shots of back-to-back scenes, Hamlet's encounter with Polonius (2.2) and Ophelia's entrance at the beginning of the nunnery scene (3.1).

Other parallels further establish the film's preoccupation with mourning and melancholy. Significantly, the two are paired as victims of abuse: as the Ghost dominates Hamlet, Hamlet dominates Ophelia, a correlation that is made through shots of both in analogous, submissive positions on the floor. Hamlet, following the Ghost's appearance (1.5), is stricken down by the commanding force of his father's spirit; Ophelia, at the close of the nunnery scene, is thrown to the floor by an angry Hamlet (3.1) (see Donaldson 1990: 41–47). Both characters remain in this position of degradation, clearly traumatized by the violence inflicted upon them. These positions signify their abnegation and tormented self-loathing. Like Hamlet, Ophelia suffers from melancholy upon the death of her father, and in her mad scenes, she links her melancholy with that of Hamlet. In a symbolic gesture, Ophelia places rosemary "for remembrance" on the empty chair of Hamlet, securing it as the film's emblem of loss and mourning.

Hamlet's behavior toward Gertrude is even more complex and ambiguous. He switches from aggressive to loving treatment of her, at once attempting to identify with his father and then with his mother in response to the paternal threat. Beyond the sensual kisses and caresses, the two seem united in a "mystical bond" (Donaldson 1990: 63), one that perhaps is sealed by Gertrude's suicide, when in this interpretation she intentionally drinks the poison meant for her son. Figuratively, Gertrude thus embodies the maternal object, the internalized loss that underlies this Hamlet's existential angst and his unrelenting self-hatred. To identify fully with his father, he would have to acknowledge her as "lost," to sever himself from her completely, and finally to substitute another object in her place. Unable to mourn her successfully, Hamlet carries her loss as an emptiness that cannot be filled, an inner void.

In the closing moments of the film, the camera positions the viewer as a "mourner" trailing Hamlet's funeral procession, followed by a repeat sequence of the film's opening shots (see Donaldson 1990: 62). Interestingly, these final shots include the infamous bed, the site of the "primal scene" (the traumatic experience of witnessing one's parents engage in sexual intercourse), and by extension, the emblem of Hamlet's own Oedipal dilemma. Following the bed, other objects appear in successive shots: Hamlet's "mourning" chair, Ophelia's room, and the chapel. Through the use of these emblems, Olivier closes the film with a final emphasis on Hamlet's failed mourning, his unsuccessful attempt to come to terms with death and separation, which lies at the root of his inner longings and Oedipal impulses.

In contrast to Olivier's film, with its emphasis on Hamlet's unconscious desire and loss, Zeffirelli's *Hamlet* focuses instead on Gertrude's overwhelming passion and its consuming effect on others. Although Zeffirelli's adaptation opens with a scene of mourning, or insufficient mourning, it clearly gives way to the predominate issue at stake in this *Hamlet* – the overpowering desire of the mother and the anxiety it produces in those who seek to fulfill it, namely Hamlet and Claudius. In this initial funeral scene, Gertrude's grief as she weeps over her husband's dead body instantly transforms into a look of sexual longing directed at Claudius, which emblematically presents the film's departure from Olivier's *Hamlet*: mourning gives way to Gertrude's desire. In further contrast to Olivier, Zeffirelli makes no attempt to reveal Hamlet's unconscious, or to deal with desire on anything other than a conscious, literal level. The appropriation of psychoanalysis in this film is obvious and literal, counter to Freud's emphasis on the unconscious and repression and more in line with Lacan's theory in that "Oedipus is not so much distanced by repression as too close for comfort" in *Hamlet* (Lupton and Reinhard 1993: 76). According to Lacan, the Oedipal dilemma and desire itself are openly dramatized and explored in Shakespeare's *Hamlet*, not buried and detached from conscious action, as Freud had argued.[7]

Zeffirelli's literal rendering of the Oedipal scenario resembles Lacan's interpretation of *Hamlet* as a play about the workings of desire and its relationship to mourning and lack (Lupton and Reinhard 1993: 82–84). Lacan's Hamlet has "lost the way of his [own] desire" (Lacan 1993: 12), as he is enmeshed in the desire of the (m)Other.[8] For Lacan,

> This desire, of the mother, is essentially manifested in the fact that, confronted on one hand with an eminent, idealized, exalted object – his father – and on the other with the degraded, despicable object Claudius, the criminal and adulterous brother, Hamlet does not choose.
>
> (12)

Existing only in the "time of the other" and for the fulfillment of the other's desire, this Hamlet "just doesn't know what he wants" (26). He is unable to act on his own desires, as they have become subsumed within that of his (m)Other. Within this matrix of desire, argues Lacan, Ophelia plays a key role. When she dies, Ophelia becomes an impossible "object-in-desire" for Hamlet – an object that exists for the subject only in or through desire itself. In other words, Ophelia takes on value for the subject, Hamlet, only when she is unattainable, beyond reach. According to Lacan, it is not until Ophelia becomes Hamlet's "object-in-desire" through death that he can mourn, sense his own lack and the "hole in the real," or the nothingness which the subject seeks to fill in with the "totality of the signifier," defined as the promise of transcendent meaning, or presence-in-being, that language fails to deliver (37–38).

In Zeffirelli's film, Glenn Close as Gertrude, rather than action-hero star Mel Gibson as Hamlet, dominates the screen, her force as "demanding mother" clearly registered by Hamlet and the other characters. Gibson's Hamlet appears revolted by his mother's zealous attentions and open sexuality (Lupton and Reinhard 1993: 83), and when he tops her in a violent act of mock-rape in the closet scene, the prince seems to be venting his anger and frustration in a vain attempt to dominate and control his mother's desire. Claudius also watches his wife anxiously, directing jealous glares at Gertrude as she dotes excessively on her son, clearly unable to command or satisfy his wife's desire. Ophelia as well feels the queen's domineering presence. Helena Bonham-Carter, as Ophelia, looks admiringly at the queen, who returns her gaze across the banquet table, forming a bond between the two. In her madness, Ophelia almost parodies the aggressiveness of Gertrude in her lewd sexual behavior directed at the castle guard and also in *her* sarcastic demand of the demanding (m)Other queen: "Where is the beauteous queen of Denmark?" (4.5.21). Through this affinity, Ophelia reverses the play of desire when, as Gertrude's substitute, she functions as Hamlet's object-in-desire through her death, thereby affirming Hamlet as desiring subject. As the object rather than a stand-in for the demanding (m)Other, Ophelia becomes more of a contrasting foil than a double to Gertrude. Ophelia's transformation is effected visually through the filming of her drowning – a long shot view of a green landscape resembling a Pre-Raphaelite painting, Ophelia's body only a small, distant object floating on the water. In this brief moment, Ophelia is transformed into an abstract, sublime object, which is further emphasized when her body, draped in white, is featured in the foreground of the funeral scene.

Each of these films figures within multiple cultural contexts that intertextually frame their appropriations of psychoanalysis and *Hamlet*; psychoanalytic film theory provides a means by which these interactions can be read. From this perspective, argues Laura Mulvey, one can read the cinema as a "massive screen on which collective fantasy, anxiety, fear and their effects can be projected," for visually "it speaks the blind-spots of a culture and finds forms that make manifest socially traumatic material, through distortion, defence and disguise" (Mulvey 1996: 12). In this sense, the filmed *Hamlets*, through their appropriation of psychoanalytic theory, reveal much about the obsessions and anxieties of their particular cultural and historical moments. Olivier's adaptation self-consciously responds to post-World War II existentialist thought, which was deeply enmeshed in psychoanalytic theory, especially in its depiction of the subject's angst at facing the inner void or lack. Zeffirelli's version, by contrast, could be read as a *Hamlet* that grew out of the 1980s–90s backlash against feminism common in many popular Hollywood films, which portray powerful female figures as either "bitches" or neurotics. Glenn Close's physical presence in *Hamlet* derives significance from these contexts, through the "cinematic unconscious" – the intertextual meanings generated by Close's other roles, in such films as Adrian Lyne's *Fatal Attraction*, in which she plays a neurotic other woman who obsessively stalks her married ex-lover for revenge (Lupton and Reinhard 1993: 84–86). Close's *Fatal Attraction* image as a "hysterical, violent female" contributes significantly to the cultural and ideological meanings of the maternal in Zeffirelli's *Hamlet*.

Later in the 1990s, Branagh's film continues in this conservative vein by further reinstating the Oedipal dynamic of desire. Through the representation of sexuality and the use of cinematic conventions that reinscribe dominant ideology, Branagh's film reinforces puritanical attitudes of American (and, to a lesser extent, British) culture at the close of this decade. These cultural attitudes comprise the cultural contexts framing Branagh's film in 1996 and also provide the "cultural unconscious" that informs its representational logic.

III Displaced desire in Branagh's *Hamlet*

Although Branagh's *Hamlet* emerges from the psychoanalytic tradition established by Olivier and modernized by ZeYrelli, Branagh attempts to distance it from that legacy. He avoids the problem of interpretation altogether in the "Introduction" to his screenplay, where he claims his take on Hamlet is "not an intellectual approach, but an intuitive one." For, he continues, "I cannot explain *Hamlet*, or even perhaps my own interpretation of *Hamlet*" (Branagh 1996b: xv). Branagh's anti-intellectual approach to the play underlies its lack of self-consciousness in appropriations of psychoanalytic interpretations in earlier Wlms. Oddly, though his Wlm is curiously and ostensibly positioned *against* its inherited psychoanalytic legacy (see Andrews 1996: 53, 62, 66, 76), Branagh refers to it as "simply the passionate expression of a dream ... that has preoccupied me for so many years," one that "I cannot really explain" (Branagh 1996b: xv), strangely echoing and inviting a psychoanalytic reading of his production. If there is a concept at work in his *Hamlet*, Branagh implies, it resides in his own unconscious mind, inaccessible even to himself.

Although Branagh denies any intellectual frame or influence, his film ironically enacts the Freud/Jones Oedipal reading more closely than any previous adaptation, revealing in its avoidance of the unconscious and the maternal the workings of cultural repression and the effects of the paternal law. Branagh's film is set in the late nineteenth century, correlating its period with that of Freud; moreover, through its iconography, it suggests figuratively the shift in Freud's own writings on *Hamlet*. Branagh's *Hamlet* represses the maternal (melancholy) to focus on the ambivalent identification with fathers (Oedipal), thereby duplicating the move made by Freud himself in his own reading of Shakespeare's tragedy.

The look of Branagh's *Hamlet* itself serves as a metaphor for its approach to maternal loss. Visually, its art direction suggests the containment of the mother, the desire to "box her up" as in Freud's dream, to internalize her presence as absence until her very memory has been consumed by the conflict of Oedipal rivalry. Freud thus "figures maternal absence through a projective displacement; maternal loss, however, returns as the ghostly father and his law of lack" (Lupton and Reinhard 1993: 28), the law based on division and separation. Once mourned, the maternal can only be viewed through the lens of paternal law, for, as Lupton and Reinhard explain, "the screen memory [or internalized image] of maternal loss already takes place in the court of paternal law; pre-Oedipal catastrophe is both imagined and effaced from the symbolic retrospection of the Oedipal triangle" (19). In other words, once the maternal image is mourned and imagined as lost, the subject has already rejected the pre-Oedipal stage, when its being was merged with that of the mother. In the Oedipal stage, the child severs that earlier bond and effectively obliterates its existence from conscious memory to enter into the Symbolic order, in accordance with the laws and ideology that constitute human social identity (ego or *moi*). This same maneuver can be seen in Branagh's *Hamlet*, in which the maternal is effaced in favor of the paternal "and his law of lack." Unlike Olivier's intense, carefully crafted, black-and-white version of *Hamlet* – reminiscent of German Expressionist cinema with its dark, brooding atmosphere, winding staircases, empty rooms and chairs – Branagh's adaptation is the epitome of Hollywood excess. It features bright, white, expansive exteriors; lavish, lush-colored and decorated interiors, filled with crowds of extras; elaborate costumes; sweeping cameras; melodramatic flashbacks; extreme special effects (particularly with the Ghost); a ubiquitous and obtrusive soundtrack; and an all-star cast. These features – along with the film's claim to the "complete text" – seem to fulfill a compensatory need to fill in a lack, to deflect from what is missing in this full-length *Hamlet*.

From this perspective, this missing element in Branagh's film is the maternal, whose loss is deflected through this excess, a move that reveals an "aesthetic of disavowal," in Mulvey's terms, which "can easily provide a formal basis for a displacement which moves signification considerably further away from the problem of reference" (Mulvey 1996: 13). In this case, the problem of reference resides in the maternal/melancholic reading of *Hamlet*, the trace remainder of the Freud/Jones Oedipal reading. The frigid, stark whiteness of the film's landscape and the expansive, clinically bright interiors of the palace, draped with blood red fabrics, all suggest a cold, virginal vastness of space, diametrically opposed to the dark and claustrophobic interiors featured in Olivier's and Zeffirelli's versions. Through its iconography, Branagh's *Hamlet* averts the subject of mourning and the memory of maternal loss, thereby escaping the dilemma it poses for the male subject and eliminating any impediments to the construction of masculinity and sexuality in accordance with the paternal law, the legacy of the Oedipal myth.

In contrast to earlier filmed *Hamlets*, Branagh's prince and Julie Christie's queen refrain from excessive embraces or lingering kisses; and although the two play out the closet scene with Gertrude at first seated alone on her bed, they do not engage in imagined or mimed sexual intercourse. Instead, Branagh's Hamlet speaks to his mother "as if he were a priest about to pronounce eternal damnation," as indicated in his screenplay (Branagh 1996b: 105). As the scene progresses, the two end up seated on a sofa "like two lost children," as Branagh describes them (112). This staging, although it rejects the popularized psychoanalytic interpretation, ironically suggests the scene of analysis itself. If anything, Branagh plays Hamlet-as-analyst in a closet scene that more closely resembles a frustrated therapy session than a passionate encounter.

No longer Lacan's demanding (m)Other, Christie's Gertrude fades into the blank white background, her own desires obscured by those of Claudius and Hamlet. Her appearance in a wedding gown with Claudius in the opening scene at court suggests the symbolic "incorporation" of her and the maternal in *Hamlet.* Gertrude only exists as an object in relation to Claudius, an object-of-(his)-desire, as is visually illustrated in the flashbacks that accompany the Ghost's exposition speech. In a brief clip designed to connote the queen's sexuality, the camera, shot from Claudius's perspective, shows Christie's back as he lustfully unlaces her corset from behind. Otherwise, the film shifts its focus from Gertrude to Ophelia as the object of Hamlet's desire. As in Zeffirelli's *Hamlet*, Christie's Gertrude and Kate Winslet's Ophelia are linked in Branagh's version by their similarity in physical appearance, if not age, and also through sympathetic looks exchanged between them at key moments, such as Ophelia's reading of Hamlet's letter before the king and queen. Only after Ophelia's mad scene, when Claudius orders his wife to "[g]ive her good watch" (4.5.71), a command designated for Horatio in the play text, does Gertrude disobey his commands, which implies that Ophelia's distracted behavior has profoundly affected her.

This connection between Gertrude and Ophelia serves other uses as well. To downplay and to offset any hint of erotic attraction between son and mother, Branagh displaces Hamlet's sexual yearnings from Gertrude to Ophelia through the use of flashbacks, all but one explicitly marked as deriving from Ophelia's memory. As Ophelia agrees to obey her father's wishes in rejecting Hamlet's romantic advances, she remembers making love with him in memories that resemble the most typical Hollywood love/sex scenes; from body positioning to lighting and filming, Ophelia is clearly the object of her lover's desire. Branagh also has Ophelia, instead of Polonius, read Hamlet's love letter to the king and queen. When she runs out of the room in distress, Polonius finishes the letter, juxtaposed with flashback shots of Hamlet reading Ophelia amorous verses in bed. These flashbacks reappear in Ophelia's mad scene, when she apparently visualizes Hamlet making love to her as she parodies the act of sexual intercourse, lying supine, thrusting her pelvis up and down while chanting, "before you tumbled me, / You promised me to wed" (4.5.61–62).

These flashbacks underwrite the nunnery scene as well, where the relationship between Ophelia and Hamlet is unmistakable. Hamlet's cruelty to Ophelia in this version is greatly mitigated, even more so than in most performances. Hamlet shows his romantic feelings for Ophelia through his gentle speech and passionate kiss, his mood changing to anger only when he feels wounded by her perceived rejection and betrayal. He treats Ophelia in an abusive manner only after becoming aware of Polonius's and Claudius's presence behind the mirrored door. Hamlet's interest in "mettle more attractive" than his mother (3.2.99) is fully realized when he reveals his love for the lost Ophelia, now the impossible object of desire through death.

In a subsequent move to de-emphasize the relationship between mother and son, Branagh stresses instead scenes involving Hamlet and Claudius. Therefore, Branagh's *Hamlet* becomes the story of step-father/uncle and son, in a relationship that is intense and emotionally charged. The obvious similarity in physical appearance of both actors and intertextual, biographical connections between the two – Jacobi was Branagh's inspirational mentor and the major "paternal" influence in his acting training (Branagh 1990: 36, 84) – highlight this Oedipal conflict even more. Further emphasis on the father–son relationship over that of the mother–son is achieved through an exchange of looks in key scenes, as well as through camera shots and body positioning. When Gertrude pleads with her son to "let thine eye look like a friend on Denmark" (1.2.69), Hamlet ignores her gesture and reciprocates intense glares with Claudius, who, in a fatherly manner, twice places his arm around Hamlet's shoulders when warning of the dangers of mourning. Despite the directorial notes provided in Branagh's screenplay, which describe Claudius's behavior here as "chilling," the effect in performance is the opposite (Branagh 1996b: 14–15). Jacobi's Claudius appears as if he sincerely wishes to become Hamlet's paternal substitute, as if he wants to claim not only the affection of his brother's wife, but also the filial devotion of his brother's son. In Hamlet's soliloquy that follows, the nature of the triangular relationship is apparent: Branagh throws away the line "frailty thy name is woman" (1.2.146) to stress, instead, that Gertrude "married with mine uncle, / My father's brother" (1.2.151–52), accentuating Hamlet's hostility toward Claudius over his disgust with Gertrude. These early scenes set the pace for the entire film, in which Jacobi's Claudius emerges as the prominent figure, second only to Branagh's Hamlet.

The paternal emphasis of Branagh's *Hamlet* is introduced even earlier, during the film's opening credits, when the title *Hamlet* appears engraved on the gigantic statue of Hamlet, Sr. This film thus announces itself as a *Hamlet* about fathers right from the start – both the literal father and the figurative "Law-of-the-Father," or the law that governs the Symbolic order in Lacanian theory. According to Lacan, once the human subject enters into the social order, it is forced into laws of division and repression instituted through language, which employs the male sign as its governing principle. In Branagh's film, both the father and the Law-of-the-Father are symbolically embodied in the huge stone memorial of the dead king. As the film continues, this stone sculpture transforms into an enormous Ghost, played by the fleshy Brian Blessed. In his scene with Hamlet, the monstrous specter pushes his son to his knees and then accosts him face-to-face, the phantom's piercing blue eyes appearing wolf-like in their stare. As he speaks the lines "Revenge his foul and most unnatural murder" (1.5.25), the camera zooms in for an extreme close-up of Blessed's mouth, creating a bizarre effect of exaggerating his speech, emphasizing every syllable of his commands. Overblown and exaggerated, the spirit of Hamlet, Sr. signifies the paternal law, not just the lost father. At the film's close, this statue is ceremoniously decapitated on the heels of Fortinbras's victory, an obvious image of castration signifying the usurpation of the father by the "son," young Fortinbras, and the ushering in of his new law of martial prowess. Hamlet's Oedipal dilemma is then framed by a larger father–son conflict, which reinstates the Oedipal succession of sons who challenge the authority of their fathers.

The paternal law also figures in less obvious ways in Branagh's *Hamlet*, particularly in its representation of sexuality. In compliance with the paternal taboo against incest and homoerotic desire, Branagh avoids any gesture toward non-normative sexuality. The flashbacks of the Hollywood love scenes between Hamlet and Ophelia invest Branagh with the screen image of a "healthy" hetero-Hamlet, who exemplifies normative ideals of masculinity and sexuality. To construct this image, Branagh eschews not only the hint of incestuous desire between Hamlet and Gertrude or even sexual anxiety on Hamlet's part, but also any indication of Hamlet's "femininity" or affiliation with homoeroticism.

Branagh's "masculinization" of Hamlet is created through directorial choices in the casting and interpretations of various secondary characters in this all-star film, such as Robin Williams's portrayal of Osric in stereotypical "fag joke" fashion. In this scene, both Hamlet and Horatio are positioned as "regular guys," in contrast to the exaggeratedly effeminate Osric. Williams's portrayal of Osric, combined with Branagh's delivery of Hamlet's jibes, strongly homophobic in their cultural resonances, derisively present a stereotypical image of male homosexuality, once again defensively situating Branagh's Hamlet in "safe" hetero-male territory.

A similar gesture to "sanitize" Hamlet and *Hamlet* is made in the scenes with the players. Instead of the all-male troupe of actors featured in Olivier's and Zeffirelli's films, Branagh's nineteenth-century players are a "wholesome," middle-class family, complete with father, mother, and children. To support his "family guy" image, Branagh's Hamlet delivers his acting advice to the little boy player in a sweet and affectionate manner. Not surprisingly, the head of this nuclear unit is played by none other than Charlton Heston. As an icon, Heston brings ideologically charged meanings to the film, via its "cinematic unconscious." The Father extraordinaire of Classic Hollywood Cinema (Ben Hur/Moses/God), the National Rifle Association, and American conservative politics, Heston provides the intertextual authority of the paternal law, the embodiment of the Law-of-the-Father in cinematic and cultural iconography.

As a text that supports the dominant fiction of the Oedipal fantasy, Branagh's *Hamlet* is a "squeaky clean" adaptation of Shakespeare's tragedy, one that reinforces conservative ideology and cultural values. The links forged between Heston as the white-bearded, "good Father"/Player, Blessed as the enormous Ghost, and Jacobi as the father-Claudius in Branagh's version make it the most Oedipal of all *Hamlets* on screen, despite its director's denials. The Father and the Name-of-the-Father completely dominate Branagh's *Hamlet*, a film that resituates Shakespeare's text in a new age of taboos and repression, symptoms, and traumas. This adaptation represses the maternal in *Hamlet*, featured in disparate ways in both Olivier's and Zeffirelli's films, and valorizes instead the paternal law and its dictates for normalcy through visual disavowals and displacements. Branagh's *Hamlet* delivers more than it promises through its "complete text" of Shakespeare's play; it reinscribes – in an unself-conscious and therefore insidious way – the dominant fiction of Freud's family romance, along with its repressive ideology.

Notes

1 I would like to thank Courtney Lehmann for her helpful commentary, particularly for her insights on "Hamlet-as-analyst" in Branagh's *Hamlet*.

2 For a more comprehensive discussion of Freud's work on mourning and *Hamlet*, see Lupton and Reinhard 1993: 11–33.

3 Freud's commentary on *Hamlet* was included as a footnote in the first edition of *The Interpretation of Dreams*, then as part of the text in later printings after 1914.

4 Freud undercuts a biographical reading of *Hamlet* later on by denying Shakespearean authorship in a 1930 footnote.

5 Jones makes only brief mentions of melancholy in his book, first in reference to earlier views of Hamlet's delay (1954: 74) and second in discussion of Hamlet's suicidal impulse (100).

6 Olivier never cites Freud as a source for his production (see Olivier 1982 and Donaldson 1990: 32).

7 For an extended explication of Lacan's reading of *Hamlet*, see Žižek (1989: 120–21).

8 The psychoanalytic term "(m)Other", conflating "mother" and "Other," refers to the abstract concept of the mother as the primary Other against which the human subject must define itself. Separation from the mother is necessary before a human being can begin to see itself as a separate entity. From this initial break, the human subject constitutes its identity in relation to that which it is not, that which is the Other, or "not me." Therefore, the mother, in a figurative sense, becomes *the* Other from which human identity is formed.

10

Disney cites Shakespeare: The limits of appropriation

RICHARD FINKELSTEIN

I

By 1938, Walt Disney had received honorary degrees from Harvard, Yale, and the University of Southern California for his innovations in animation technology and aesthetics, what one citation called his "one touch of nature [that] makes the whole world kin."[1] Until the 1940s, critical reception of Disney's work saw him as a great reconciler – joining art and commerce, high and low art, easily acceptable fare and innovative work (Smoodin 1993: 98–101 and *passim*). During subsequent decades, however, the praise changed to disdain and outright hostility. Condescension, especially toward Disney's minor family-values films of the 1950s, became antagonism toward the political and cultural implications of his work. Because of its penetration into several converging media markets, Walt Disney Corporation is now used to exemplify theories, originating with the Frankfurt School, about the increasing power of commercial culture and the subsequent impoverishment of citizens.[2] Instead of celebrating Disney for creating a world family, critics excoriate him as a patriarchal imperialist (Dorfman and Mattelart 1975), and for creating a family in which no one participates. Others charge that his films commodify memory by substituting orchestrated fictions, simulacra, for a history that he helped to fracture (Fjellman 1992: 32, 57; Giroux 1994: 29–31; Project on Disney 1995: 65).

Where Disney is concerned, the academy discerns a clear line between two kinds of culture, similar to, but not exactly synonymous with, the distinction between high and low culture that is dismissed by Herbert Gans (1974) and interrogated historically by Lawrence Levine (1988). Scholars resent industrialized, mechanistic culture, whose products are based on intensive market research and produced in vast quantities, resulting in a standardization of taste among consumers. (Barbie dolls are a good example.) Academicians prefer projects with a local, individual origin that do not depend on marketing calculations, are available in limited quantities, and bear evidence of either an artisan's hand or a set of signs identifying the product with a culturally distinct group, place, or era. Most non-business writers about Disney share Theodor Adorno's and Max Horkheimer's resentment that the modern world has imposed science and technology – artificial systems – on the natural experience of pleasure. (Adorno, for instance, inveighs against even seventeenth-century writer Francis Bacon for subduing nature with human machinery.) Many writers, including the Project on Disney and Fjellman, focus their criticism on Disney World and the Epcot Center, associating all of Disney's output with a mechanical reproduction that deprives original texts of their "aura," defined by Walter Benjamin (1969) as an authenticity or essence that includes the history that works themselves experience.

Resentment of Disney is thus resentment of its brand of appropriation – not just of literary works for its movies, but also of history and memory, pleasure and bodies, nature and origins. Cultural critics dislike Disney less because they see its products as "low culture" than because they are skeptical about its modernist methods of appropriation. This corporation is now the most powerful cultural communicator of twentieth-century "modern" values, which Eric Smoodin describes as stressing fluidity rather than difference and breaking down national and global boundaries to de-emphasize local ontologies (1994: 9). Disney's most recent films also promote essentialist models of self that strip persons and texts of their histories. In this sense they are both modern and *modernist*.[3]

Pierre Bourdieu's concept of cultural capital (1984: 53–57, 70–71) implicitly describes many of Disney's calculations for appropriating a wide range of sources. The company recognizes that in the game of culture, having access to certain ideas not only expresses the virtues of the dominant class, but also brings that class more "credit" and power and, I would argue, a privileged position in the social sphere. As Bourdieu suggests, gaining this special place gives aesthetic products a veil of "objectivity." From its animated fairy tales, set in vague historical settings so that they will not become dated, to movies such as *Peter Pan*, *Alice in Wonderland*, *Sleeping Beauty*, and *The Jungle Book*, Disney has always used "high art" for feature-length animation. High art provides a kind of cultural capital that distinguishes Disney products in two ways. In combination with animation, this art enables the corporation to please both educated and uneducated audiences. Walt Disney's appropriation of "timeless" sources also masked his very specific conservative politics. Even when Walt himself was involved in small-time surveillance activities (Smoodin 1993: 140–68), his films seemed to occupy an apolitical sphere because he adapted "timeless" classics that themselves appeared to transcend immediate concerns.

Since the late 1980s, Disney has quietly absorbed Shakespeare into its family. Following the involvement of Michael Eisner, Chief Executive Officer, and Jeffrey Katzenberg, Chairman of Disney Studios until 1994, its animated films have been sprinkled with references to Shakespeare's plays. Disney's Miramax division has distributed *Shakespeare in Love*, a prelude to its upcoming distribution of three astutely targeted films from Kenneth Branagh's "Shakespeare Film Company": a musical *Love's Labour's Lost* with Alicia Silverstone; a *Macbeth* played on Wall Street; and an *As You Like It* set in Kyoto. Among the films created in house, *The Lion King* and *The Little Mermaid*, in particular, not only make isolated allusions to Shakespeare, but also involve plot structures and characters that consistently borrow from his works. Although names change or get reassigned, characters owe their dramatic and ideological functions within their plots to specific Shakespearean predecessors. As journalistic critics have noted, *The Lion King* takes its plot and characters from *Hamlet* (Klass 1994). Less noted is the fact that its prince also follows the prodigal son story from *1 Henry IV* and that *The Little Mermaid* rewrites Hans Christian Andersen by using *The Tempest*.

The Lion King follows Prince Simba from his anxious, conflicted childhood through an irresponsible adolescence to his triumphant reclamation of his kingdom. Simba's uncle Scar, who has a pack of sinister hyenas secretly in his service, causes a massive stampede in the pridelands in order to assault the realm of King Mufasa, Simba's wise and heroic father. When Mufasa is wounded rescuing

Simba from the onrush of animals, Scar throws the King down to his death, then blames Simba. Stricken by guilt, Simba flees the pridelands and grows up under the influence of the meercat Timon, who teaches him to avoid all cares and worries. When Nala, Simba's childhood fiancée, rediscovers Simba, she shames him for avoiding responsibility. After seeing the image of his father in the stars and facing the past, Simba returns to defeat his uncle, now the King, marry Nala, and ascend Mufasa's mountain triumphantly with his own child.

The heroine of *The Little Mermaid* goes after her desires from the film's start and never wavers in the disciplined pursuit of her goals. Ariel the mermaid yearns to experience the human world that her father, King Triton, has forbidden her to enter. She rescues the drowning Prince Eric after his boat breaks up in a storm, but leaves him before he fully revives; he, however, remembers the mysterious song she had sung to him. Eager to join Eric, Ariel trades her voice to the sea witch, Ursula, for a pair of legs. But if Ariel cannot win a kiss from the Prince before the end of three days, she will become one of Ursula's eternal prisoners. Before Ariel can succeed, Ursula transforms herself into a woman named Vanessa and, using Ariel's voice and song, wins the Prince. With the help of friends, Ariel stops the Prince's wedding, an elaborate sea battle ensues, the witch is destroyed, and finally, King Triton drops his opposition and blesses his daughter's wedding to Prince Eric.

Although not the first animated feature from the new Disney corporate culture created by Eisner and Katzenberg, *The Little Mermaid* (1989) was its largest success before *The Lion King* (1994). *Mermaid* took in $84 million at the box office and sold 9 million videos, making it second in sales only to *E.T.* Perhaps most importantly, *The Little Mermaid* gave Disney its first successful promotional character for spin-off products (Grover 1991: 132). Figures from *The Lion King* were developed and marketed just as profitably. By studying the corporation's two most successful films, or product launches, that draw on Shakespeare, we can expose its recent strategies for standardizing the consumption patterns of the largest possible public in order to dominate the marketplace. When Disney appropriates Shakespeare, we are reminded of the uncomfortably easy fit between Shakespeare and corporate objectives, and perhaps of Shakespeare's own role in the scientific, mechanistic project critiqued by Adorno in his complaints about Bacon.

II

Shakespeare's presence in *The Lion King* and *The Little Mermaid* provides Disney with cultural capital that puts its entertainment products in a position to win the approval of critics – recently, even Broadway critics – and thus the tickets of upper-middle-class, educated parents who bring their children to the theater and must sit through the presentation. Approval by the affluent also brings good public relations and political influence for the company. Hence, Disney has contributed to the revival of New York City's 42nd Street with its stage production of *The Lion King* and with the renovation of a theater in which to perform it. Michael Eisner has also allied the company with the architectural vanguard, having gained much publicity for appointing Michael Graves, Robert Stern, Charles Moore, and Helmut Jahn to major assignments for the corporation. All of these activities have brought extensive and free, favorable press coverage.

Particularly in *The Little Mermaid* and *The Lion King*, Shakespeare also strengthens Disney's bottom line less directly. Shakespeare's presence in these two films helps to make Disney taste and thus, a Disney view of human development, become the standards by which other entertainment products are measured. For Disney, Shakespeare authorizes essentialist, puritan models of development that tie growth to the acquisition of discipline and the taming of rebellious, simplistically defined Oedipal impulses. The heroic young people in Disney's films overcome threatening obstacles to supplant parental power with their own. But implicitly in *The Lion King* and explicitly in *The Little Mermaid*, only discipline, culture, and the subduing of natural pleasures can bring the acquisition of either *things* or power.

In struggling to organize some of the most private elements of experience, both films regulate desire and pleasure. As Jean Baudrillard fears, consumption becomes an organized extension of production (1988: 43). It is not just that audiences come to desire Disney products; it is that they are alienated from the experience of liberating pleasures, of pleasures not shaped by the mechanistic requirements of capital formation. Both films thus use Shakespeare to authorize their arguments, to tame their characters, and in the process, to standardize audiences' consumption of their products.

Disney's *Little Mermaid* preserves, even intensifies, the kind of Puritan presentation of female maturation that Andersen imposed on his sources for a Calvinist audience (Zipes 1983: 71–94). The two versions differ greatly, however, in large part because the filmmakers splice a Shakespearean structure and characterizations into Andersen's plot. The characters of "A Little Mermaid" inhabit a female-dominated world. While the Mer-King is barely mentioned, the mermaids are founts of inspiration and independence for the heroine; the enticing stories of the human world that she hears, for instance, come from a grandmother. Mer-women, however, are also the source of destructive powers. The witch, who gives the Mermaid feet at the cost of her tongue, doubles the grandmother or the absent mother. Both promote separation, but independence is also associated with danger: the grandmother talks of the forest and the witch lives in one (Soracco 1990: 409). Andersen therefore presents female independence as threatening, and ultimately praises the Little Mermaid for letting her body dissolve into sea foam.

While in the end Disney's *Little Mermaid* is equally conservative on the subject of female empowerment, the film complicates its puritan message by restructuring Andersen's fairy tale according to the logic of Shakespearean comedy, in which the younger generation triumphs over the older. In Andersen's tale, swimming up to the ocean surface is a female rite of passage that each mermaid sister undergoes when she turns fifteen. In Disney, this ritual becomes a more generalized romance quest in which the adolescent heroine must overcome blocks to her happiness. First, she must act against the wishes of her father, who opposes relationships with humans. Then, she must compete with a displaced version of the father, the vindictive sea witch Ursula, who wants her voice and her Prince. The two most important changes to "The Little Mermaid" story are to the characters of the mermaid's father and the witch, both of them barriers to Ariel's happiness. The Mer-King gains a vastly increased presence and a name: he is King Triton, who, like Shakespeare's powerful father Prospero, wields storm and tempest to manage his realm. (The film begins with a scene that is not found in Andersen, but resembles closely the first scene of *The Tempest*, which opens with an argument – while a storm is sinking the ship – about whether a prominent ducal counselor or the sailors themselves should decide nautical conduct. In a similar vein, before the credits of *The Little Mermaid* appear, a dark boat tosses violently on stormy seas, while its occupants engage in a class-inflected discussion. Sailors attribute their problems to King Triton, and are surly when the Prince and his trusted advisor say that they have never heard of him.) Ursula the sea witch has also grown in presence and power. In Andersen's story, the Little Mermaid ultimately loses the Prince to a human Princess; in Disney's film, Ursula transforms herself into a slender young woman and almost succeeds, as Ariel's rival, in marrying Prince Eric. *The Little Mermaid* finally ends festively. Where Andersen's mermaid only gains hope for salvation after 300 years of selfless work, Ariel gets a splendid dress and a big wedding, attended by both mer-people and humans.

The addition to Andersen's story of certain features – parental blocks, the festive ending, the movement in and out of an enticing, but dangerous place beyond the law – all suggest that Disney's writers are familiar with Northrop Frye's influential analysis of Shakespearean comedy (1949).[4] Frye observes that Shakespeare's comic plots, modeled on Roman New Comedy, work to remove blocks to youthful desire according to a basically Oedipal pattern. The blocks are embodied in a *senex* or representative of the older generation, who often competes with a young man for a young woman. In Shakespeare, the *senex* may appear as the young woman's father. He insists that she follow his wishes for her sexual choice, but need not overtly compete for physical possession of her. After the young lovers undergo a journey, the blocking laws and values of the *senex* give way to those of the "green world" sympathetic to the younger generation's desires.

The quest of Disney's Ariel follows closely the implicitly Oedipal pattern of Frye's "The Argument of Comedy." *The Little Mermaid*'s opening minutes establish that Ariel has strong desires that contest her father's plans for her. The crab Sebastian, like Philostrate in *A Midsummer Night's Dream*, is orchestrating performances for his lord, King Triton. They are to feature Ariel singing for her father, but she is instead busy exploring a sunken human ship. Her absence angers the King. Although many journalists note Ariel's desire for human *things*, for material possessions, Ariel says she has many things already, but that she wants *more*. To this extent, she is driven by desire itself more than by consumerism. Accordingly, the Calvinist restrictions on desire that lead to a loss of body for Andersen's mermaid become, in Disney, the father's prohibition on mixing with the human world. Sebastian sums up her father's blocking action with a deceptively charming calypso song that ends, "Someone needs to nail that girl's fins to the floor."

The comic structure of *The Little Mermaid* suggests Shakespeare generally, but the characters of Ariel the mermaid and other figures point specifically to *The Tempest*. Shakespeare's Ariel is a sprite, not unlike the ethereal mermaid of Andersen's version. But in fact, Disney has efficiently mixed Andersen's character with a pair of Shakespearean figures. As the central image of youth struggling for independence, the corporate mermaid Ariel conflates Shakespeare's Miranda with his fairy Ariel in her innocence, her announced desire for freedom, her wish for knowledge, and again, her position with regard to her father. Like Miranda (with the exception of her father), Ariel has never seen a man before and has little knowledge of humans; she mistakes forks for combs, for instance, and believes her friend when he calls the forks "dingelhoppers." The desires that Ariel's father so opposes, and about which Shakespeare's Prospero is ambivalent, present themselves in her signature song: Ariel wants feet so that she can walk, dance, run, see the sun, explore, "know what people know," and become part of the human world. In short, Ariel's desire is defined by *difference from her father*, and integration into a brave new world of knowledge and relationships.

Not only Ariel, but also Ursula the sea witch, derives specifically from *The Tempest*. Caliban, Prospero's central antagonist, is absent from *The Little Mermaid*. King Triton, and then Ariel, fight instead against Ursula, whom Disney creates by inflating the role of Caliban's absent mother, Sycorax, and by conflating Sycorax with her son. Ursula wars with King Triton for control of the undersea domain, as Sycorax once fought with Prospero for the island. While Ursula doubles Triton as a member of the older generation standing in the way of young desire, she herself also stands for transgressive desire. Like the rebellious Caliban, Ursula provides a negative version of the child's rebellious, maturing desires; she also supplies Ariel with the means for gaining them. The first image of Ursula shows her putting on lipstick; she also wears an enormous amount of eye shadow. When Ariel is frightened about being left voiceless, with thrusting hips the witch tells her, "Use your body language." Although Ariel at first follows Ursula's advice, batting her eyelashes and looking innocently seductive, the film ultimately shows that discipline, hard work, and purity of voice bring a man.

Paradoxically, the use of Shakespearean comic structure in Disney's *The Little Mermaid* allows the film to circumscribe female desire – for independence, possessions, and sexuality – under the guise of celebrating the triumph of young people over the old. According to Frye's "Argument of Comedy," while the blocks to young desire are overcome, the transgressors are also reintegrated into society, usually through marriage. Peter Erickson (1985) and Lynda Boose (1982) have shown that Shakespeare's comic heroines accommodate themselves to a society in which the husband's role replicates that of the father. Disney's Ariel, after resisting the authority of her male parent with energetic independence, accordingly subordinates herself to the male authority of her husband: she learns to follow the rules and manners of his world. Joining this new patriarchal order in the human realm means subduing all that Ursula represents and winning a sexualized competition with her for Prince Eric, and for larger goals – to prevent the witch from emasculating the King and, by taking his Triton, dominating his realm. Disney uses Shakespeare's text and structure to focus more on the disciplining of Ursula and of female bodies than on the exchange of Triton's patriarchal system for that of Ariel's husband. Indeed, youth and patriarchy are reconciled only after the inflation and explosion of Ursula's body during the final battle. Not until Ursula's body, and the female sexual energies it signifies, are gone can Ariel successfully join Eric's class-inflected patriarchy.

Shakespeare enables Disney to bring female bodily pleasure into alignment with standardized social orders. Cynthia Serz, in *People Magazine*, quotes Pat Carroll, who provided the voice of Ursula, as saying that she played the sea witch "as a has-been Shakespearean actress." Whether or not so directed by the writers, Carroll was speaking to Shakespeare's position as a double signifier when quoted by late-twentieth-century popular films: he displays cultural capital by signifying "high-culture" taste or "objective" standards; but used episodically to denote character, he also signifies theatricality and its transgressiveness. To rein in transgressive sexualities, including female desire, Disney uses Shakespeare, often against himself. This dynamic informs not only *The Little Mermaid*, but also *The Lion King*.

In *The Lion King*, Ursula's spiritual brothers, Scar and Timon, signify Shakespearean transgression. Although he is very genial and his fate is happier than Ursula's, Timon's influence as a facilitator of desire is as short-lived as hers. In the film, Prince Simba is weighed down by guilt because he mistakenly believes that he killed his father. But when young Simba runs from his past and denies his royal duties, he moves from *Hamlet* to *1 Henry IV* via *Timon of Athens*. A comic version of the philosophy found in Shakespeare's tragic *Timon of Athens* enters *The Lion King* through the misanthrope's Disney namesake, the meercat Timon, who fittingly teaches Simba that "when the past turns its back on you, you need to turn your back on it." While Shakespeare's tragic hero enacts this attitude by turning from Athens and cursing his friends, Disney's Timon imparts the message jovially, as a means of encouraging Prince Simba to forget his worries. The Disney Timon becomes, like Falstaff to Prince Hal in *1 Henry IV*, a substitute father to Simba. Timon is also like Falstaff because he has no memory or knowledge of time. He acts histrionically, and even quotes Shakespeare in his famous song, "Hakuna Matata," which contains the words "What's in a name?" from the balcony scene of *Romeo and Juliet* (2.1.85). Specifically, the character of Timon offers an alternative sexual identity. By the time of *The Lion King*'s appearance, Nathan Lane, the voice of Timon, had played the role of an aging gay man in *The Birdcage*, and the campiest gay role in the stage version of *Love! Valour! Compassion!* Timon thus signifies gayness, or at least, Simba's unsettled adolescent sexuality. Although Timon's values are positive forces for pleasure, they must be overcome in order for Simba to regain his kingdom.

Disney uses *1 Henry IV* both to establish Simba's and Timon's transgressive natures and to restrict them. The corporation ultimately disciplines these characters' desires for behavioral diversity by closing the movie with marriage and childbirth, the culmination of Frye's festive pattern. The gay-inflected Timon is present at Simba's ritual celebration of his new son. But in marrying, fathering a child, assuming the mantle of power, and literally stepping into the role of his father, King Mufasa, when he repeats the ritual of ascending the mountain, Simba gives up the irresponsibility nurtured by Timon and proves his own heterosexuality. Unlike Ursula of *The Little Mermaid*, Timon is not eradicated, suggesting in part that theatrical selves and transgressive bodies may be tolerated, although their influence recedes. Similarly, although Falstaff's influence has "fallen away" (3.3.1) after Prince Hal joins with the King during the second half of *1 Henry IV*, Hal continues to countenance the disorderly Knight. *The Lion King*, though, can only tolerate Timon's disreputable presence because heterosexuality seems to be the central source of power. In fact, the catalyst to Simba's re-emergence is his fiancée, Nala. When she pressures him to return home, he says, "You're starting to sound like my father." In *The Lion King* the ingénue is already an agent for patriarchy.

It is not just the enshrinement of Simba's heterosexuality that enables *The Lion King* to tolerate Timon. Disney also manages the threat to discipline that Timon poses by splitting the disruptive aspects of the outsider's histrionic personality between Timon and the vain, posing, villain Scar. Scar's death provides a warning against violent transgression *within* centers of power. With anxiety deflected from the court, the film conservatively presents its "Prince Hal" as a beneficent figure, whose political self-fashioning does not share a continuum with ambition.

Gender difference provides another reason why *The Lion King* tolerates Timon, while *The Little Mermaid* demonizes Andersen's witch. Although some of Ursula's traits are generic to female villains, Disney invests them with a misogynist ideology by framing them within *The Tempest*'s arrangement of characters. In transforming Caliban into Ursula, the American patriarchal corporation re-genders a Shakespearean scheme, making the patriarch's opponent not merely feminized, but feminine.

As Patricia Parker (1987) has shown, writers, including Shakespeare, have since biblical times identified women with "fatness": with a lack of sexual discipline and with inflation, multiplication, and proliferation, including especially the proliferation of texts and words. Ursula tells Ariel in song that men do not like girls who talk:

> Men don't like a lot of blabber
> They think a girl who gossips is a bore …
> It's she who holds her tongue who gets her man.

Yet Ursula, who has multiple octopus "legs," is also a copious speaker. She is, more specifically, a puritan nightmare of the female sexual body. When singing "Poor Unfortunate Souls," Ursula jiggles her breasts and swings her wide hips to underscore her points. The film marks Ursula's temporary triumph near the end by having her blow herself up to gigantic proportions, while lightning, storm, and fireworks issue from her. The triumph of Eric and Ariel, the creations of a large patriarchal corporation, over Ursula is the disciplining of the female "fatness" she represents. Created out of Shakespearean discourse, Ursula, like Scar and Timon, demonstrates how easily Shakespeare can be coopted by large *corporate* bodies for the imposition of marketplace control.

III

By appropriating Shakespeare, *The Lion King* and *The Little Mermaid* – as films targeted at children, adolescents, and their parents – manage not just patterns of desire, but also cultural attitudes towards "growing up" and entering culture. Michiko Kakutani provides a high-concept summary of *The Lion King*: "Simba, the conflicted lion cub … overcomes his feelings of guilt and inadequacy to accept the responsibilities of adulthood" (1998: 8). Substitute one name for another, and Kakutani could be describing *Hamlet.* Disney gains enormous currency from this appropriation: it generates product placement, including a half-page color picture and front-page article connecting Shakespeare and Disney in *The New York Times,* Arts and Leisure section. But the corporation also enlists Shakespeare to lend credibility to its simplistically Oedipal model of development, recognizable as a popularized version of Ernest Jones's (1954; first published 1949) dated analysis of Prince Hamlet, which identifies Claudius as a displaced version of Hamlet's father and diagnoses the Prince's failure to act as deriving from unresolved, conflicted feelings about his parents.

Although Bourdieu's model of cultural distinction implies that appropriation transfers value unidirectionally, from a source to a new receptacle for cultural capital, Disney's use of Shakespeare shows that worth flows in two directions. Revaluing one currency in turn alters the standard currency by which it is measured. While Shakespeare lends credibility to the Oedipal schemes of *Mermaid* and *The Lion King,* the Disney films also perpetuate popular notions about Shakespeare's plays, especially with regard to Hamlet's "Oedipal complex." Unlike the elder Hamlet, Simba's father, King Mufasa, is alive when the action begins. In one of his father–son advice sessions, he shows Simba a shadowy, menacing place beyond the borders of his kingdom, where we see threatening animals lurk. (We later discover them among Scar's henchmen.) Simba imagines that being King means thinking, as Scar himself later says, "I'm the King and I can do whatever I want." This youthful grandiosity gets Simba in trouble with his powerful father. When Mufasa observes Simba visiting the shadowy dangerous regions, he punishes his son strictly.

These father–son dynamics leave Simba unable to resolve an implied set of internal conflicts. Simba feels stirred in an unsanctioned manner; he feels aggressive and ready to replace his father; yet he also feels small next to the grand, powerful father he loves. When Simba avoids all effective action by living with Timon in the forest, he seems immobilized, like Jones's Hamlet, by psychological conflicts originating in guilt over his father's death. Intimidated by his father's greatness and physical strength, Simba in many ways wears an Oedipal "scar," even before it is deepened by his Uncle Scar's accusations.

Disney's Oedipal plot for Simba therefore defines not just masculine development, but also the order of culture to which concepts of growth contribute. To depict the relationship between these orders, Disney adapts popular attitudes about Shakespeare's views on social organization. Although Mufasa teaches Simba that nature requires a delicate balance between respecting creatures and eating them in the "great circle of life," the group in the shadows seems outside this scheme. Mufasa's depiction of a natural food chain borrows from the "great chain of being," popularized by E. M. W. Tillyard's *Elizabethan World Picture* (1943). (Hamlet himself gestures to the concept when speaking to Rosencrantz and Guildenstern. Before he recognizes that his friends have betrayed his trust, he declares of man: "How noble in reason, how infinite in faculty, in form and moving how express and admirable, in action how like an angel, in apprehension how like a god – the beauty of the world, the paragon of animals!" [2.2.293–97]). Disney reifies Tillyard's now-discarded metaphysical construct by giving it a visual, horizontal geography. As in *Troilus and Cressida* or even *Henry V*, Shakespeare never presents concepts of natural order without questioning the motives of his speakers. Disney, however, erases Shakespeare's contingencies, presenting him to the modern marketplace as a believer in natural orders.

Beyond the chain or circle, Scar and his henchmen are represented as outside culture through gender inversion: once they take over, the males send the lionesses out to hunt food while they remain at home. As a histrionic, vaguely Wildeian figure whose style contrasts with the hyper-masculinity of his brother Mufasa, even Scar's name more than hints at castration. Because of his ambiguously gay mannerisms, the film makes him a figure both of Simba's Oedipal crisis and of forbidden adolescent eroticism. Gazing at Scar's troops in the shadowy world beyond the kingdom's geographic borders, Simba seems to be acting on a fluidity of desire. When his father punishes him for it, we see the film colluding with parents' desires for regulation: erotized curiosity is outside culture. The film thus replicates Shakespeare's supposedly Oedipal design to authorize the discipline of transgressive adolescent desires. At the same time, it offers a high-concept reading of *Hamlet*: a young Prince is prevented from taking his place in the masculine world of action and politics because of improper longings. The double appropriation of Shakespeare and Freud/Jones gives credence to the developmental scheme that Disney presents, in which male children risk being scarred and emasculated if they stray beyond the boundaries of discipline, desire, and dominance. With Simba restored to his father's role, the ending of *The Lion King* therefore narrows Shakespeare's double signifying: initially a sign of transgression *and* authority, by the end of the film Shakespeare as dramatist signifies only the discipline of culture. While Shakespeare reifies Disney's products, Disney in turn alters or fixes Shakespearean economies of reception.

Discipline asserts itself differently when Disney surveys Oedipal development in girls or women. Differences between Ariel's struggle and Simba's "Oedipal" plight arise partly from an intersection between contemporary American and early modern cultural attitudes. In *The Little Mermaid*, as in Shakespeare, maternal sexual desire is dangerous. Ursula's largest sin is, in fact, combining sexuality with the maternal instincts of Shakespearean women such as Gertrude (*Hamlet*) and Tamora (*Titus Andronicus*). When two of her eel-servants are killed by Eric in the grand, final battle, Ursula whimpers, "Babies ... my poor little poopsies." Ursula's stylized breasts, and hips in particular, present her body in terms of maternity. Visual clues suggest, however, that this mother wants her children never to grow up or separate, much like Tamora in *Titus Andronicus*, who finally (although unintentionally) consumes her children. People swim into Ursula's lair through vaginal-looking tunnels. She imprisons captives there after reducing them to small but large-headed creatures with tiny, thin tails. Their appearance recalls that of tadpoles, even sperm. Either way, we see Ursula as a mother who wants her "children" to regress, even to the point of returning to the womb.[5] In a pattern that Janet Adelman (1992) finds to be pervasive in Shakespeare, the film links a mother's expression of her sexual desire with destructiveness to her children. *The Little Mermaid* therefore encourages us to believe, with Hamlet, that a mother's blood should be tame (3.4.68), a point he makes to Gertrude in the closet scene when he warns her away from Claudius's bed. The film's misogyny therefore lies in making Ariel's triumph over a competitive, sexualized maternal figure a prerequisite to maturity. This scheme of development conforms to the ideology of a puritan, American market: while depicting an independent, physically flirtatious girl in a sea-shell bra, the film reassures audiences that it respects domestically bounded desire. *The Little Mermaid*'s rearrangement of *The Tempest*, particularly the assignment of Caliban's role to a woman, makes this dynamic possible.

The Little Mermaid also reconfigures Shakespeare by de-politicizing his play, neglecting or rejecting a postcolonial reading of *The Tempest* that sympathizes with Caliban, seeing him as a feminized "other" whose evil is not essential, like Ursula's, but culturally constructed. It is not surprising that during the same years in which Shakespeare scholars found "good" figures in *The Tempest* increasingly suspect – the Reagan–Bush 1980s – Disney produced a film reifying their sunny natures and demonizing their opponents. *The Little Mermaid* therefore participates in a larger cultural project to reclaim Shakespearean themes – even Shakespeare himself – for the conservative structure of the multinational marketplace.

The general effects of animated appropriation on Shakespearean reception are *structurally* conservative because viewers principally understand the borrowings by relying on general, familiar patterns of plots and characters. Structurally conservative appropriation is the end to which Disney films put both Frye's model for Shakespearean structure and psychoanalytic patterns of development. However animators may be using Shakespeare, the typical viewer brings to the theater popular paraphrases that circulate through many sectors of culture. As evidenced by Disney's other quotations of Shakespeare (e.g., Iago as a bird in *Aladdin*, and isolated lines), popular culture focuses more on character than other elements. (Everyone knew what it meant to call Mario Cuomo "Hamlet on the Hudson," but audiences have to be told about the sources of movie plots such as Orson Welles's *Chimes at Midnight*.) This fact pushes appropriations of Shakespeare toward the personal, and toward psychological allegory.

Disney's appropriation of Shakespeare thus promotes a corporate agenda that, with regard to cultural difference, coincides with modernist projects. It borrows Shakespeare to authorize essentialist models of the heroic self, to discipline bodies and the transgressive tendencies they represent, and to seem apolitical by bringing together sources rooted in temporally and geographically disparate cultures. Although its size, brand recognition, and market penetration magnify Disney's visibility, the conflation between corporate and modernist agenda is inevitable within our late capitalist environment, which is connected by an interlocking system of mass communications, like the one Leo Bogart (1995) describes. This environment, constantly reshaping and reshaped by rapid shifts in the international distribution of wealth and technology, encourages renegotiations of the distinction between elite and haut-bourgeois culture as different groups claim their worth. Consumers buy what they know, but they also want *standards*. Since appropriation both reifies and conservatively affirms familiar interpretations or opinions, it is extremely profitable. Appropriation helps to standardize desire by giving people the market standards they demand, but as a currency, it actually floats within markets.

Appropriation thus participates in those inevitable historical movements in which, as Lawrence Levine points out, what is elite and what is popular are always being redefined (1991: 230). Walt Disney showed that he himself understood the dynamics of appropriation when, speaking of *Fantasia*, he said, "Gee, this'll make Beethoven!" (cited in Schickel 1968: 244). Although probably joking, Disney was intuitively aware that cultural capital moves bi-directionally: that his sources lent him cultural authority, but that he also changed the nature of their marketing and popularity. Perhaps Walt Disney also understood that he renegotiated the meaning of individual works and the signifying of authorial names.

IV

Thinking about how a major Disney animated film uses Shakespeare leads to an interrogation of the phenomenon of appropriation itself. When appropriation informs a film's overall structure and set of characterizations, as in *The Little Mermaid* and *Lion King*, it serves the kinds of rhetorical goals that we have seen. But in corporately made animations, where appropriation tends toward allegory, resemblances to Shakespeare can seem generic or coincidental. Why, for instance, quote Hamlet's Yorick speech in *The Quest for Camelot* or give Iago's name (from *Othello*) to a bird in *Aladdin*? In such brief quotations, modernist transcendence is less a goal than a transient effect. When, as in *The Quest for Camelot*, flourish seems the main end, we perceive mainly trivialization, personal indulgence by the creators, and creative fatigue.

Sometimes we forget that corporate entities are composed of individual people, making personal judgments *based on*, but not mechanically generated by, market assessments that derive from education and even taste. Despite its dispersion into a variety of corporate products, Disney's conglomerate is run by *individuals*, including a very "hands-on" Chief Executive Officer with direct influence on what animated blockbusters get made, and how they appear.[6] As Herbert Gans has shown (1974: 23–27), we cannot assume that "low-culture" creators write less to please themselves than "high-culture" ones do. Since the ascension of Michael Eisner, Disney has carefully blurred the cultural boundaries between high and low with the development of Touchstone and Miramax. Market strategies have driven the changes at Disney but some shifts derive from personal difference: Eisner has steered a company led no longer by Horatio Algers, but by prep school, liberal arts college graduates from very affluent origins.[7] Disney, therefore, may not be entirely a mechanical entity that imposes itself on culture. Instead, Disney may be a forceful mechanical means for imposing the private visions of a limited few.

Resented and feared for its role in erasing memory, Disney's enterprise provides a paradigm for the process by which simulacra substitute for real-life experiences and communities. Because even the most postmodernist critics of Shakespeare recognize in his name an effective signifier for memory, Disney's appropriations threaten to erase all opponents, to wipe out Culture. Yet Shakespeare and Disney are not polar opposites. As the extant sketch for *Titus Andronicus* shows, Shakespeare himself regularly erases difference and obscures memory. *Troilus and Cressida* openly questions the contingency of a self constructed through remembered reputation; heroes such as Henry V manipulate national memories.[8] As the second tetralogy generally shows, appropriating memory for personal ends is a messy, readily contested process. Disney therefore erases the memory of a cultural icon who himself destabilizes culture by reporting on this postmodern process. In the present moment, then, Disney generates cultural anxiety by drawing attention to the process by which corporations and the Shakespeare Industry authorize one another and those groups who "want more."

Notes

1 William Lyon Phelps, of Yale, quoted in Schickel 1968: 231.

2 By mid-century, Theodor Adorno and Max Horkheimer (1988), associated with the Frankfurt School, had identified consumer culture as an extension of production and thus controlled, classified, organized, and labeled by forces that dominate the marketplace. Jean Baudrillard develops their ideas in "The System of Objects" (1988). Like Dorfman and Mattelart (1975), he fears that even affect and emotions will become signs and thus subject to control. In *America* (Baudrillard 1989: 55), Baudrillard openly fears that Disneyland figures the degeneration of American culture as a whole.

3 Richard Halpern (1997: 1–14) delineates the strongly dehistoricizing impulse of modernism, particularly in T. S. Eliot's criticism and what Halpern calls "academic modernism."

4 Written in the late 1940s, Frye's analysis of comedy dominated English departments for at least a generation. It is unlikely that college-educated writers would be unfamiliar with interpretations of Shakespeare influenced by it.

5 Laura Sells labels the imagery surrounding Ursula "gynophobic," intended to sanitize Ariel's loss of power (1995: 181).

6 Flower quotes sources who refer to Michael Eisner as "more hands-on than Mother Theresa" (1991: 145). He also documents Eisner's direct involvement in creating *The Little Mermaid* (178).

7 Michael Eisner became an undergraduate major in Theater at Denison University in Ohio after boarding at the Lawrenceville School in New Jersey. At Denison, Eisner tried his hand at writing plays (Flower 1991: 37). While growing up, like Eisner, on Park Avenue, Jeffrey Katzenberg attended Horace Mann, a distinguished New York City independent school, and then New York University before he dropped out. Frank Wells, Eisner's first President and Chief Operating Officer, had the highest grade point average in his class at Pomona, a prominent liberal arts college in Los Angeles, before becoming a Rhodes Scholar at Oxford and returning to Stanford Law School. Eisner met Michael Graves during a performance at the Metropolitan Opera; his affection for Broadway theater dates to his childhood, and he grew up with a Picasso hanging in his bedroom. Trained in "the classics," Katzenberg and Eisner have broad tastes: the first film for Touchstone Pictures that they produced (*Down and Out in Beverly Hills*) was based on a 1932 film by the French director, Jean Renoir; Eisner approved the idea for *Footloose* because it reminded him of *The Scarlet Letter* and "The Maypole of Merrymount" (Grover 1991: 31–33, 53, 86, 219).

8 Here I am relying on readings by Jonathan Baldo of *Henry V* (1996) and Linda Charnes of *Troilus and Cressida* (1993).

11
Afterword: The incredible shrinking Bard

GARY TAYLOR

Size does matter.

Shakespeareans all know this. It matters that Shakespeare has been elected "Briton of the millennium," that his works are studied by twenty million American schoolchildren every year, that Baz Luhrmann's *Romeo & Juliet* was the number one grossing film in America the weekend it opened, that *Shakespeare in Love* received more Academy Awards than any other 1998 film. Shakespeare accumulates superlatives: the greatest X, the most widely Y, the most often Z.

I come to measure Shakespeare, not to praise him, because I imagine myself as a cultural historian, not a cheerleader. Shakespeare's reputation has a history (Taylor 1989; Bate 1998). More important, that history – however we tell it – is only one item in a much larger category. All reputations evolve; all reputations are subject to the mechanisms of biological and artificial memory, to the laws of stimulus, representation, and recollection (Taylor 1996). All reputations, even the most powerful, at some point begin to diminish. According to my measurements, Shakespeare's reputation peaked in the reign of Queen Victoria, and is now shrinking.

This declaration will almost certainly be greeted, in many quarters, with snorts of derision and with a flood of counter-examples. "At the end of the twentieth century, Shakespeare is not retreating, but colonizing new territory – Shakespeare on video, Shakespeare on CD-ROM, Shakespeare on the Internet, Shakespeare on hypertext. Harold Bloom has just published a 745-page book entitled *Shakespeare: The Invention of the Human* (1998b). The cover story of the November 1998 issue of *Lingua Franca* – an empathetic review of Bloom by another major scholar of his generation, William Kerrigan – is entitled 'The Case for Bardolatry.' How, at this particular cultural moment, could anyone sane claim that Shakespeare's reputation is shrinking?"

Different critics might cite different counter-examples, but the technique of refutation would remain the same: a statistical claim is countered by citing individual cases that contradict it. Such refutations are illogical, because the statistical claim has already included the evidence of the alleged counter-examples. I do not claim that Shakespeare's reputation has disappeared; I claim only that it has passed its peak of expansion, and begun to decline. Such a claim can only be tested by looking beyond individual examples of appropriation to a larger pattern, which includes both positive and negative evidence. But Shakespeareans, almost by definition, never look at negative evidence: evidence of the absence of Shakespeare, where one might expect his presence. That is, Shakespeareans look for evidence that would confirm the hypothesis of his ubiquitous and expanding cultural mass; they do not look for evidence that would falsify that hypothesis. But falsification is an essential component in the construction of valid theories about the world (Popper 1959, 1963).

From this perspective, look again at the alleged counter-examples. Video, CD-ROM, and the Internet are not really expanding the Shakespearean domain; they just provide an alternative way to satisfy the existing Bard market. They replace textbooks. Shakespeareans are not leading the digital revolution; they are just trying to preserve their market share in an increasingly demanding educational environment, where they must ward off hostile incursions from technologized multiculturalism. In 1996, the World Shakespeare Congress heard a self-congratulatory description of the development of new electronic, hypertext, and Internet editions of Shakespeare (Werstine 1998). This assessment ignored a fundamental historical shift in the balance of intellectual power. Specialists in Shakespeare and the English Renaissance dominated Anglo-American editorial practice and theory from the eighteenth century through McKerrow, Greg, Hinman, and Bowers. Terence

Hawkes here legitimately criticizes the editorial practice of Quiller-Couch and Dover Wilson, but their New Shakespeare series was riding the crest of a pioneering and pivotal intellectual development, the New Bibliography. By contrast, at the end of the twentieth century, our dominant editorial theorists are D. C. Greetham, co-founder and executive director of the Society of Textual Scholarship (Greetham 1992, 1995, 1997, 1999), and Jerome McGann, editor of Byron and Rossetti, author of *A Critique of Modern Textual Criticism* and *The Textual Condition* (McGann 1980–93, 1983, 1985, 1991). Greetham specializes in medieval literature, McGann in the nineteenth century. The internecine battles of Shakespeare editing may be as vicious as ever, but their victors do not command as much cultural authority as they once did.

This decline in cultural authority is also relevant to the other counter-examples. Why does Kerrigan believe that he needs to justify his bardolatry? Kerrigan's case for Shakespeare – subtitled "Rescuing Shakespeare from the Critics" – entails an attack on every major Shakespeare scholar of the last two decades. At the end of the twentieth century Shakespeare enthusiasts assume, for perhaps the first time since the end of the eighteenth century, that Shakespeare needs defending, that his genius is not universally appreciated, that his supremacy is contested. In particular, his defenders assume that Shakespeare is now appreciated primarily by an older generation of critics who are losing power in the academy. Ivo Kamps is right that, whether or not this assessment is correct, it positions Shakespeare not as a shared possession, but as the icon of one academic faction in its struggle with another. To the extent that Shakespeare is associated – by both his defenders and his critics – with political and cultural conservatism, even the most impassioned praise of his work will be seen not as an objective assessment, but as mere partisan rhetoric. Thus, when Kerrigan proclaims that the only appropriate response to Shakespeare is "adulation" and Bloom asserts that Shakespeare's intelligence is "limitless," they indulge in a kind of hyperbole that most professional scholars disdain.

But maybe that is the problem; maybe academic Shakespeareans are an isolated and inbred minority, at odds with the rest of Western society. The fact that some of us are giving less time to Shakespeare, and more to Toni Morrison and Thomas Middleton, might not accurately represent Shakespeare's status in the larger world. But the postmodern appropriations of Shakespeare separately examined in this book tell the same story. Novelists such as Gloria Naylor and Jane Smiley now write *against* Shakespeare, either denying his influence altogether, or openly resisting it; they see him as a conservative figure. So too does Hollywood, although Disney and Kenneth Branagh capitalize on his cultural conservatism rather than resisting it. Romance novelists, at the bottom of the cultural food chain, continue to mine Shakespeare for authority-by-association; but even in that most despised of contemporary literary forms, Shakespeare synecdochically represents a patriarchal social order.

Things are not any better when we leave the classroom for the green room. Shakespeareans may protest: what about the new Globe Theatre, yet another monument to Shakespeare in the heart of Europe's largest city? But that new monument to Shakespeare in its 1998 season offered only two plays from the Shakespeare canon – alongside two from the Middleton canon. The Middleton plays got better reviews.

Well, what about the Royal Shakespeare Company? Charles Spencer, reviewing the 1998 season of that "beleaguered, debt-ridden company," asks, "Is the RSC bored with Shakespeare? … once again the Shakespeare productions range from the adequate to the disgraceful" (Spencer 1998). Another reviewer describes most recent Stratford productions as "routine and dismal: either bored novelty-for-novelty's-sake (like the current *Twelfth Night*) or echoing empty middle-of-the-road fare (like the current *Merchant of Venice*)" (P. Taylor 1998). Virtually the same complaints were being made at the same time about "the other Stratford." Wildly praised in the 1990s for its productions of plays like *Long Day's Journey into Night* and *Waiting for Godot*, Ontario's Stratford Festival has been stridently attacked for "pedestrian" or "outrageously overproduced" Shakespeare (Coulbourne 1998; K. Taylor 1998). For the Stratford Festival, as for the RSC, the mid-1980s represented a decisive turning point, a crisis of decline after two decades of expansion. Our most prestigious Shakespearean theaters have both been overwhelmed by the mechanical demand to re-produce the same plays, over and over again. Audiences seem to be interested in only a limited number of Shakespeare's works, but they also get tired of seeing those plays performed *ad nauseam* (Taylor 1999).

This problem is not limited to the two major companies. Increasingly, members of the American Association of Shakespeare Festivals are having to confine themselves to the dozen plays with name recognition. The Alabama Shakespeare Festival, with the largest endowment of any U.S. company, performs only three Shakespeare plays a year, and whenever it wants to do something ambitious like *Antony and Cleopatra*, the company has to balance it with an old war-horse like *The Taming of the Shrew*. And what spectators, when asked, remember from 1998's very successful production of *Shrew* is the end of the performance, when Kate stripped to a spandex body suit and jumped onto the driver's seat of Petruccio's Harley-Davidson – a detail somehow unaccountably omitted from most of the editions of Shakespeare. In other words, even when Shakespeare's plays are good box office, what makes them good box office is not exactly Shakespeare.

This is also relevant to the recent flurry of Shakespearean activity at another kind of box office. For the corporate accountants of Hollywood, every new Shakespeare film has some of the built-in safety of any other remake, particularly if it is a remake of one of the handful of best-known plays, such as *A Midsummer Night's Dream*, *Much Ado about Nothing*, or *Romeo and Juliet*. Nevertheless, most of the Shakespeare films released in the 1990s were art films with limited distribution. Trevor Nunn's *Twelfth Night*, for instance, played on only one screen in the entire Boston metropolitan area; Branagh's *Hamlet*, like his early *Henry V*, had to offer theaters willing to show it a monopoly, so that for several weeks they were guaranteed to be the only retailer in a city of more than a million people; *Looking for Richard* is still hard to find, even in video stores. Most Shakespeare films make a profit, not in theatrical release, but in video rentals and sales, particularly in the educational market; advertisements for such videos have become a routine component of the junk mail that crosses every Shakespeare teacher's desk, every semester.

The chief exception to this dreary commercial history, Baz Luhrmann's *Romeo & Juliet*, confirms the intrinsic difficulty of selling Shakespeare to America. Ask yourself: were all those teenagers going to see Shakespeare, or going to see Claire Danes and Leonardo DiCaprio? Contrast the marketing of Luhrmann's *Romeo & Juliet* with the marketing of Franco Zeffirelli's, a generation earlier. Zeffirelli's romantic leads were complete unknowns; Luhrmann's were already teen idols, and Luhrmann himself best known for directing music videos, also aimed primarily at a teen market; indeed, Luhrmann's was the first Shakespeare film to present a rock soundtrack "filled with popular songs containing *lyrics*" (Guenther forthcoming). In the movie, the words of the Butthole Surfers overlap with the Bard's; in the marketplace, the soundtrack stayed on the charts long after the movie closed. Luhrmann marketed his Shakespeare to pop-culture-addict adolescents because he recognized that every American teenager is required to read *Romeo and Juliet.* Hence its exploitation in another Hollywood success story, 1998's *Shakespeare in Love*, an adaptation of *Romeo and Juliet* which has the further advantage of reproducing only the most famous bits of Shakespeare's play, suspended in a solution of anachronistic romantic comedy, real breasts, chase scenes, and gorgeous costumes. Shakespeare in starland is indeed "neither more nor less essential to consumers than Bugs Bunny" (Bristol 1996: 233).

But unlike Bugs Bunny, Shakespeare receives a massive government subsidy. In 1765, Samuel Johnson cited as the best evidence for Shakespeare's genius the fact that his works were then "read without any other reason than the desire of pleasure" and were "therefore praised only as pleasure is obtained"; the author's reputation was "unassisted by interest or passion" (1958: 7: 61). This is, of course, no longer true. Shakespeare is now usually read "without any other reason than the desire" for a passing grade, and his reputation is continually assisted by the self-interest and passion of Shakespearean *apparatchiks* – cultural bureaucrats who, like myself, make a living off his reputation. A text can only belong to everybody if everybody is forced to adopt it. Universality, never the product of free choice, can only be imposed by totalitarian means. And that very imposition of a text itself creates resistance to it. As a result, even when Shakespeare is taught, he doesn't stick. People don't internalize him, the way they used to.

Most Americans know by heart a few tags from Shakespeare's plays, even if they have not read them. A man on the street interviewed in New York by Al Pacino for his documentary *Looking for Richard*, or a Congressman in Washington D.C. providing sound bites for the six o'clock news, can quote or parody the same rusty speech from *Hamlet* ("B2, or not B2"). But neither the man on the street nor the politician trying to impress the man on the street would be likely to quote Virgil, Ovid, or Seneca, as Shakespeare did. The Greek and Roman classics have become less quotable, not because their style has changed, or their genius diminished, but simply because their readership has declined; their phrases are no longer in circulation. And Shakespeare's own good words are planted in fewer memories than they once were: he has become, like caviar, familiar to the General but arcane in the ranks.

It was not always so. In 1752, William Dodd published the first of many anthologies of *The Beauties of Shakespear* (1971); for the next century and a half the quoting of Shakespeare was pandemic. It has been convincingly argued that, by 1764, Shakespeare was becoming in many ways a religious cult figure, an object of pilgrimage and of quasi-transcendental authority, his works accorded many of the attributes of sacred scripture (Dávidházi 1998). Certainly, in nineteenth-century Britain and its empire – as Robert Sawyer, Sudipto Chatterjee and Jyotsna G. Singh, and Georgianna Ziegler here demonstrate – appropriations of Shakespeare pervaded the public sphere, from book illustration and gender debate to the rhetoric of poetic self-legitimation and imperial racism. The great Romantic essayist William Hazlitt quoted Shakespeare more than 2,400 times in his published prose (Bate 1984: 26); William Blake could label an image "Jocund Day" (from *Romeo and Juliet* 3.5.9) or "Fiery Pegasus" (from *1 Henry IV* 4.1.110) and expect just two words to recall their Shakespearean context (Taylor 1989: 107). In 1831, Alexis de Tocqueville, visiting America, reported that "There is hardly a pioneer's hut which does not contain a few odd volumes of Shakespeare" (Tocqueville 1838–40: 2: 66), and those volumes were obviously read, not just displayed on log coffee tables. In 1810, a popular burlesque entitled *Hamlet Travestie* inaugurated the dramatic subgenre of Shakespearian travesties, a genuinely "popular" form of mass entertainment that flourished in England and America for most of the nineteenth century, and presumed an audience intimately acquainted with the plots and the language of the plays (Jacobs and Johnson 1976; Wells 1978).

But never-resting time carries a backpack, wherein he puts bards for oblivion. In nineteenth-century America, Shakespeare was increasingly appropriated by "highbrow" culture (Levine 1988); the very popularity and vulgarity of the burlesques to some extent confirmed that division. At the end of the twentieth century, the comedians John Monteith and Suzanne Rand do an improvisation built upon four items suggested by the audience: a place, a person, an object, and a cliché. On the night I saw the show, the audience suggested Chicago, Al Capone, a toilet seat, and "Have a nice day." Monteith and Rand then improvised upon these details, a scene "as if written by Shakespeare." The result was screamingly funny, but I did not hear a single quotation from Shakespeare; his style was suggested, instead, by acrobatic contortions of grammar, the occasional "alas," odd "doth," and frequent "thee," incongruous mixtures of orotund polysyllables and street slang, and a singsong approximation of blank verse. So low the star is fallen.

Nor is Shakespeare any longer so important to writers intent upon legitimating themselves, certainly not as significant as he was to Browning. Consider two of the choice and master spirits of our stage, who have both won Pulitzer Prizes. Introducing his acclaimed trilogy of African American history plays, August Wilson quotes James Baldwin, Romaire Bearden, D. H. Lawrence, Pablo Picasso, and Bessie Smith; he imagines himself "sitting in the same chair as Eugene O'Neill, Tennessee Williams, Arthur Miller, Henrik Ibsen, Amiri Baraka, and Ed Bullins" (Wilson 1991: vii–xii). In a newspaper interview, Wilson claims that he has read *The Merchant of Venice* and seen *Othello* – and "that's the extent of my Shakespeare" (Wilson 1990). David Mamet has published two collections of essays, in which he quotes more than forty different authorities, from the Emperor Marcus Aurelius to the actor Richard Monette. His heroes, as writers, are Theodore Dreiser, Sherwood Anderson, Willa Cather, Sinclair Lewis, Leo Tolstoy, Edith Wharton (Mamet 1989: 66–7), and Tennessee Williams, author of "the greatest dramatic poetry in the American language" (Mamet 1986: 102). He most often quotes from Tolstoy, Stanislavski, and Thorstein Veblen. Mamet (once a college professor) has apparently read more Shakespeare than August Wilson, but he never treats Shakespeare as an artistic model. *Hamlet* is misquoted deliberately once; elsewhere, *Hamlet* is misquoted inadvertently, as are *Henry V* and *Macbeth*. "Cucullus non facit monachum" is attributed to "the Bard" and *Twelfth Night* (Mamet 1989: 60); but the phrase was proverbial, and it also occurs in *Measure for Measure*. (Shakespeare repeats himself more often than you think: see Taylor 1995.)

Stephen Jay Gould is, among scientists, of good knowledge, and literatured, and learned in the disciplines of the arts; his best-selling book, *Wonderful Life* (winner of a National Book Award), prettily and aptly quotes Robert Frost, Omar Khayyam, Stephen King, George Orwell, Alexander Pope, Robert Louis Stevenson, Mark Twain, and Kurt Vonnegut (Gould 1989: 28, 43, 44, 45, 98, 130, 285–86, 291). Although Gould quotes Shakespeare four times (27, 60, 321), Shakespeare is not listed in his index, presumably because Gould's indexer did not recognize the author of the unattributed quotations. The four Shakespeare quotations, moreover, are utterly predictable: two come from "the most famous soliloquy of all time" (which grows something stale by now), a third from another ward of the same Danish prison (*Hamlet* 1.3.59 ff.), and the fourth from *The Tempest* (or Aldous Huxley): "O brave – and improbable – new world, that has such people in it!" (referring to 5.1.186–87). This last exclamation (slightly misquoted) is virtually the climax of the book; we are not invited to remember Prospero's sardonic rejoinder, "'Tis new to thee" (5.1.188). If even learned clerks and witty writers quote Shakespeare less inventively, less accurately, and less often than of yore, you may imagine how his price has fallen in vulgar company.

The Shakespeare industry will no doubt dismiss Wilson, Mamet, and Gould as in some way "unrepresentative" of our time. They have to be, because Shakespeare is "immortal." He has been repeatedly declared so since 1623, when Ben Jonson claimed that Shakespeare's plays were "not of an age, but for all time!" (Shakespeare 1986: xlv). "All time" is a long time. Will Shakespeare's plays last longer than the earth? Longer than the sun? Five billion years? Five million? Five thousand? Next to five billion, five thousand may sound trivial, but the works of Homer are not even three thousand years old. Shakespeare, as yet, hasn't even lasted five *hundred*.

I come to measure Shakespeare, not to bury him. Here is my end-of-millennium prophecy: as long as the English language survives, people will be reading or listening to Shakespeare. They will be doing to Shakespeare what Shakespeare did to Plautus in *The Comedy of Errors*, expropriating what they can use, often without acknowledgment. But the number of people attending to Shakespeare, the intensity of their attention, the frequency and complexity of their appropriations, will inevitably diminish. Even now, if Shakespeare were not so massively supported by corporate capital and government subsidy, if he were not forced upon schoolchildren, would he still loom so large in our culture? Or would he collapse to the status of Chaucer? A great writer, admired by specialists, but paid little attention by the larger world.

The collapse of Shakespeare is hard to imagine. But then, who could have imagined how easily the Berlin Wall would collapse? Who could have imagined, twenty years ago, the shrinking of the Soviet Union? Already in our classical theaters the shrinking of Shakespeare has created more room for other playwrights. As Shakespeare gets smaller, the available cultural space for other writers – for Gloria Naylor, or Jane Smiley, or Thomas Middleton – gets bigger. Why should we confine our admiration to a single writer?

Polybardolatry, anyone?

Further reading
MATT KOZUSKO

I Critical works and collections

Bate, Jonathan (1989) *Shakespearean Constitutions: Politics, Theatre, Criticism 1730–1830*, Oxford: Clarendon Press. Examines the reciprocal influences of Georgian England on Shakespeare and of Shakespeare on Georgian England; acknowledges that Shakespeare is easily appropriated, but insists that the plays can also exert their own influence on readers.

Bloom, Harold (1998) *Shakespeare: The Invention of the Human*, New York: Riverhead Books. Argues that Shakespeare is responsible both for literary character as we know it and subsequently for the understanding Westerners have of themselves as dynamic individuals.

Boose, Lynda E. and Burt, Richard (1997) (eds) *Shakespeare, the Movie: Popularizing the Plays on Film, TV, and Video*, London and New York: Routledge. Examines a range of film and television productions of Shakespeare, addressing such issues as textual authority, "popular" versus "classical" presentations, and how different film traditions transform the Shakespearean text.

Bristol, Michael D. (1990) *Shakespeare's America, America's Shakespeare*, London: Routledge. A Marxist look at Shakespeare as an institution in American criticism and popular culture.

—— (1996) *Big-Time Shakespeare*, London: Routledge. Examines how Shakespeare has become a figure of literary fame, an icon of "celebrity" status with cultural currency.

Burt, Richard (1998) *Unspeakable Shaxxxspeares: Queer Theory and American Kiddie Culture*, New York: St. Martin's. Looks at appropriations of Shakespeare in popular culture from Hollywood productions to pornographic adaptations and considers changing ideas of high and low culture.

Dobson, Michael (1992) *The Making of the National Poet: Shakespeare, Adaptation and Authorship, 1660–1769*, Oxford: Clarendon Press. Investigates the rise of Shakespeare as the national English poet from the Restoration to David Garrick's Stratford Jubilee and considers the endurance of this initial construction in later ages.

Drakakis, John (1985) (ed.) *Alternative Shakespeares*, London: Methuen. New historical and cultural materialist essays that break with traditional Shakespearean criticism by demystifying Shakespeare.

Elsom, John (1989) (ed.) *Is Shakespeare Still Our Contemporary?*, London: Routledge. Participants discuss whether Shakespeare is contemporary or "universal," considering such issues as translation, sexism, and nationalism in the plays.

Erickson, Peter (1991) *Rewriting Shakespeare, Rewriting Ourselves*, Berkeley: University of California Press. Juxtaposes analyses of the representation of women in Shakespeare's plays with women writers' representations of Shakespeare.

Grady, Hugh (1991) *The Modernist Shakespeare: Critical Texts in a Material World*, Oxford: Clarendon Press. Adamantly recognizes the "historicity"of criticism and insists that there is no "authentic" Shakespeare; surveys Shakespearean criticism from the late nineteenth century to the present, focusing on individual schools.

—— (1996) *Shakespeare's Universal Wolf: Studies in Early Modern Reification*, Oxford: Clarendon Press. Considers the notion of selfhood in Shakespeare as informed by contemporary post-structural theory.

Hawkes, Terence (1986) *That Shakespeherian Rag: Essays on a Critical Process*, London: Methuen. Drawing on Bakhtin and other notions of intertextual relations, demonstrates that we have no access to true, authoritative meanings for Shakespeare's plays.

—— (1992) *Meaning by Shakespeare*, London: Routledge. Continues the study of how Shakespeare's "meaning" is conditioned by reception and cultural context. Argues that Shakespeare's plays do not mean, but that we mean "by" Shakespeare.

—— (1996) (ed.) *Alternative Shakespeares, Volume 2*, London: Routledge. A retrospective of new historicist and materialist approaches that denies the idea of a single true Shakespeare and questions the received or inherited picture we have of Shakespeare as timeless and universal, covering issues such as gender, sexuality, and race.

Hodgdon, Barbara (1998) *The Shakespeare Trade: Performances and Appropriations*, Philadelphia: University of Pennsylvania Press. Freewheeling account of Shakespeare's cultural status at the millennium; strong on film versions of the plays.

Howard, Jean E. and O'Connor, Marion F. (1987) (eds) *Shakespeare Reproduced: The Text in History and Ideology*, New York: Methuen. Aggressively challenges traditional constructions of Shakespeare in criticism from a series of contemporary critical positions.

Kamps, Ivo (1991) (ed.) *Shakespeare Left and Right*, New York: Routledge. Part I traces a spirited exchange between "right" (traditional or conservative) and "left" (progressive or revisionist) schools of critical thought on Shakespeare. Part II deals with ideological issues in criticism and in the plays.

Kott, Jan (1964) *Shakespeare Our Contemporary*, trans. Boleslaw Taborski, Garden City, N.Y.: Doubleday. Argues for the timelessness of Shakespeare by finding archetypal analogues for twentieth-century events in the plays.

Marsden, Jean I. (1991) (ed.) *The Appropriation of Shakespeare: Post-Renaissance Reconstructions of the Works and the Myth*, New York: St. Martin's. Focuses on how post-Renaissance generations imprint their own ideology on the plays and on the myth of Shakespeare.

—— (1995) *The Re-imagined Text: Shakespeare, Adaptation, and Eighteenth-Century Literary Theory*, Lexington: University Press of Kentucky. Considers the implications of widespread adaptations of Shakespeare's plays in the seventeenth and eighteenth centuries, focusing on why adaptation became popular and why it stopped.

Novy, Marianne (1990) (ed.) *Women's Re-Visions of Shakespeare: On the Responses of Dickinson, Woolf, Rich, H. D., George Eliot, and Others*, Urbana: University of Illinois Press. Essays on women writers' identification with Shakespeare's characters and with Shakespeare himself.

—— (1993) (ed.) *Cross-Cultural Performances: Differences in Women's Re-Visions of Shakespeare*, Urbana: University of Illinois Press. Essays that challenge mainstream conceptions of Shakespeare through the lens of race and gender.

—— (1999) (ed.) *Transforming Shakespeare: Contemporary Women's Re-Visions in Literature and Performance*, New York: St. Martin's. Further studies in women's responses to Shakespeare in the twentieth century, across genres and in performance.

Taylor, Gary (1989) *Reinventing Shakespeare*, New York: Oxford University Press. Traces the rise of Shakespeare to literary and cultural eminence through productions and editions of the plays and representations of the writer as a cultural figure.

Teague, Frances (1994) (ed.) *Acting Funny: Comic Theory and Practice in Shakespeare*, Rutherford, N.J.: Fairleigh Dickinson University Press. Genre-focused collection of essays that addresses relations of literary text and performance and Shakespeare as author-function across cultures and time.

Vickers, Brian (1993) *Appropriating Shakespeare: Contemporary Critical Quarrels*, London: Yale University Press. Argues against trends in critical theory as "appropriations" of Shakespeare that sacrifice useful criticism for ideological campaigning.

II Theoretical background

Bakhtin, M. M. (1981) *The Dialogic Imagination: Four Essays*, Michael Holquist (ed.), trans. Caryl Emerson and Michael Holquist, Austin: University of Texas Press. A central study of how language, which is dialogized or replete with multiple and contradictory meanings, informs literary form. The chapter "Dialogism in the Novel" is most relevant.

Barthes, Roland (1977) "The Death of the Author," in *Image-Music-Text*, Stephen Heath (ed.) New York: Hill & Wang. A seminal essay in contemporary theory arguing that an author figure only serves to limit a text by providing a final signified; removing the author opens up a plurality of meanings.

Fish, Stanley (1980) "How to Recognize a Poem When You See One," in *Is There a Text in This Class?*, Cambridge, Mass.: Harvard University Press. Argues that literary "meaning" is the product of interpretive communities, who read texts in certain contexts to get their meanings.

Foucault, Michel (1984) "What Is an Author?," in *The Foucault Reader*, Peter Rabinow (ed.), trans. Josué V. Harari, New York: Pantheon Books. Complicates "the death of the author" as outlined by Roland Barthes by suggesting that the "author function" will persist, constraining texts in various ways. While all discourse can be appropriated, the author comes into being when discourse is transgressive and the author is therefore subject to punishment.

Greenblatt, Stephen (1989) "Towards a Poetics of Culture," in *The New Historicism*, H. Aram Veeser (ed.), New York: Routledge. A general overview of the new historicism; specifically addresses the relationship between social and aesthetic discourse.

Guillory, John (1993) *Cultural Capital: The Problem of Literary Canon Formation*, Chicago: University of Chicago Press. Analysis of literary canon formation and university curricula based on Bourdieu's notion of the circulation of cultural capital.

Orgel, Stephen (1988) "The Authentic Shakespeare," *Representations* 21: 5–25. Interrogates the idea of an "authentic" Shakespearean text by discussing what goes into critical and popular conceptions of Shakespeare; even an "original" Shakespearean text was only a working blueprint for productions.

Pechter, Edward (1987) "The New Historicism and its Discontents: Politicizing Renaissance Drama," *PMLA* 102: 292–303. Examines ideological and practical problems in the work of new historicist critics and questions the scope of new historicism's contextualization of literary works.

Taylor, Gary (1996) *Cultural Selection*, New York: Basic Books. A wide-ranging analysis of cultural value with particular attention to the construction of individual and collective memory.

References

Adelman, Janet (1992) *Suffocating Mothers: Fantasies of Maternal Origin in Shakespeare's Plays*, New York: Routledge.

Adorno, Theodor W. and Horkheimer, Max (1988) "The Culture Industry: Enlightenment as Mass Deception," in *Dialectic of Enlightenment*, trans. John Cumming, New York: Continuum.

Altick, Richard (1985) *Paintings from Books: Art and Literature in Britain, 1760–1900*, Columbus: Ohio State University Press.

Anderson, Amanda (1993) *Tainted Souls and Painted Faces: The Rhetoric of Fallenness in Victorian Culture*, Ithaca: Cornell University Press.

Andreas, James R. (1992) "Othello's African American Progeny," *South Atlantic Review*, 57: 39–57, reprinted in *Materialist Shakespeare: A History*, Ivo Kamps (ed.), New York: Verso, 181–97.

Andrews, John F. (1996) "Kenneth Branagh's *Hamlet* Launched at National Air and Space Museum," *The Shakespeare Newsletter* 46 (3): 53, 62, 66, 76.

Angelou, Maya (1970) *I Know Why the Caged Bird Sings*, New York: Random House.

Ashton, G. (1980) *Shakespeare's Heroines in the Nineteenth Century*, an exhibition catalog, Buxton: Buxton Museum.

Athenaeum (1864) Review of Robert Browning, *Dramatis Personae*, July: 765–67.

Atwood, Margaret (1994) "Gertrude Talks Back," *Good Bones and Simple Murders*, 1st edn., New York: Doubleday, 16–19.

Auden, W. H. (1948) "Brothers and Others," in *The Dyer's Hand and Other Essays*, New York: Random House.

Auerbach, Nina (1982) *Woman and the Demon*, Cambridge, Mass.: Harvard University Press.

—— (1987) *Ellen Terry: Player in Her Time*, New York: W. W. Norton.

Baker, Susan (1994) "Comic Material: Shakespeare in the Classical Detective Story," in *Acting Funny: Comic Theory and Practice in Shakespeare's Plays*, Frances Teague (ed.), Rutherford, N.J.: Fairleigh Dickinson University Press, 164–79.

Bakhtin, M. M. (1981) *The Dialogic Imagination: Four Essays*, Michael Holquist (ed.), trans. Caryl Emerson and Michael Holquist, Austin: University of Texas Press.

—— (1990) *Art and Answerability: Early Philosophical Essays by M. M. Bakhtin*, Michael Holquist and Vadim Liapunov (eds), trans. Vadim Liapunov, Austin: University of Texas Press.

Baldo, Jonathan (1996) "Wars of Memory in *Henry V*," *Shakespeare Quarterly* 47: 132–59.

Balogh, Mary (1994) *Christmas Belle*, New York: Signet.

Baraka, Amiri (1964) *"Dutchman" and "The Slave": Two Plays*, New York: Morrow.

Barker, Deborah and Kamps, Ivo (1995) (eds) *Shakespeare and Gender: A History*, New York: Verso.

Barlow, Linda and Krentz, Jayne Ann (1992) "Beneath the Surface: The Hidden Codes of Romance," in Krentz (1992a) (ed.), 19–36.

Barnet, Sylvan (1986) "*Othello* on the Stage and Screen," in Alvin Kernan (ed.) *Othello*, New York: Signet Classic.

Bate, Jonathan (1984) "Hazlitt's Shakespearean Quotations," *Prose Studies* 7: 26–37.

—— (1998) *The Genius of Shakespeare*, New York: Oxford University Press.

Baudrillard, Jean (1988) "The System of Objects," in *Selected Writings*, Mark Poster (ed.), Stanford: Stanford University Press, 10–28.

—— (1989) *America*, trans. Chris Turner, London: Verso.

Benjamin, Walter (1969) "The Work of Art in the Age of Mechanical Reproduction," in *Illuminations*, New York: Schocken Books, 217–51.

Bentham, Jeremy (1999a) "Jeremy Bentham." Online. Available HTTP: http://www.ucl.ac.uk/Bentham-Project/jb.htm.

—— (1999b) "Jeremy Bentham On-Line." Online. Available HTTP: http://doric.bart.ucl.ac.uk/web/Nina/JBentham.html.

Berdoe, Edward (1896) *Browning and the Christian Faith: The Evidences of Christianity from Browning's Point of View*, New York: Haskell House.

Beverley, Jo (1989) *The Stanforth Secrets*, New York: Avon Books.

Billington, M. (1998) "A Very British Coup," *The Guardian*, May 2.

Bloom, Harold (1973) *The Anxiety of Influence: A Theory of Poetry*, New York: Oxford University Press.

—— (1998a) Lecture to the Commonwealth Club of California, Broadcast on C-Span 2, December 12, 1998.

—— (1998b) *Shakespeare: The Invention of the Human*, New York: Riverhead Books.

Bodenstedt, Friedrich (1878) *Shakespeare's Frauencharaktere*, 3rd edn., Berlin: Hofmann.

Bogart, Leo (1995) *Commercial Culture: The Media System and the Public Interest*, New York: Oxford University Press.

Boose, Lynda (1982) "The Father and the Bride in Shakespeare," *PMLA* 97: 325–47.

Boucher, Rita (1997) *The Would-Be Witch*, New York: Signet Regency.

Bourdieu, Pierre (1984) *Distinction: A Social Critique of the Judgement of Taste*, trans. R. Nice, Cambridge, Mass.: Harvard University Press.

Bradshaw, Graham (1993) *Misrepresentations: Shakespeare and the Materialists*, Ithaca: Cornell University Press.

Branagh, Kenneth (1990) *Beginning*, New York: W. W. Norton.

—— (1996a) dir. *Hamlet*, with Kenneth Branagh and Derek Jacobi, Columbia Pictures.

—— (1996b) Screenplay and Introduction, *Hamlet*, by William Shakespeare, New York: W. W. Norton.

Bristol, Michael (1990) *Shakespeare's America, America's Shakespeare*, New York: Routledge.

—— (1996) *Big-Time Shakespeare*, New York: Routledge.

Browning, Robert (1951) *Dearest Isa: Robert Browning's Letters to Isabella Blagden*, Edward C. McAleer (ed.), Austin: University of Texas Press.

—— (1997) *Robert Browning*, Adam Roberts (ed.), Oxford: Oxford University Press.

Browning Society Papers (1966) 3 vols, London: N. Trubner, 1881–84; Liechtenstein: Kraus Rpt.

Burke, Kenneth (1969) [1950] *A Rhetoric of Motives*, Berkeley: University of California Press.

—— (1973) [1941] "The Philosophy of Literary Form," *The Philosophy of Literary Form*, Berkeley: University of California Press.

Butler, Judith P. (1990) *Gender Trouble: Feminism and the Subversion of Identity*, London: Routledge.

Byatt, A. S. (1992) "Heyer: An Honourable Escape," *Passions of the Mind: Selected Writings*, New York: Turtle Bay Press.

Calcutta Journal (1821–22) microfilm.

Campbell, Thomas (1834) *Life of Mrs. Siddons*, 2 vols, London: Effingham Wilson.

Camper, Petrius (1821) *Works of the Late Professor Camper*, London: J. Hearne, Priestly, Weale, E. Butler, W. Mason.

Carroll, Susan (1986) *The Lady Who Hated Shakespeare*, New York: Fawcett Crest.

Casteras, Susan P. (1987) *Images of Victorian Womanhood in English Art*, London and Toronto: Associated University Presses.

Césaire, Aimé (1985) *A Tempest*, trans. Richard Miller, New York: Ubu Repertory Theater Productions.

Charles, Prince of Wales (1989) "Bad English Rubs Charles," *Trenton Times*, 20 December.

Charnes, Linda (1993) *Notorious Identity: Materializing the Subject in Shakespeare*, Cambridge, Mass.: Harvard University Press.

—— (1998) "The Hamlet Formerly Known as Prince." Unpublished paper read at the annual meeting of the Shakespeare Association of America, Cleveland, Ohio.

Chase, Loretta (1988) *The Vagabond Viscount*, New York: Avon Books.

—— (1989) *The Devil's Delilah*, New York: Fawcett Crest.

Chesnutt, Charles W. (1993) *The Journals of Charles W. Chesnutt*, Richard H. Brodhead (ed.), Durham: Duke University Press.

Clarke, Mary Cowden (1850–52) *The Girlhood of Shakespeare's Heroines*, London: W. H. Smith.

—— (1887) "Shakespeare as the Girl's Friend," *The Girl's Own Paper*, June 8, 562–64.

Conlogue, R. (1998) "Troubled Times for Classic Theatre," *Globe and Mail*, July 11.

Cook, Carol (1995) "'The Sign and Semblance of her Honor': Reading Gender Difference in *Much Ado About Nothing*," in Barker and Kamps (eds), 75–103.

Costigan, Giovanni (1967) *Makers of Modern England: The Force of Individual Genius in History*, New York: Macmillan.

Coulbourne, J. (1998) "Stratford Needs to Take New Direction," *Toronto Sun*, July 26.

Cowper, William (1926) *The Poetical Works of William Cowper*, H. S. Milford (ed.), London: Oxford University Press.

Crawford, Robert (1998) (ed.) *The Scottish Invention of English Literature*, Cambridge: Cambridge University Press.

Daily Telegraph [London] (1879) June 16.

Dangerfield, George (1961) *The Strange Death of Liberal England, 1910–1914*, New York: Capricorn Books.

Dash, Julie (1992) *Daughters of the Dust: The Making of an African American Woman's Film*, New York: New Press.

Dávidházi, Péter (1998) *The Romantic Cult of Shakespeare: Literary Reception in Anthropological Perspective*, New York: St. Martin's.

Davies, H. (1998) "Wronged Hillary Takes Revenge in Dramatic Fashion," in *Electronic Telegraph*, issue 1271. Online. Available HTTP: http://www.telegraph.co.uk (November 17).

Derrida, Jacques (1986) "Racism's Last Word," in *"Race," Writing, and Difference*, Henry Louis Gates, Jr. (ed.), Chicago: University of Chicago Press, 329–38.

Desmet, Christy (1990) "'Intercepting the Dew-Drop': Female Readers and Readings in Anna Jameson's Shakespearean Criticism," in *Women's Re-Visions of Shakespeare*, Marianne Novy (ed.), Urbana: University of Illinois Press, 41–57.

—— (1992) *Reading Shakespeare's Characters: Rhetoric, Ethics, and Identity*, Amherst: University of Massachusetts Press.

De Vane, William Clyde (1955) *A Browning Handbook*, 2nd edn., New York: Appleton-Century-Crofts.

Dijkstra, Bram (1986) *Idols of Perversity: Fantasies of Feminine Evil in Fin-de-Siècle Culture*, New York and Oxford: Oxford University Press.

Dodd, Christina (1994) *The Greatest Lover in All England*, New York: HarperCollins.

Dodd, William (1971) (ed.) *The Beauties of Shakespear, Regularly Selected from Each Play*, 2 vols, [1752]; London: Frank Cass & Co.

Dollimore, Jonathan (1985) "Shakespeare, Cultural Materialism and the New Historicism," in *Political Shakespeare: New Essays in Cultural Materialism*, Jonathan Dollimore and Alan Sinfield (eds), Ithaca: Cornell University Press, 2–18.

Donaldson, Peter S. (1990) *Shakespearean Films/Shakespearean Directors*, Boston: Unwin Hyman.

Dorfman, Ariel and Mattelart, Armand (1975) *How to Read Donald Duck: Imperialist Ideology in the Disney Comic*, trans. David Kunzle, New York: International General.

Dowden, Edward (1901) *Shakspere: A Critical Study of His Mind and Art*, 12th edn., London: Kegan Paul.

Dunn, L. (1998) "Practicing Safe Shakespeare in *In and Out*." Unpublished paper presented in the seminar on "Citing Shakespeare in American Popular Culture" at the annual meeting of the Shakespeare Association of America, Cleveland, Ohio.

Eagleton, Terry (1986) *William Shakespeare*, New York: Basil Blackwell.

Ellis, Sarah Stickney (1839) *The Women of England*, London: Fischer.

Ellison, Ralph (1952) *Invisible Man*, New York: Random House.

—— (1995) *The Collected Essays of Ralph Ellison*, John F. Callahan (ed.), New York: Modern Library.

Erickson, Peter (1985) *Patriarchal Structures in Shakespeare's Drama*, Berkeley: University of California Press.

—— (1991) *Rewriting Shakespeare, Rewriting Ourselves*, Berkeley: University of California Press.

—— (1993) "'Shakespeare's Black?': The Role of Shakespeare in Naylor's Novels," in Gates and Appiah (eds), 231–48.

"Essay Writing on a Great English Author – My Favorite Heroine from Shakespeare" (1888) *Girl's Own Paper*, March 10, 380–81.

Evans, Malcolm (1986) *Signifying Nothing: Truth's True Contents in Shakespeare's Text*, Brighton: Harvester Press.

Ewen, Stuart and Ewen, Elizabeth (1992) *Channels of Desire: Mass Images and the Shaping of American Consciousness*, Minneapolis: University of Minnesota Press.

Faulkner, William (1930) *As I Lay Dying*, New York: J. Cape, H. Smith.

Fjellman, Stephen (1992) *Vinyl Leaves: Walt Disney World and America*, Boulder: Westview Press.

Fletcher, M. (1993) "Hillary Clinton Rejects Lady Macbeth Image," *The Times* [London], June 11, A: 9.

Flower, Joe (1991) *Prince of the Magic Kingdom: Michael Eisner and the Re-Making of Disney*, New York: Wiley.

Foner, Philip S. (1978) (ed.) *Paul Robeson Speaks: Writings, Speeches, Interviews, 1918–1974*, New York: Brunner-Mazel.

Foucault, Michel (1984) "What Is an Author?," in *The Foucault Reader*, Peter Rabinow (ed.), trans. Josué V. Harari, New York: Pantheon Books.

Fowler, Virginia C. (1996) *Gloria Naylor: In Search of Sanctuary*, New York: Twayne Publishers.

Freud, Sigmund (1974) *The Standard Edition of the Complete Psychological Works*, James Strachey *et al.*, ed. and trans., 24 vols, London: Hogarth Press.

—— (1985) *The Complete Letters of Sigmund Freud to Wilhelm Fliess, 1887–1904*, Jeffrey Moussaieff Masson, ed. and trans., Cambridge, Mass.: Harvard University Press.

Frye, Northrop (1949) "The Argument of Comedy," in *English Institute Essays, 1948, 1949*, New York: Columbia University Press.

Gans, Herbert J. (1974) *Popular Culture and High Culture: An Analysis and Evaluation of Taste*, New York: Basic Books.

Garwood, Julie (1994) *Prince Charming*, New York: Simon & Schuster.

Gates, Henry Louis, Jr. (1988) *The Signifying Monkey: A Theory of Afro-American Literary Criticism*, Oxford: Oxford University Press.

—— (1993) "Preface," in Gates and Appiah (eds), ix–xii.

Gates, Henry Louis, Jr. and Appiah, K. A. (1993) (eds) *Gloria Naylor: Critical Perspectives Past and Present*, New York: Amistad Press.

Gervinus, G. G. (1883) *Shakespeare Commentaries*, trans. F. E. Bunnett, London: Smith, Elder.

Giroux, Henry (1994) *Disturbing Pleasures: Learning Popular Culture*, New York: Routledge.

Givhan, Robin (1998) "Model Behavior: Cover Girl Hillary Clinton, Getting Her Due in Vogue," *The Washington Post*, November 16: B: 1.

Gore-Langton, R. (1998) "The Tempest," *Daily Express*, March 1.

Gould, Stephen Jay (1989) *Wonderful Life: The Burgess Shale and the Nature of History*, New York: W. W. Norton.

Grady, Hugh (1991) *The Modernist Shakespeare: Critical Texts in a Material World*, Oxford: Clarendon Press.

—— (1996) *Shakespeare's Universal Wolf: Studies in Early Modern Reification*, Oxford: Clarendon Press.

Greenblatt, Stephen J. (1980) *Renaissance Self-Fashioning: From More to Shakespeare*, Chicago: University of Chicago Press.

—— (1988) *Shakespearean Negotiations: The Circulation of Social Energy in Renaissance England*, Berkeley: University of California Press.

Greetham, D. C. (1992) *Textual Scholarship: An Introduction*, New York: Garland.

—— (1995) (ed.) *Scholarly Editing: A Guide to Research*, New York: Modern Language Association.

—— (1997) (ed.) *The Margins of the Text*, Ann Arbor: University of Michigan Press.

—— (1999) *Theories of the Text*, Oxford: Clarendon Press.

Gross, John (1973) *The Rise and Fall of the Man of Letters*, Harmondsworth: Pelican Books.

Grover, Ron (1991) *The Disney Touch: How a Daring Management Team Revived an Entertainment Empire*, New York: Irwin.

Guenther, Leah (forthcoming) "Luhrmann's Top Forty Shakespeare and the Crises of Shakespearean Consumption," *Journal of American Culture*.

Guillory, John (1993) *Cultural Capital: The Problem of Literary Canon Formation*, Chicago: University of Chicago Press.

Guizot, M. (1852) *Shakespeare and His Times*, London: Bentley.

Halpern, Richard (1997) *Shakespeare among the Moderns*, Ithaca: Cornell University Press.

Hamilton, Charles (1985) *In Search of Shakespeare: A Reconnaissance into the Poet's Life and Handwriting*, New York: Harcourt Brace Jovanovich.

Hawkes, Terence (1986) *That Shakespeherian Rag: Essays on a Critical Process*, London: Methuen.

—— (1992) *Meaning by Shakespeare*, London: Routledge.

—— (1996) *Alternative Shakespeares Vol. 2*, London: Routledge.

Hazlitt, William (1817) *Characters of Shakespear's Plays*, London: C. H. Reynell for R. Hunter and C. and J. Ollier.

Heath, Charles (1836–37) *The Shakspeare Gallery, Containing the Principal Female Characters in the Plays of the Great Poet*, London: Charles Tilt.

Heine, Heinrich (1891) "Shakespeare's Maidens and Women," in *Florentine Nights*, in *The Works of Heinrich Heine*, trans. C. G. Leland, New York: John W. Lovell. First published in German in 1839.

Heroines of Shakespeare (1848) London and New York: The London Printing and Publishing Company.

Hersey, Heloise E. (1890) "Browning in America," *New England Magazine* 1: 543.

Heyer, Georgette (1944) *Friday's Child*, London: Heinemann.

—— (1956) *Sprig Muslin*, London: Heinemann.

—— (1958) *Venetia*, London: Heinemann.

—— (1959) *The Unknown Ajax*, London: Heinemann.

—— (1967) *Black Sheep*, London: Bodley Head.

Heyerlist (1998) Online. Available HTTP: http://www.heyerlist.org/

Hiatt, Brenda (1992) *The Ugly Duckling*, New York: Harlequin Books.

Hodgdon, Barbara (1998) *The Shakespeare Trade: Performances and Appropriations*, Philadelphia: University of Pennsylvania Press.

Homans, Margaret (1993) "To the Queen's Private Apartments: Royal Family Portraiture and the Construction of Victoria's Sovereign Obedience," *Victorian Studies* 37: 1–41.

Honan, Park (1964) "Browning's Testimony on his Essay on Shelley in 'Sheperd v. Francis,'" *English Language Notes* 2: 27–31.

Honour, Hugh (1979) *Romanticism*, New York: Harper & Row.

Hugo, Victor (1887) *William Shakespeare*, trans. Melville B. Anderson, Chicago: McClung.

Hurston, Zora Neale (1937) *Their Eyes Were Watching God*, New York: Negro Universities Press.

Irvine, William and Honan, Park (1974) *The Book, the Ring and the Poet: A Biography of Robert Browning*, New York: McGraw-Hill.

Jacobs, Henry E. and Johnson, Claudia D. (1976) *An Annotated Bibliography of Shakespearean Burlesques, Parodies, and Travesties*, New York: Garland.

James, Deanna (1992a) *Acts of Love*, New York: Zebra Books.

—— (1992b) *Acts of Passion*, New York: Zebra Books.

Jameson, Anna (1854) *Characteristics of Women, Moral, Poetical, and Historical*, Boston: Phillips, Sampson, & Co.

Jenkin, H. C. F. (1915) *Mrs. Siddons as Lady Macbeth and as Queen Katharine*, Papers on Acting III, New York: Dramatic Museum of Columbia University.

Johnson, Samuel (1958) "Preface to Shakespeare, 1765" in *The Yale Edition of the Works of Samuel Johnson*, Arthur Sherbo (ed.), 26 vols, New Haven and London: Yale University Press.

Jones, Ernest (1954) *Hamlet and Oedipus*, New York: Doubleday.

Jong, Erica (1986) *Shylock's Daughter*, New York: Harper Paperbacks.

Jorgensen, Paul A. (1967) *Lear's Self-Discovery*, Berkeley: University of California Press.

Kahn, Coppélia (1986) "The Absent Mother in *King Lear*," in *Rewriting the Renaissance: The Discourses of Sexual Difference in Early Modern Europe*, Margaret W. Ferguson, Maureen Quilligan, and Nancy J. Vickers (eds), Chicago: University of Chicago Press, 33–49.

—— (1995) "The Rape in Shakespeare's *Lucrece*," in Barker and Kamps (eds), 22–46.

Kakutani, Michiko (1998) "The Mouse Once Roared," *New York Times Magazine*, January 4, 8–10.

Kaul, Mythili (1996) (ed.) *Othello: New Essays by Black Writers*, Washington, D.C.: Howard University Press.

Kelly, Carla (1992) *Miss Grimsley's Oxford Career*, New York: Signet.

—— (1993) *Miss Billings Treads the Boards*, New York: Signet.

Kernan, Alvin (1990) *The Death of Literature*, New Haven: Yale University Press.

—— (1995) *Shakespeare, the King's Playwright: Theater in the Stuart Court, 1603–1613*, New Haven: Yale University Press.

—— (1997a) "Introduction: Change in the Humanities and Higher Education," in Kernan 1997b (ed.), 3–13.

—— (1997b) (ed.) *What's Happened to the Humanities?*, Princeton: Princeton University Press.

Kerrigan, William H. (1998) "The Case for Bardolatry: Rescuing Shakespeare from the Critics," *Lingua Franca*, 8 (8): 28–37.

Kingsley, Ben (1988) "Othello," in *Players of Shakespeare 2: Further Essays in Shakespearean Performance by Players with the Royal Shakespeare Company*, Russell Jackson and Robert Smallwood (eds), Cambridge: Cambridge University Press, 167–77.

Klass, P. (1994) "A 'Bambi' for the 90s, Via Shakespeare," *New York Times*, Arts and Leisure Section, June 19, 1: 20.

Krentz, Jayne Ann (1992a) (ed.) *Dangerous Men and Adventurous Women:*

Romance Writers on the Appeal of the Romance, Philadelphia: University of Pennsylvania Press.

—— (1992b) "Trying to Tame the Romance: Critics and Correctness," in Krentz (1992a) (ed.), 131–40.

Lacan, Jacques (1993) "Desire and the Interpretation of Desire in *Hamlet*," in *Literature and Psychoanalysis – The Question of Reading: Otherwise*, Shoshana Felman (ed.), Baltimore and London: Johns Hopkins University Press, 11–52.

Layton, Edith (1988) *The Game of Love*, New York: Signet Super Regency.

Leigh-Noel, M. (1884) *Lady Macbeth: A Study*, London: Wyman & Sons.

—— (1885) *Shakspeare's Garden of Girls*, London: Remington & Co.

Le Sueur, Meridel (1982) "The Ancient People and the Newly Come," in *Ripening: Selected Work, 1927–1980*, Elaine Hedges (ed.), New York: Feminist Press, 39–62.

Levin, Richard (1979) *New Readings vs. Old Plays: Recent Trends in the Reinterpretation of English Renaissance Drama*, Chicago: University of Chicago Press.

—— (1988) "Feminist Thematics and Shakespearean Tragedy," *PMLA* 103: 125–33.

—— (1990) "The Poetics and Politics of Bardicide," *PMLA* 105: 491–504.

—— (1997) "(Re)Thinking Unthinkable Thoughts," *New Literary History* 28: 525–37.

—— (1998) "Capitalism and the Marxist Imaginary at Yale (and Elsewhere)," *Journal x* 3 (1): 39–49.

Levine, Lawrence W. (1988) *Highbrow/Lowbrow: The Emergence of Cultural Hierarchy in America*, Cambridge, Mass.: Harvard University Press.

—— (1991) "William Shakespeare and the American People: A Study in Cultural Transformation," in *Rethinking Popular Culture: Contemporary Perspectives in Cultural Studies*, Chandra Mukerji and Michael Schudson (eds), Berkeley: University of California Press.

Lewes, Louis (1895) *The Women of Shakespeare*, trans. Helen Zimmern, New York: G. P. Putnam's.

The Lion King (1994) dir. Rob Minkoff and Roger Allers, Disney.

The Little Mermaid (1989) dir. John Musker and Ron Clements, Disney.

Litzinger, Boyd and Smalley, Donald (1970) (eds) *Browning: The Critical Heritage*, New York: Barnes & Noble.

Lodge, David (1978) *Changing Places*, Harmondsworth: Penguin.

Lootens, Tricia (1996) *Lost Saints: Silence, Gender, and Victorian Literary Canonization*, Charlottesville and London: University Press of Virginia.

Loucks, James F. (1979) (ed.) *Robert Browning's Poetry: Authoritative Texts, Criticism*, New York: W. W. Norton.

Luhrmann, Baz (1996) dir. *William Shakespeare's Romeo & Juliet*, with Claire Danes and Leonardo DiCaprio, 20th Century Fox.

Lupton, Julia Reinhard and Reinhard, Kenneth (1993) *After Oedipus: Shakespeare in Psychoanalysis*, Ithaca and London: Cornell University Press.

McGann, Jerome J. (1980–93) (ed.) *Lord Byron: The Complete Poetical Works*, 7 vols, Oxford: Clarendon Press.

—— (1983) *A Critique of Modern Textual Criticism*, Chicago: University of Chicago Press.

—— (1985) (ed.) *Textual Criticism and Literary Interpretation*, Chicago: University of Chicago Press.

—— (1991) *The Textual Condition*, Princeton: Princeton University Press.

McPherson, Heather (forthcoming) "Masculinity, Femininity, and the Tragic Sublime: Reinventing Lady Macbeth," *Studies in Eighteenth-Century Culture.*

Mamet, David (1986) *Writing in Restaurants*, New York: Viking Penguin.

—— (1989) *Some Freaks*, New York: Viking Penguin.

Mansfield, Elizabeth (1996) *Matched Pairs*, New York: Jove.

Martin, Michelle (1993) *The Hampshire Hoyden*, New York: Fawcett Crest Books.

Maynard, John (1977) *Browning's Youth*, Cambridge, Mass.: Harvard University Press.

Meadows, Kenneth (1895) Illustrations to *Macbeth*, in *The Complete Works of Shakspere*, Barry Cornwall (ed.), vol. 2, *Tragedies*, London and New York: Printing and Publishing Co.

Michaels, Kasey (1982) *The Tenacious Miss Tamerlane*, New York: Avon Books.

—— (1988) *The Playful Lady Penelope*, New York: Avon Books.

—— (1992) *The Haunted Miss Hampshire*, New York: Avon Books.

Milsand, Joseph (1856) Review of Robert Browning, *Men and Women*, in *Revue Contemporaine*, September, 545–46.

Mitra, Amal (1967) *Kalkātāy Bideśī Raṅgālay* [Foreign Theatres in Calcutta], Calcutta: Prakāś Bhaban.

Morley, S. (1998) "Much Ado about Nothing," *The Spectator*, February 28.

Morris, William (1856) Unsigned review of Robert Browning, *Men and Women*, in *Oxford and Cambridge Magazine*, 1: 162–72.

Morrison, Toni (1981) *Tar Baby*, New York: Knopf.

—— (1992) *Playing in the Dark: Whiteness and the Literary Imagination*, Cambridge, Mass.: Harvard University Press.

Mulhern, Francis (1979) *The Moment of "Scrutiny,"* London: New Left Books.

Mulvey, Laura (1996) *Fetishism and Curiosity*, Bloomington: Indiana University Press.

Murfin, Ross C. (1978) *Swinburne, Hardy, Lawrence and the Burden of Belief*, Chicago: University of Chicago Press.

Myrdal, Gunnar (1944) *An American Dilemma: The Negro Problem and Modern Democracy*, New York: Harper.

Naylor, Gloria (1985) *Linden Hills*, New York: Ticknor & Fields.

—— (1989) *Mama Day*, New York: Random House.

Nead, Lynda (1988) *Myths of Sexuality: Representations of Women in Victorian Britain*, Oxford: Basil Blackwell.

Neill, Michael (1989) "Unproper Beds: Race, Adultery, and the Hideous in *Othello*," *Shakespeare Quarterly* 40: 383–412.

—— (1998) "'Mulattos,' 'Blacks,' and 'Indian Moors': *Othello* and Early Modern Constructions of Human Difference," *Shakespeare Quarterly* 49: 361–74.

Newman, Karen (1987) "'And Wash the Ethiope White': Femininity and the Monstrous in *Othello*," in *Shakespeare Reproduced: The Text in History and Ideology*, Jean E. Howard and Marion F. O'Connor (eds), London: Methuen, 141–62.

Novy, Marianne (1984) *Love's Argument: Gender Relations in Shakespeare*, Chapel Hill: University of North Carolina Press.

Olivier, Laurence (1948) dir. and prod. *Hamlet*, with Laurence Olivier and Eileen Herlie, Two Cities Films.

— (1982) *Confessions of an Actor*, New York: Simon & Schuster.

Orkin, Martin (1998) "Possessing the Book and Peopling the Text," in *Post-Colonial Shakespeares*, Ania Loomba and Martin Orkin (eds), London: Routledge, 164–85.

Osborne, Laurie (1997) "*Fool's Masquerade*." Online. E-mail: leosborn@colby.edu, October 12, 1997.

—— (1998) "Shakespeare Romances by Play." Online. Available HTTP: http://www.colby.edu/personal/leosborn/popshak.htm

O'Sullivan, Daniel (n.d.) "Lady Macbeth," in *Galerie des Femmes de Shakespeare: Collection de 45 Portraits*, Paris: O.-P. Dufour et Mulat, 177–80.

Overfield, Joan (1992) *The Spirited Bluestocking*, New York: Zebra Books.

Parker, Patricia (1987) *Literary Fat Ladies: Rhetoric, Gender, Property*, New York: Methuen.

Pequigney, Joseph (1985) *Such Is My Love: A Study of Shakespeare's Sonnets*, Chicago: University of Chicago Press.

Peterson, William S. (1969) *Interrogating the Oracle: A History of the London Browning Society*, Athens, Ohio: Ohio University Press.

Phillips, K. (1993) "If Looks Could Kill," *Tatler*, December: 46–48, 51.

Poole, J. (1810) *Hamlet Travestie*, London: Thomas Hailes Lacy.

Popper, Karl (1959) *The Logic of Scientific Discovery*, London: Hutchinson.

—— (1963) *Conjectures and Refutations: The Growth of Scientific Knowledge*, London: Routledge & Kegan Paul.

Porter, Margaret Evans (1993) *Toast of the Town*, New York: Signet.

Pressly, William L. (1993) *A Catalogue of Paintings in the Folger Shakespeare Library*, New Haven: Yale University Press.

Project on Disney (Klugman, Karen; Kuenz, Jan; Waldrep, Shelton; and Willis, Susan) (1995) *Inside the Mouse: Work and Play at Disney World*, Durham: Duke University Press.

Quiller-Couch, Arthur (1918) *Shakespeare's Workmanship*, London: T. Fisher Unwin.

—— (1921) *On the Art of Reading*, Cambridge: Cambridge University Press.

—— (1944) *Memories and Opinions: An Unfinished Autobiography*, S. C. Roberts (ed.), Cambridge: Cambridge University Press.

—— and John Dover Wilson (1921) (eds) *The Tempest*, Cambridge: Cambridge University Press.

—— and John Dover Wilson (1926) (eds) *As You Like It*, Cambridge: Cambridge University Press.

Radway, Janice A. (1984) *Reading the Romance: Women, Patriarchy, and Popular Literature*, Chapel Hill: University of North Carolina Press.

Rich, Adrienne (1979) "When We Dead Awaken: Writing as Re-Vision," in *On Lies, Secrets, and Silence: Selected Prose*, New York: W. W. Norton, 33–49.

Roberts, Helene E. (1972) "Marriage, Redundancy or Sin: The Painter's View of Women in the First Twenty-Five Years of Victoria's Reign," in *Suffer and Be Still: Women in the Victorian Age*, Martha Vicinus (ed.), Bloomington: Indiana University Press, 45–76.

Robeson, Paul (1992) *The Odyssey of Paul Robeson*, Omega Classics, OCD 3007.

Rooksby, Rikky (1997) *A. C. Swinburne: A Poet's Life*, Hants, Eng.: Scolar Press.

Rowell, George (1978) *Queen Victoria Goes to the Theatre*, London: Paul Elek.

Royal Shakespeare Company (1987) *111th Report to the Council*, Stratford-upon-Avon.

Rozett, Martha Tuck (1994) *Talking Back to Shakespeare*, Newark: University of Delaware Press.

RRA-L (Romance Readers List) (1998). Online. Available e-mail: bit.listserv.rra-l

Ruskin, John (1891) "Of Queens' Gardens," in *Sesame and Lilies*, introduction C. E. Norton, New York: Charles E. Merrill; rpt. St. Clair Shores, Mich.: Scholarly Press, 1972.

Russell, Anne E. (1991) "'History and Real Life': Anna Jameson, *Shakespeare's Heroines* and Victorian Women," *Victorian Review* 17: 35–49.

Sabin, Margery (1997) "Evolution and Revolution: Change in the Literary Humanities, 1968–1995," in Kernan (1997b) (ed.), 84–103.

Sānyāl, Kouśik (1997) "Nabīn Basur Thieṭār" [Nabīn Basu's Theatre], Anuṣṭup: Calcutta.

Sawyer, Robert (1997) "Mid-Victorian Appropriations of Shakespeare: George Eliot, Robert Browning, and A. C. Swinburne," unpublished Ph.D. dissertation, University of Georgia.

Schanzer, Ernest (1960) "The Marriage-Contracts in *Measure for Measure*," *Shakespeare Survey* 13: 81–89.

Schickel, Richard (1968) *The Disney Version: The Life, Times, Art and Commerce of Walt Disney*, London: Pavilion.

Schlegel, A. W. (1833) *A Course of Lectures on Dramatic Art and Literature*, trans. John Black, Philadelphia: Hogan & Thompson.

Seidel, Kathleen Gilles (1992) "Judge Me by the Joy I Bring," in Krentz (1992a) (ed.), 220–26.

Sells, Laura (1995) "'Where Do the Mermaids Stand?' Voice and Body in *The Little Mermaid*," in *From Mouse to Mermaid: The Politics of Film, Gender, and Culture*, Elizabeth Bell, Lynda Haas, and Laura Sells (eds), Bloomington: Indiana University Press, 175–92.

Serz, Cynthia (1989) "Those Faces! Those Voices! Behind the Box Office Splash Are Some Surprising Folks," *People Magazine*, 11 December, 123–25.

Shakespeare, William (1986) *The Complete Works*, (gen. eds) S. W. Wells and G. Taylor, Oxford: Clarendon Press.

—— (1997) *The Norton Shakespeare*, Stephen Greenblatt *et al.* (eds), New York: W. W. Norton.

Shakespeare in Love (1998) dir. John Madden, with Gwyneth Paltrow and Joseph Fiennes, Miramax.

Shaw, W. David (1968) *The Dialectical Temper: The Rhetorical Art of Robert Browning*, Ithaca: Cornell University Press.

Showalter, Elaine (1991) *Sister's Choice: Tradition and Change in American Women's Writing*, Oxford: Clarendon Press.

Siddons, Sarah (1834) "Remarks on the Character of Lady Macbeth," in Thomas Campbell, *Life of Mrs. Siddons*, 2 vols, 2: 10–39.

Singh, Jyotsna (1994) "Othello's Identity, Postcolonial Theory and Contemporary African Rewritings of *Othello*," in *Women, "Race," and Writing in the Early Modern Period*, Margo Hendricks and Patricia Parker (eds), London: Routledge, 287–99.

Smiley, Jane (1991) *A Thousand Acres*, New York: Fawcett Columbine.

—— (1998) "Shakespeare in Iceland," in *Shakespeare and the Twentieth Century: The Selected Proceedings of the International Shakespeare Association World Congress, Los Angeles, 1996*, Jonathan Bate, Jill L. Levenson, and Dieter Mehl (eds), Newark: University of Delaware Press, 41–59.

Smoodin, Eric (1993) *Animating Culture: Hollywood Cartoons from the Sound Era*, Brunswick, N.J.: Rutgers University Press.

—— (1994) (ed.) *Disney Discourse: Producing the Magic Kingdom*, New York: Routledge.

Snitnow, Ann Barr (1983) "Mass Market Romance: Pornography for Women Is Different," in *Powers of Desire: The Politics of Sexuality*, Ann Snitnow, Christine Stansell, and Sharon Thompson (eds), New York: Monthly Review Press, 245–63.

Soracco, S. (1990) "Splash! Six Views of *The Little Mermaid* – A Psychoanalytic Approach," *Scandinavian Studies* 62: 408–12.

Spencer, Charles (1998) "Dispiriting Plod through the RSC's Theatrical No-man's-land," *Daily Telegraph*, May 5.

Spencer, Theodore (1949) *Shakespeare and the Nature of Man*, 2nd edn., New York: Macmillan.

Springer, Marlene (1977) "Angels and Other Women in Victorian Literature," in *What Manner of Woman*, Marlene Springer (ed.), New York: New York University Press, 124–59.

Stoppard, Tom (1967) *Rosencrantz & Guildenstern Are Dead*, New York: Grove Press.

—— (1976) *The Fifteen Minute Hamlet*, London: Samuel French.

Taylor, Gary (1989) *Reinventing Shakespeare: A Cultural History from the Restoration to the Present*, New York: Oxford University Press.

—— (1995) "Shakespeare and Others: The Authorship of *Henry the Sixth, Part One*," *Medieval and Renaissance Drama in England* 7: 145–205.

—— (1996) *Cultural Selection*, New York: Basic Books.

—— (1999) "Shakespeare in Context: The 1998 Stratford Festival," *Shakespeare Quarterly*.

—— (forthcoming) "c:\wp\file.txt 05: 41 10–07–98," in *Renaissance Text*, A. D. Murphy (ed.), Manchester: Manchester University Press.

Taylor, K. (1998) "Saving Stratford from the Excesses of Success," *Globe and Mail*, July 18.

Taylor, P. (1998) *The Independent*, February 27.

Terry, Ellen (1932) "The Pathetic Women," in *Four Lectures on Shakespeare*, C. St. John (ed.), London: Martin Hopkinson.

Thompson, Ann and Roberts, Sasha (1997) (eds) *Women Reading Shakespeare, 1660–1900*, Manchester and New York: Manchester University Press.

Thurston, Carol (1987) *The Romance Revolution: Erotic Novels for Women and the Quest for a New Sexual Identity*, Urbana: University of Illinois Press.

Tillyard, E. M. W. (1943) *The Elizabethan World Picture*, London: Chatto & Windus.

—— (1958) *The Muse Unchained*, London: Bowes & Bowes.

Tocqueville, Alexis de (1838–40) *Democracy in America*, vol. 2, trans. H. Reeve, London: Saunders & Otley.

Traub, Valerie (1993) "Rainbows of Darkness: Deconstructing Shakespeare in the Work of Gloria Naylor and Zora Neale Hurston," in *Cross-Cultural Performances: Differences in Women's Re-Visions of Shakespeare*, Marianne Novy (ed.), Urbana: University of Illinois Press, 150–64.

Treuherz, Julian (1993) *Victorian Painting*, London and New York: Thames & Hudson.

Ulrici, Hermann (1846) *Shakspeare's Dramatic Art*, London: Chapman. Published originally as *Shakspeare's Dramatische Kunst* in 1839.

Vaughan, Virginia Mason (1994) *Othello: A Contextual History*, Cambridge: Cambridge University Press .

Vaughan, W. H. T. (1996) "Shakespeare Compared: Boydell and Retzsch," in *The Boydell Shakespeare Gallery*, W. Pape and F. Burwick (eds), Bottrop: Peter Pomp, 175–83.

Veryan, Patricia (1987) *Love Alters Not*, New York: St. Martin's.

—— (1989) *Men Were Deceivers Ever*, New York: Harlequin Regency Romance.

—— (1994) *A Shadow's Bliss*, New York: St. Martin's.

Vickers, Brian (1993) *Appropriating Shakespeare: Contemporary Critical Quarrels*, New Haven: Yale University Press.

Watson, Nicola J. (1997) "Gloriana Victoriana: Victoria and the Cultural Memory of Elizabeth I," in *Remaking Queen Victoria*, Margaret Homans and Adrienne Munich (eds), Cambridge: Cambridge University Press, 79–104.

Watts, Steven (1997) *The Magic Kingdom: Walt Disney and the American Way of Life*, Boston: Houghton Mifflin.

Wells, Stanley (1978) *Nineteenth-Century Shakespeare Burlesques*, 5 vols, Wilmington: Michael Glazier.

Werstine, Paul (1998) "Hypertext as Editorial Horizon," in *Shakespeare and the Twentieth Century: The Selected Proceedings of the International Shakespeare Association World Congress, Los Angeles, 1996*, Jonathan Bate, Jill L. Levenson, and Dieter Mehl (eds), Newark: University of Delaware Press, 248–57.

Westminster Review (1869) January 1, 298–300.

Wideman, John Edgar (1990) *Philadelphia Fire*, New York: Holt.

—— (1994) *Fatheralong: A Meditation on Fathers and Sons, Race and Society*, New York: Pantheon Books.

Wilde, Oscar (1890) "The True Function of Criticism," *Nineteenth Century* 38: 123–47.

Will, George F. (1991) "Literary Politics," *Newsweek*, April 22, 72.

Willey, Basil (1968) *Cambridge and Other Memories*, London: Chatto & Windus.

Williams, Anne (1983) "Browning's 'Childe Roland,' Apprentice for Night," *Victorian Poetry* 21: 27–42.

Williams, Simon (1990) *Shakespeare on the German Stage*, vol. 1, 1586–1914, Cambridge: Cambridge University Press.

Wilson, A. N. (1983) *The Life of John Milton*, Oxford: Oxford University Press.

Wilson, August (1990) "An Interview with August Wilson," *City Paper*, Washington D.C.

—— (1991) *Three Plays*, Pittsburgh: University of Pittsburgh Press.

Wolf, Joan (1980) *The Counterfeit Marriage*, New York: Signet.

—— (1981) *A London Season*, New York: Signet.

—— (1982) *His Lordship's Mistress*, New York: Signet.

—— (1984) *Fool's Masquerade*, New York: Signet.

Woodbridge, Linda (1991) "Poetics from the Barrel of a Gun," in *Shakespeare Right and Left*, Ivo Kamps (ed.), New York: Routledge, 285–98.

Woolford, John and Karlin, Daniel (1996) *Robert Browning*, London: Longman.

Wordsworth, William (1917) *The Poetical Works of William Wordsworth*, Thomas Hutchinson (ed.), London: Oxford University Press.

Wright, Richard (1940) *Native Son*, New York and London: Harper.

Zeffirelli, Franco (1991) dir. *Hamlet*, with Mel Gibson and Glenn Close, Warner Bros.

Ziegler, Georgianna (1997) (ed.) with Frances E. Dolan and Jeanne Addison Roberts, *Shakespeare's Unruly Women*, Washington, D.C.: Folger Shakespeare Library.

Zipes, Jack David (1983) *Fairy Tales and the Art of Subversion: The Classical Genre for Children and the Process of Civilization*, New York: Methuen.

Žižek, Slavoj (1989) *The Sublime Object of Ideology*, London: Verso.

Index

Lightning Source UK Ltd.
Milton Keynes UK
UKOW031015110912

198821UK00011B/42/P